TROUBLED RELATIONS

Kenton Clymer

TROUBLED RELATIONS

THE UNITED STATES
AND CAMBODIA
SINCE 1870

NORTHERN

ILLINOIS

UNIVERSITY

PRESS

DeKalb

Based on *The United States and Cambodia, 1870–1969:*
From Curiosity to Confrontation and *The United States and Cambodia, 1969–2000:*
A Troubled Relationship (Routledge, 2004). Published with permission.

Library of Congress Cataloging-in-Publication Data

Clymer, Kenton J.

Troubled relations : the United States and Cambodia since 1870 / Kenton J. Clymer.

p. cm.

Includes bibliographical references and index.

ISBN 978-0-87580-615-0 (pbk. : alk. paper)

1. United States—Foreign relations—Cambodia. 2. Cambodia—Foreign relations—United
States. 3. United States—Foreign relations—1865–. 4. Presidents—United States—History
—19th century. 5. Presidents—United States—History—20th century. I. Title.

E183.8.C15C568 2007   327.73059609'034—dc22

2007004624

Cover photo of Angkor Wat by Marlee Clymer

To grandsons

Ethan Kenton Clymer and

Matthew Nolan Clymer

and to the people of Cambodia

Contents

Preface and Acknowledgments

ABOUT THE ONLY POSITIVE CONSEQUENCE of the American war in Vietnam was the explosion of scholarship on American relations with Southeast Asia. Books on Vietnam now number in the thousands, and accounts of American relations with other parts of Southeast Asia have also increased. There are several fine works about American relations with Cambodia, but most of them concentrate on the relationship during the Vietnam War when for the first time Cambodia became etched in the minds of Americans as successive tragedies engulfed that small country—tragedies that, though certainly not entirely the result of American actions, nevertheless derived in part from American policy. With the release of thousands of relevant documents, it is now possible to trace American policy and actions in greater depth than before. But the Cambodian-American relationship encompasses more than simply the war years, important as they were. This work covers the entire relationship from the 1870s into the first decade of the twenty-first century.

I am very grateful to Northern Illinois University Press and its director, Mary Lincoln, for seeing the value in bringing out a one-volume, updated, abridged paperback version of my earlier study, originally published by Routledge Publishers. This paperback retains the core arguments and essential detail; it appears with the permission of Routledge. The notations have been limited largely to direct quotations. The new edition has also allowed me to correct minor errors. Those wishing a more fully documented account are invited to consult the original books: *The United States and Cambodia, 1870–1969: From Curiosity to Confrontation* and *The United States and Cambodia, 1969–2000: A Troubled Relationship*.

In this edition, I would like to reiterate my deep appreciation of a number of persons and institutions whose support was essential in writing these books. The study's inspiration goes back to 1988 when John McAuliffe, director of the U.S.–Indochina Reconciliation Project, invited me to be part of a group visiting Laos, Vietnam, and Cambodia. I am also deeply grateful to Bill Herod, who as director of Indochina Project, then a program of the Fund for Peace in Washington, DC, invited me to work with him during the summer of 1989. Later Bill was instrumental in obtaining permission for me to do research in the Cambodian National Archives.

Several Cambodian scholars—especially David Chandler, Craig Etcheson, Steve Heder, and Ben Kiernan—generously responded to inquiries and read draft chapters, papers, and articles. Judy Ledgerwood and Kheang Un (colleagues at Northern Illinois University) and Ambassador Julio Jeldres shared their extensive knowledge of contemporary Cambodia. Ambassador Jeldres, King Sihanouk's official biographer, also provided several photographs that are reproduced in the book, for which I am most grateful. Several non-Cambodian specialists also commented on various parts of the manuscript, including Pamela Sodhy, Bradford Perkins, Carl T. Jackson, David L. Anderson, Zhai Qiang, David Schalk, Cary Fraser, Gary Hess, Ross Marley, Nick Cullather, and Charles Ambler. William C. Trimble Jr. kindly provided information about his late father, Ambassador William Cattell Trimble. The late Noël St. Clair Deschamps, Australian Ambassador to Cambodia in the 1960s, flew from Melbourne to Canberra so that I could interview him for parts of two days. U.S. Ambassador to Cambodia Charles Twining took time from his busy schedule for an interview in Phnom Penh, while Ambassador Kenneth Quinn critiqued portions of my manuscript and responded to numerous inquiries. Sorya Sim of the Cambodian Documentation Project in Phnom Penh graciously shared with me many relevant documents from the project's collection. Sally Benson discussed recent Cambodian developments and shared documents with me. Carlos Cartlidge, who served in Vietnam with the Special Forces, discussed his experiences with me and shared photographs of Khmer Serei soldiers. While teaching in Germany in 1992–1993 my able assistant, Volker Depkat, photocopied numerous clippings for me. Cindy Flores, a student at the University of Texas at El Paso, brought my attention to articles about the Khmer Rouge. The late Ruth Arrowsmith sent me many newspaper clippings of value. David Hackett answered my numerous computer questions. To all these people I express my most profound gratitude.

No history books can be written without the use of archives and libraries. In the United States I am most grateful to the National Archives II staff (and particularly to archivist Milt Gustafson), as well as to the staffs at the Truman, Eisenhower, Kennedy, Johnson, Ford, and Carter libraries. Similarly the staffs at the Seeley Mudd Library at Princeton University and the Christian and Missionary Alliance Archives in Colorado Springs were most helpful. I was ably assisted in Cambodia by Lim Ky at the Cambodian National Archives. I want to single out Gay Hogan of the National Archives of Australia for her dedicated assistance during my three visits to Canberra and her persistence in calling my attention to relevant materials.

I am also grateful to the several funding agencies that helped defray the costs of research. These include the National Endowment for the Humanities, which provided both a Summer Stipend and a year-long Grant for College Teachers; the Rockefeller Foundation, which invited my wife and me, as well as Sorya Sim, to spend a month at the foundation's beautiful Bellagio Study Center in Italy; and the Truman, Eisenhower, Kennedy, and Ford libraries, which provided travel grants. A Fulbright grant to teach at the University of Indonesia in 1990–1991 allowed me to gain Southeast Asian perspectives on the intense efforts to arrive at a settlement in Cambodia, in part by reading the considerable coverage of the events in the *Jakarta Post*. The University of Texas at El Paso, my academic home when most of the research was conducted, assisted me in numerous ways, most notably with a year-long Faculty Development Grant.

An earlier version of chapter 2 appeared as "Decolonization, Nationalism, and Anti-Communism: United States Relations with Cambodia, 1945–1954," *Journal of American–East Asian Relations* 6 (Sum./Fall 1997): 91–124. Earlier versions of the first half of chapter 4 appeared as "The Perils of Neutrality: The Break in U.S.–Cambodian Relations," *Diplomatic History* 23 (Fall 1999): 609–31, and as "A Casualty of War: The Break in American Relations with Cambodia, 1965," in Marilyn Young and Robert Buzzanco, eds., *A Companion to the Vietnam War* (Oxford: Blackwell Publishers Limited, 2002), 198–228. Another portion of chapter 4 appeared as "Ambassador William Cattell Trimble and Cambodia, 1959–1962," in David L. Anderson, ed., *The Human Tradition in the Vietnam Era* (Wilmington, DE: Scholarly Resources, 2000). An earlier version of chapter 9 appeared previously as "Jimmy Carter, Human Rights, and Cambodia," *Diplomatic History* 27 (April 2003): 145–78. All are included here with permission.

Finally, I am as always grateful to my wife, Marlee, who has not only lived with this project for years but has read draft after draft, assisted with research, and given me encouragement along the way.

TROUBLED RELATIONS

Cambodia

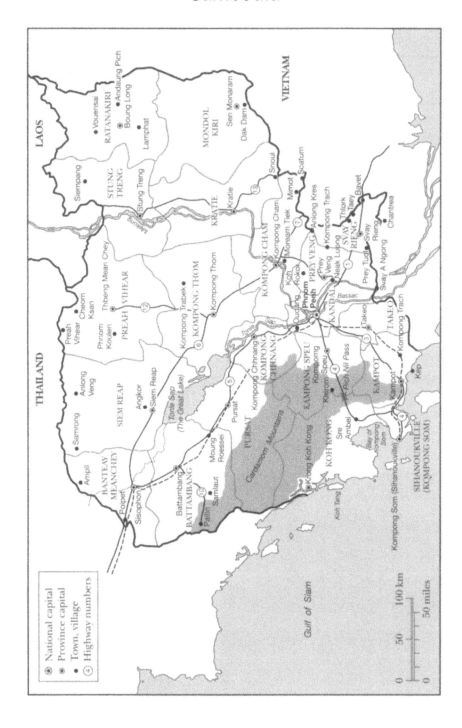

Nineteenth- and Early Twentieth-Century Encounters

"No one should die before they see Angkor."—Somerset Maugham

FOR MOST AMERICANS who lived in the last half of the twentieth century, Cambodia became a household word only in 1970 when President Richard Nixon ordered an invasion of that country to destroy Vietnamese Communist sanctuaries. That action, which led to dramatic protests and the deaths of students at Kent State and Jackson State universities, brought Cambodia into the war in neighboring Vietnam in a major way for the first time. It led to successive tragedies inside Cambodia itself as hundreds of thousands died in a civil war that raged from 1970 to 1975, followed by three years of the almost unbelievable savagery of Pol Pot's Khmer Rouge, who ruled until the end of 1978, when Vietnamese troops drove them from power. Many Americans and Europeans concluded that the United States was largely responsible for destroying what had hitherto been an idyllic, unchanging land of happy peasants.

There was truth in the assertion that the United States bore considerable responsibility for Cambodia's destruction, but the stereotype of Cambodia was a distortion. Cambodia, though in some respects deeply conservative and traditional, was hardly immune to larger historical developments and had undergone considerable change over the centuries. Nor was it an entirely peaceful society, as anyone who has seen the bas-reliefs on the late twelfth- /early thirteenth-century Bayon temple at Angkor Thom can attest.

Like other societies of Southeast Asia, Cambodia's people—the Khmer—had their own culture that descended from prehistoric times. But early in the Christian era, outside influences, primarily from India, merged with the indigenous culture and animistic religion and, at least on the surface, became dominant. A similar pattern of cultural change occurred in most areas of Southeast Asia outside of Vietnam. Mahayana Buddhism came to Southeast Asia very early, but Hinduism was more widespread. The first of the famous Angkor temples, begun in the ninth century, were Hindu. Later some of them became Buddhist or combined Hinduism and Buddhism. The most famous temple of them all, Angkor Wat, built in the twelfth century, was dedicated to the Hindu god Vishnu, but the slightly later Bayon is a Mayahana Buddhist monument. Later in the thirteenth century, Theravada Buddhism, a stricter, more "puritanical" form of the religion, came to dominate Cambodia, in part due to missionary influences from Siam and elsewhere.

The first recorded kingdom in Southeast Asia, called Funan by the Chinese, developed in the early Christian era in what is now Cambodia and southern Vietnam. While it was long thought to have been a major state, new evidence suggests that it may not have been as unified or as significant as the Chinese, and later the French, sought to portray it; and it may be that early Cambodia, like other parts of Southeast Asia, was composed of small city-states that occasionally joined together for specific purposes. By the eighth century, however, Cambodia was becoming more consolidated politically into a kingdom (or perhaps two kingdoms) called Chenla.

Cambodia's greatness as a state began in the following century when the "Angkorian period" began. Usually said to have begun in 802 and lasting until 1431, Angkor (located near present-day Siem Reap) at times dominated much of mainland Southeast Asia. During this period of great creativity, several hundred temples and other buildings were erected that displayed, as Milton Osborne puts it, "a richness of iconography and symbolism to rival anything to be found in the great cathedrals of Europe."[1] A system of reservoirs and canals allowed large harvests of rice that supported an urbanized population of close to one million people.

It was not, however, a peaceful period, as the Khmers fought fierce wars with the Siamese (Thais) to the west, the Vietnamese to the northeast, and the Chams to the south. By the fifteenth century, the kingdom's influence was waning, and a Thai invasion in 1431 is traditionally said to have marked the end of the Angkorian state. In fact, the situation was more complex than that. Although no one can say for certain why the court left Angkor to establish a new capital in the vicinity of Phnom Penh, the growing. significance of international trade may explain the move, since two major river systems converged at Phnom Penh.

Although the capital had moved, Cambodia did not escape external pressures, and the country found itself caught between the Thais and the Vietnamese. At times Cambodia became a semivassal of one side or the other, or even of both at the same time. In the sixteenth century the king even appealed to Spain for protection and promised to convert to Christianity. Late in the century Spanish officials, soldiers, and missionaries lived in Cambodia and were given Cambodian bureaucratic titles, though they had no lasting influence.

Despite the outside pressures, Cambodia in the seventeenth century was reasonably independent. But by the nineteenth century its independence was little more than a shell. Initially the Vietnamese absorbed significant amounts of its territory. The Siamese also attacked Cambodia; in 1772 they burned down Phnom Penh. The Cambodian king was no longer able to protect his people, and his popularity declined. Cambodia had become a poor state, often under foreign sway, with a mostly subsistence economy. By 1808 European visitors had to request Vietnamese permission to visit Phnom Penh. The Vietnamese considered Cambodians barbarians and wanted to civilize them, even to the point of telling them what to wear and how to conduct themselves. It was not unlike the subsequent French *mission civilisatrice*. Only in the 1840s did a semblance of independence return, in part due to a Thai military expedition against Vietnam.

In 1853 Cambodia's King Duang sought French protection against the Thais. The Thais prevented this for the moment, but within a decade the French had begun to establish themselves in the kingdom, as well as in Vietnam. By the beginning of the twentieth century, French protection had become French control, symbolized by the installation of several French *résidents* and a *résident supérieur* who were in complete control of the country. Cambodia was a part of the French colony of Indochina.

In 1907 French authorities managed to get Siam to cede back to Cambodia important territories taken years earlier, including Angkor. For this, Cambodians were immensely grateful, and thereafter French savants and Cambodian laborers worked together to restore the temples. There was some resistance to the French. But, while a major revolutionary movement began in neighboring Vietnam, Cambodia remained largely quiescent until after World War II.

Prior to the arrival of the French, no Americans seem to have entered Cambodia. The United States had no diplomatic or consular representatives in the kingdom until 1950. The earliest semipermanent Americans to reside in Cambodia were Protestant missionaries from the Christian and Missionary Alliance, who received permission to enter Cambodia in 1922. Prior to that time, the only Americans to visit the kingdom were intrepid adventurers (followed later by tourists), big game hunters, and scientists. Some of these early adventurers wrote books and articles about their travels, and from their accounts interested Americans learned something about the kingdom.

The first American account of Cambodia was Frank Vincent Jr.'s book, *The Land of the White Elephant,* first published in 1872. The author's main interest was to visit the fabled temples of Angkor, which the French naturalist Henri Mouhot had "discovered" roughly a decade earlier. The book, with Vincent's account of traveling from Bangkok to Angkor by boat, horse, bullock cart, and elephant was immensely popular and within twelve years had gone through four editions. It continued to remain in print during the twentieth century.

The remarkably well illustrated book revealed Vincent's sense of wonderment and awe. But there was a paradox: Vincent, like most Westerners of that age, considered non-Western societies incapable of great accomplishments. Although his book was not viciously racist, Vincent, like the Vietnamese and the French, considered ordinary Cambodians "degenerate" and "lazy," incapable of conceptualizing and constructing the magnificent temples.[2]

Theories about who might have built the monuments ranged from the lost tribes of Israel to the Romans, with ancient Burmese, Javanese, and Indians as other possible candidates. Vincent himself was partial to the Assyrians and Persians; they might even have built some of the Mayan monuments in the Western Hemisphere, he hypothesized.

There were few if any other accounts by Americans in the nineteenth century and almost no official interest in the kingdom. The United States established a consulate at Saigon in 1889, but this did not contribute much to understanding what Americans thought about Cambodia. Until 1906 all of the consular agents were non-Americans, mostly French. For many years they seem to have made no reports about Cambodia at all. Their accounts of the importation of American kerosene, timber, rice, flour, and a few other goods, however, indicate that there was a modest American commercial interest in Indochina. Kerosene, produced by the Standard Oil Company, was the most important of the imports, and doubtless some of it was sold in Phnom Penh and other areas of Cambodia.

Late in 1911, however, a former American consul at Saigon, Jacob E. Conner, traveled to Angkor, apparently one of the very few Americans to have visited the ruins since Vincent's famous trip several decades earlier. By then it was no longer necessary to travel by elephant, but the trip was still difficult. Conner went by train from Saigon to Mytho, then by a steamboat with minimal accommodations for a twenty-four-hour voyage up the Mekong to Phnom Penh. Another day took the party up the Tonle Sap River to Kompong Chhnang, where they entered the Great Lake (the Tonle Sap). At midnight, passengers transferred to sampans for a five-hour trip powered by oarsmen up the Siem Reap River to Siem Reap town. There they boarded bullock carts for the final three or four miles to Angkor. Once there they found no hotel, only a rest house "consisting of roof, floor, and walls, and that is all." No food was available. Anticipating this, Conner had brought with him "a steamer-trunk full of tropical clothing, a steamer-rug, a camp-bed, a Cambodian mattress (splendid thing for comfort), a supply of provisions, and a Chinese cook."[3]

Conner made a few condescending observations about contemporary Cambodia. King Sisowath, then in his sixties, was portrayed as a kind of pretend, childlike monarch. In contrast to other Asian societies the women, he thought, were not exploited. Finally, like most observers he speculated about who had built the temples and other structures at Angkor. He did note that the figures carved in the bas-reliefs resembled contemporary Cambodians. But he suspected that the real founders of the kingdom came from India in the fourth century and wondered if the fabulous wealth they brought with them might have been the riches sought by Christopher Columbus in the fifteenth century.

Accounts of Angkor like Conner's soon created considerable interest in travel there, and by the early 1920s a tourist industry was beginning to flourish. Well-to-do tourists could now board a boat in Saigon and travel up the Mekong River and through the Great Lake. Automobiles had replaced the bullock carts for the short ride to Angkor, where visitors now stayed in bungalows near Angkor Wat itself. (They could still tour the ruins by elephant, however.)

Among those Americans to take the trip in the mid 1920s were two important writers: Helen Churchill Candee, a wealthy New Yorker who in 1912 was one of the first-class passengers on the ill-fated *Titanic* to have survived the disaster; and Harry A. Franck, a prolific and very popular travel writer. At the time of her visit to Cambodia, Candee was well into her sixties. By the time she traveled to Cambodia there was a much better understanding of when Angkor had been built, but at least in the popular imagination there remained much question about who had built the temples. Vincent's theory about the Assyrians and Persians had fortunately never caught on, but whether the ancient Khmers were related to the present-day Cambodians remained an issue. Candee doubted that they were. Franck, by contrast, was convinced that the builders were Khmers, but he felt that their civilization had collapsed and could never again regain its former grandeur. Nevertheless, both writers were less certain about western superiority (Candee pointed to the savagery of World War I) and found much that was good in Khmer culture, with Franck even writing that, as the only people of Indochina to have left "enduring works of their intellectual past," the Khmers deserved to be counted among "the great races of mankind."[4]

Meanwhile, for the first time official American representatives in Indochina began to take some interest in Cambodian developments. In 1924, for example, Lt. Col. John A. Hambleton applied for permission to hunt big game, but part of his mission was to gather intelligence for the War Department about aviation. Hambleton's was not the last effort to gather military intelligence. In 1930 the American military attaché in Peiping requested information about aviation, including military aviation, in Indochina. The next year the consul replied to an inquiry from the military attaché in Paris about the "combat value" of Indochinese forces.[5]

However, the primary concern of the American consuls was to pursue American economic interests in Indochina. In June 1922 the American consul in Saigon, Leland L. Smith, produced what was apparently the first comprehensive report on Cambodia. Accompanied (not insignificantly) by the manager of the Standard Oil Company, Smith visited Phnom Penh and consulted with various French officials. He came away with a sense that Cambodia had great economic potential and far exceeded Cochin China (the southern part of Vietnam) in its resource base.

Subsequent reports indicated a continuing interest in possible markets for American products in Indochina, as well as limited investment opportunities. With the development of excellent new roads, for example, the consulate urged American automobile manufacturers to compete. At some point American car dealerships developed. By at least 1938 the Societé Coloniale d'Automobiles was the Ford Motor Company's agency in Cochin China, Cambodia, and southern Annam (central Vietnam).[6] International Harvester was present by at least 1930, and Standard Oil had significant operations in the country.

American firms operated at a disadvantage, since the French placed various obstacles in the way of foreign concerns. Obstacles to land ownership posed another problem. Aside from French restrictions, there was another perceived drawback to the country's potential economic development: Cambodians, Consul Smith observed in his report, were "lazy."[7] Initially enthusiastic about Cambodia's future, Smith's reports became increasingly pessimistic due to his assessment of the people. "The Cambodians and the Annamites are among the laziest people in the world," he reported in 1923. A year later the consul had arrived at an even lower estimate of the Cambodians: they were "even lazier than the Annamites."[8]

One thing that all observers agreed upon was that the French colonial government was building an excellent network of new roads. The ability to penetrate deeper into Indochina increased big game hunting. Indeed, by the 1930s hunting had taken such a toll that it was difficult to locate the previously numerous wild water buffalo. The popularity of hunting resulted in many dispatches from the American consulate about hunting regulations, how to import guns, and so forth.

The new roads also made it easier to get to Angkor, and by the mid 1920s travel to Angkor was less taxing. What had taken Helen Candee five days was now a mere matter of hours by automobile. Among the first Americans to take advantage of this route was Robert Casey. A prolific writer who had wanted to visit the temples ever since seeing a picture of them while serving in the trenches in World War I, Casey finally got his chance in 1927 when the National Geographic Society sent him to Cambodia. His report first appeared in the society's well-known magazine in September 1928 and was followed the next year by a lengthy book detailing his travels, *Four Faces of Siva: The Detective Story of a Vanished Race*.

Like all observers, Casey was awestruck by the magnificence of Angkor. The builders were more advanced than any Europeans at the time, he reported. But as the book's subtitle suggests, Casey, like previous authors, found it difficult to believe that ancient Khmers of Angkor were related to the present-day Cambodians, who were "very close to savagery." Even if, as some scholars had argued, they were of the same race, they "are no more the same people who built Angkor than the rock piles of Verdun are the town that stood by the Meuse before 1914." Civilized people, he believed, would not have lapsed "into savagery merely because of a change of address." Therefore, if they were descendants, the only explanation was that a slave rebellion had destroyed Angkorian civilization, including the intelligentsia. The revolutionists then quickly returned "to the primitive life of the jungle."[9]

To be sure, Americans did have some contrary images of Cambodia to consider. Not only were Candee's and Franck's accounts more nuanced, but those few published accounts in the 1930s tended to describe Angkor without disparaging comments about the present-day population. Given the persistence of negative racial stereotypes in American culture at that time, however, it seems likely that the view of Cambodia as a land with a generally degraded population living with a comic opera court continued to predominate. Such was certainly the American perception of neighboring Vietnam, as Mark Philip Bradley has demonstrated so convincingly.[10]

"They are spiritually dead, but they do not know it."
—E. F. Irwin, *With Christ in Indo-China*[11]

Although Cambodia was overwhelmingly a Buddhist society, Christianity had had some presence ever since the first contacts with Portuguese and Spanish adventurers and traders in the sixteenth century. In the following century French Jesuits, having been expelled from Japan, moved into Vietnam. They, along with other Catholic missionaries who had established work in Siam, soon moved into Cambodia. As the Vietnamese and Siamese exerted increasing influence in Cambodia in the eighteenth century, the missionaries increased their presence in the increasingly weak kingdom. When the French incorporated Cambodia into Indochina, French Catholicism had unhindered access to the people. But in fact only a handful of Khmers seems to have been converted. There was no Protestant presence at all until American missionaries from the Christian and Missionary Alliance arrived in the 1920s.

The Alliance served in Indochina as a result of a comity agreement with other Protestant missionary societies that divided the world among them, and by the 1920s Indochina was the organization's most populous field. Until well into the twentieth century, therefore, the Alliance was the only mainline Protestant mission in the region, except for a small Swedish Brethren presence in Laos. In the early days there may also have been a few Seventh Day Adventists.

Since the late nineteenth century, the Alliance had viewed Indochina as a place that needed a Protestant presence. Finally, in 1911 Alliance missionaries went into Vietnam (having expanded there from established work in southern China), but French authorities were hostile to their expansion into Cambodia. When a new and more sympathetic French interim *résident supérieur* took over temporarily in Phnom Penh, he told missionaries E. F. Irwin and Arthur L. Hammond, who had traveled from Saigon in 1922 to request permission to begin work, that they could do so. "You will have no success," he added quickly, "but you can try if you like."[12]

In January 1923 Hammond and his wife, Esther King Hammond, moved to the capital. In October David E. and Muriel Harrison Ellison moved to Battambang where, in 1925, they established a Bible school. The Hammonds and the Ellisons appear to have been the first permanent American residents of the kingdom. Five new missionaries arrived in 1926 but some soon moved to other locations. For most of the time, the Alliance mission in Cambodia included only two or three couples.

At first, Alliance gains were small. Indeed, most of the society's work initially was among the Vietnamese and Chinese inhabitants, who then outnumbered the Khmers in Phnom Penh. There were two Cambodian converts in 1923, and only a few more in 1924.

Gradually the mission managed to increase its converts. By the end of 1925 the missionaries claimed eighty, and by 1929 there were said to be between 200 and 300 Protestant Christians in Cambodia. Over the years the Alliance established new mission stations, and in 1939 the missionaries reported "a real turning to God" as sixty-four people were baptized and 1,000 more converted or nearly so.[13] In addition to seeking conversions directly, the missionaries laboriously translated the Bible into Khmer, finally completing the task in 1940. Sometime thereafter, presumably in 1941, the missionaries presented a special copy to the newly installed eighteen-year-old king, Norodom Sihanouk. According to an Alliance account, the king "showed genuine interest" in the project, asked numerous questions about its production, and professed to read the Bible daily.[14]

Stories of success, however, were overstated. Hints of the difficulties the missionaries faced appeared in their weekly magazine and the annual reports. One missionary reported in 1928 that the work in Phnom Penh was "difficult," that the missionaries often found their chapel entirely empty, and that "the very forces of hell" opposed them.[15] The *Annual Report* for 1930 stated that there was "no natural enthusiasm on the part of the Cambodians to accept a new religion." There were no graduates of the Bible School until 1947. As late as the 1950s the only freestanding church building was in Battambang.[16]

The missionaries regularly complained that "persecution" of one kind or another interfered with their efforts, persecution that more often affected their converts than themselves. Occasionally they complained of opposition from Roman Catholics and Muslims, but usually they found that the "bigoted" nature of Buddhism created the most difficulties for them. Buddhism, which the missionaries thought was evidence of the devil's work in the world, was so ingrained in the populace that it was difficult to gain a hearing for Christianity.

One form of "persecution" affected missionary efforts directly: the "rigid restrictions" imposed by French government officials. Actually, the missionaries were generally very positive in their assessment of the benefits of "modern civilization" that the French had brought to Cambodia: an excellent telegraph system, new roads and railroads, and in general an efficient administration. But they nevertheless found most French officials hostile to their work. French opposition was not based directly on religious considerations. Throughout Indochina the French were concerned about real and potential subversive movements and therefore discouraged any associations that might promote solidarity among the people, regardless of how nonpolitical or innocuous they seemed. As David Chandler explains cogently, "the French preferred to deal with a society that was . . . arranged vertically rather than horizontally."[17] Some French officials also considered the mission to be the vanguard of an American political conquest of the region. In any event, there was sufficient friction with the government that the American consul in Saigon reported in 1924, "some difficulty has been had with the authorities on account of American missionaries who have been credited with political actions."[18] As a result, missionaries in most of Indochina worked under various restrictions.

Part of the government's concern was the considerable attraction of the new Cao Dai religion. Founded in 1926 and centered in Chaudoc, Vietnam, the practitioners worshiped Jesus, Buddha, Jean-Jacques Rousseau, and Victor Hugo. It spread so quickly into Cambodia that in 1930 the king formally forbade all religious practices in Cambodia, except for Buddhism and Roman Catholicism. The Protestants, however, refused to comply with this decree and continued to preach and establish small churches. In 1932 the government decided that the missionaries could continue their work in already established stations but could not evangelize outside of those areas. Cambodians were officially forbidden to become Christians, although those already converted were not forced to give up their new religion. By the late 1930s restrictions appear to have lessened. But for most of the decade the missionaries labored under various limitations.

In any event, while the missionaries had established a few churches, printed the scriptures in local languages, sold and distributed thousands of tracts and other religious works, established several mission stations, and opened a Bible

School in Battambang, the number of actual converts remained relatively small. As an Alliance historian put it, "it was not until the early 1970s that large numbers of Cambodians began to move toward the Saviour."[19]

Were missionary views of Cambodia any different from those of the tourists and diplomats who occasionally set foot in the country? Did long residence there make any difference? Aside from the religious state of the people, the available missionary records reveal surprisingly little about Cambodia. Even physical descriptions of the countryside are rare. Angkor itself is scarcely mentioned. The accomplishment of a pagan society, it probably held little attraction for most missionaries.

Almost nothing appears in the missionaries' published comments about internal political or social matters, and, aside from some positive remarks about the benefits the French had brought to Indochina, there is little comment about government, except when authorities restricted evangelization. Nor is there much about the Cambodian people themselves. The people had a "bigoted" culture, were "steeped in heathen idolatry and superstition," and were "wicked." Cambodia was "Satan's back yard." But these were terms that Alliance missionaries used to describe persons or cultures anywhere that resisted Christianity.

It seems likely that, at least to some degree, the missionaries shared the sense of superiority common to most Westerners. Hints of this appear in their publications, such as when David Ellison described "the Cambodian" as "indolent," though also "faithful and loyal to those who succeed in winning his confidence." Another missionary, describing a gathering of Cambodians (and these were Christians), was struck by the "queer, native smell—a mixture of life-long worn rags, native food, babies, and general staleness. There were lots of flies, especially on the running sores of various members of the congregation." More telling, Arthur Hammond recalled that the French preferred the "keener intellects" of the Vietnamese for government work (a judgment that Hammond accepted), and in 1936 an Alliance publication referred to the Cambodians as "excessively lethargic and lazy."[20] But generally speaking (though with the exception of the strongly negative views of the so-called tribal peoples who lived in remote areas), published missionary comments about the people were less likely to reflect the condescending, often racist, assessments made by other observers.

The relative dearth of missionary observations on secular society probably results in part from the fact that they were writing for a church publication designed for home consumption. The focus was on the religious state of the people, and readers wanted to know about religious advances—souls saved, lives redeemed, challenges overcome. Private correspondence, were it available, might include broader observations and analyses; indeed Arthur Hammond's retrospective "Manuscript History" of the Alliance mission in Cambodia includes numerous observations on everyday life. However, as the Alliance's Foreign Secretary put it, "the purpose of this ministry is *salvation*," and the missionaries were driven by a belief that those who died without accepting Christ were condemned for eternity. As one missionary put it, commenting upon the death of a non-Christian, "one more soul has passed on from the darkness of heathenism to the more intense darkness of a hopeless eternity. . . . The longer we tarry with the Gospel, the more such deaths there will be."[21] Focusing almost exclusively on the task of evangelization, the Alliance was less interested than some other missionary groups in seeking social justice or bettering the society. Given their otherworldly focus, there was simply less interest in reporting on physical surroundings or secular developments.

In sum, then, the American image of Cambodia prior to World War II was of an exotic land of pleasant but lazy natives. The country admittedly contained some of the most impressive archaeological sites in the entire world, but it was hard to imagine that the present-day Cambodians were related to the ancient Khmers who had built Angkor. If they were, there had been a dramatic decline in their civilization over the centuries. More recently, the French had brought many improvements to the country, including an excellent system of highways and railroads, and Cambodia, with its numerous natural resources, had much potential. But the very nature of the inhabitants made economic and social development problematic, and the king ruled a comic opera court without authority. This picture of Cambodia inevitably influenced some of those Americans who in the near future would have official responsibilities for American policy toward the region.

Cambodia

THE VIEW FROM THE UNITED STATES, 1940–1954

"The passion in Cambodia in terms of independence at that time was extraordinary. I remember getting up in the very early morning and seeing hundreds of men walking around with wooden rifles, parading and drilling with obvious enthusiasm."—Frank Valeo, Secretary of the U.S. Senate, recalling events in 1953

LATE IN 1940 the Siamese, taking advantage of French weakness caused by the Japanese movement into Southeast Asia, moved to recover Battambang and other areas of Cambodia that the French had taken from them in 1907. The Siamese and the French fought each other, and air raids over Battambang caused many casualties. The Japanese, who already occupied the northern portion of Indochina, had made their peace with the new Vichy French government, and fearing embarrassment to Pibul Songgram's pro-Japanese administration in Bangkok, forced a settlement. The French managed to hold on to Angkor for Cambodia, but they had to give up Battambang and other areas of northern and western Cambodia. The settlement so angered King Monivong that he never again met with French officials; he died in April 1941. In the middle of 1941 the French withdrew from Battambang "with drooping flags." The Thais, in contrast, entered the city with "pageantry and pomp."[1]

The French still retained nominal control of a truncated Indochina (although ultimately the Japanese called the shots). In October 1941 they installed eighteen-year-old Norodom Sihanouk as the new Cambodian monarch. In December the Japanese not only bombed Pearl Harbor and the Philippines but also invaded and quickly subdued Thailand. Soon they were in control of virtually all of Southeast Asia.

During World War II several significant events took place in Cambodia that prepared the ground for eventual independence, but these were almost unknown in the United States. Sihanouk's installation did not merit the attention of the *New York Times* nor of any of the American news magazines. During the war, few if any American troops or intelligence agents served in Cambodia. Missionaries who remained in Indochina found initially that little had changed in their day-to-day activities. Things "were just about normal," Floyd Peterson wrote in June 1942. He could travel wherever he wanted, and there was plenty of food. "You would never think a war was going on," he stated. However in 1943 there was a change, and all of the missionaries in Indochina and their families were interned at Mytho, Vietnam. They remained there until the end of the war.[2]

If Cambodia almost totally disappeared from the radar screen of most Americans, the Franklin D. Roosevelt administration did not ignore Indochina, since the president hoped the country would be the testing ground for international trusteeships that he wanted to establish after the war, trusteeships that would lead to independence. Opposed to old-fashioned colonialism, he especially felt that France, which he believed had behaved in a cowardly fashion during the war, should be stripped of its empire. But when Roosevelt and others spoke of Indochina, they were thinking mostly about Vietnam. Prior to the war, after all, the United States had had consular representation only in Vietnam, and American officials probably shared the general Western view of Cambodia and Laos as backwater areas. Still, during the war some images specifically of Cambodia emerged in official circles. One of the earliest impressions was that the Cambodians accommodated quickly to whatever colonial power happened to be in charge. With the defeat of Japan, therefore, some Americans, relying primarily on French sources for their information, thought that the Cambodians would welcome a French return to Indochina, in part because they feared Siamese and Vietnamese ambitions. Other Americans were more skeptical, reflecting both a residual anticolonialist perspective and a different assessment of the state of internal Cambodian opinion.

There was some evidence on both sides of the argument. There were, for example, a number of Francophiles in the Cambodian court. But the evidence of discontent with the French return was more apparent. Even Sihanouk informed the French that Cambodia had already achieved its independence, and others, such as Son Ngoc Thanh, a leading Cambodian nationalist, made vague plans to resist forcibly any French attempt to return. When the French did return they arrested Thanh and put him on trial, suggesting that they feared his influence. Thanh may have been temporarily silenced, but as early as 1945 some Americans, such as Charles Yost, the perceptive American political adviser in the American embassy in

Bangkok, predicted that armed resistance would greet the French return nonetheless. He was right. Before the year was out, reports of isolated incidents of violence in Cambodia arrived in Washington.

In 1946 and 1947 reports multiplied of growing resistance to the French and to the Sihanouk government that was now cooperating with the French. An Alliance publication stated that in 1946 the French and Cambodian government controlled the roads and cities by day, but at night the Khmer Issaraks (rebels) "were in complete control of everything outside the principal towns."[3] The Issaraks represented the most violent response to French rule, but legal opposition was also in evidence. Although the French hoped to return to the prewar status quo (Charles DeGaulle once wondered aloud to whom Indochina could belong if not to France), they found they had to negotiate. They assured the Americans that French rule would now be solicitous of Cambodian opinion. On 7 January 1946 France and Cambodia signed a modus vivendi (a temporary agreement) regulating relations between them until a final accord was reached. There would be fewer than fifty French officials in Cambodia, down from several hundred in the prewar days. The first elections following the modus vivendi took place in September 1946, which the nationalistic Democratic Party won. On 30 April 1947 Sihanouk promulgated Cambodia's first constitution which, he said, made Cambodia a "Free State associated with France." Sovereignty, he insisted, had now reverted to the Cambodian government and people. But despite the new constitution France retained ultimate influence. In December 1947 Charles Reed, the American consul in Saigon, stated bluntly that the French Commission in Phnom Penh actually ran the country.

Elections held in December 1947 further demonstrated discontent with French rule when the Democratic Party won another victory. There is little evidence that American observers understood that the Democrats were, as historian Ben Kiernan puts it, "the biggest force representing Khmer nationalism"—even more so at this time than the Issaraks—or that both the monarchy and the French were working to undercut them.[4] But American diplomats were aware of Cambodian dissatisfaction with the French, including irritation at the lack of any constitutional progress toward greater autonomy. Despite French professions that the modus vivendi of January 1946 was only a first step, an agreement clarifying the relationship between France and Cambodia had not yet been negotiated. Franco-Cambodian discussions took place in 1948, and in June Sihanouk announced that an accord was near, a pronouncement that was met with (apparently deserved) ringing skepticism in the nationalist press of Vietnam. Finally on 21 December 1948 the French proclaimed Cambodia independent within the French Union. Only in April 1949 did the French Union Assembly narrowly approve a new statute that replaced the modus vivendi, and a final agreement was not signed until late in the year. Sihanouk later said that the treaty gave Cambodia only "50 percent independence,"[5] and it is doubtful that this settlement had widespread support.

All of these developments led American officials in the region to become increasingly critical of the French—although they resisted calls for any direct American involvement to bring about a settlement. In June 1948 American diplomats meeting in Bangkok concluded that "over half a century of pre-war French misrule and oppression" had left "a legacy of hate." Nor could a military victory be expected. On the other hand, there was little American enthusiasm for the Issaraks. The Bangkok conference report described them as "a pack of conceited prima-donnas whose sole objective is the seizure of power for their own personal benefit." Their "typical patriotic activities" were "cattle rustling, highway robbery, village looting and occasional assassination," supplemented by gun-running and drug smuggling.[6]

The Americans also believed that Ho Chi Minh's Communist-led Viet Minh, which was fighting an increasingly bloody (and successful) war against the French in neighboring Vietnam, was sustaining the Issaraks. Communism had of course been a worrisome matter since the end of World War II, but over time the seriousness of the threat seemed to grow—at least from the American perspective. By the middle of 1949, with a Communist victory in China certain, the issue of Communist expansion had come to overshadow all other considerations for the United States. Should Southeast Asia fall to Communism, the National Security Council (NSC) concluded, "we shall have suffered a major political rout the repercussions of which will be felt throughout the rest of the world."[7]

In fact, there was a growing Communist movement in Cambodia. As Kiernan writes, by the end of 1949 "the groundwork for a communist movement had been laid, and the trend towards colonial emancipation was also irresistible. . . . The longer the French attempted to maintain their control of Indo-China by force, the stronger the communist elements in the independence movements there would become."[8] Apparent Communist ascendancy made American support for the French more likely, but it did not mean that the United States would support them without question. Indeed, as Kiernan noted, French intransigence could be viewed as playing into the hands of the Communists. Furthermore, some appreciation of the importance of nationalism continued to inform American judgments. NSC-51, approved in July 1949, concluded that nationalism was "the most potent idea in SEA," something the French failed to recognize.[9] There would, therefore, be tensions with the French. But for the Americans, preventing the further spread of Communism in Southeast Asia remained paramount.

Nong Kimny, the first Cambodian diplomat assigned to Washington, D.C. is welcomed at Union Station by John F. Simmons, chief of protocol of the Department of State, 6 April 1951. Department of State photo, courtesy of the National Archives and Records Administration.

This was apparent when on 7 February 1950, shortly after the French Assembly declared that the three countries of Indochina were autonomous states within the French Union, the United States recognized the newly "independent" governments in Cambodia, Laos, and Vietnam and tried to get other states to do so as well. Indian Prime Minister Jawaharlal Nehru had urged Secretary of State Dean Acheson in the strongest terms not to do this. And after the fact the distinguished Philippine statesman, Carlos Romulo, asserted that recognition of the French-dominated Bao Dai government in Vietnam was counterproductive since the United States was now directly associated with the "iniquity of colonial imperialism."[10] But the final Communist victory in China and the decision of the Soviet Union in January 1950 to recognize Ho Chi Minh's government in Vietnam convinced the United States that it had no choice.

Recognition was the first major step toward a more concerted American effort to contain Communism in Southeast Asia. The ink was scarcely dry on the instruments of recognition when the French ambassador to the United States, Henri Bonnet, began to press for military and economic assistance for use in Indochina. The perceived need to act quickly made it unlikely that the United States would be able to secure French concessions toward Indochinese nationalist sentiments in return for the aid. On 10 March President Harry S. Truman approved aid to Indochina (including Cambodia) in principle, and in May he made the final decision to provide $20 million in aid for the remaining six weeks in the fiscal year, with more to come later. No French concessions were demanded.

The North Korean invasion of South Korea on 25 June 1950 led to an immediate decision to increase military aid to Indochina. To implement this Truman authorized a special mission to Southeast Asia headed by John F. Melby, special assistant to Dean Rusk, the assistant secretary for Far Eastern affairs. The Melby mission, which spent several weeks in the region, encountered considerable skepticism among American diplomats that American aid would do much good. Many thought Indochina a "nightmare." Most pessimistic was Ambassador to Thailand Edwin F. Stanton, who opposed all but token military aid to Southeast Asia because he considered the game already "lost and there is no point in kidding ourselves about it." An equally pessimistic (and in retrospect realistic and thoughtful) appraisal came not from Southeast Asia but from George Kennan, who told Acheson that the situation in Indochina was "basically hopeless" and that the United States should encourage the French to withdraw from the region and let events take their own course, even if this meant Viet Minh control of Vietnam. Melby disagreed, but neither he nor anyone else thought that the situation was susceptible to a military solution.[11]

In light of the newly established policy, along with growing criticism from Republicans that the Truman administration had not been sufficiently tough on the Communists, the doubters had no impact on policy. In December the United States signed a mutual defense assistance agreement with Cambodia and the other countries of French Indochina, and over the next four years the United States provided Cambodia with at least $7,800,000 in economic and military assistance.

Meanwhile, now that the State Department finally had a diplomat stationed in Phnom Penh, the United States was getting much more informed reports of developments there. Politically, relations between the French and Cambodians were tense. Also, rebel activity was once again beginning to pose a serious threat. Don V. Catlett, the American chargé d'affaires ad interim in Phnom Penh, reported that there were bands of Issaraks and Viet Minh at large and certain areas were unsafe. "Any person who has traveled on the railroad from Phnom Penh to Battambang and has seen the burned-out rail stations along the route will not agree that Cambodia is entirely peaceful," he wrote.[12] Such reports were on target. The dissidents—Communist and non-Communist alike—had increased their control over rural areas of Cambodia (they claimed to control one-third of the country). In April 1950 about 200 delegates from various rebel groups met to form the Samakhum Khmer Issarak, or Unified Issarak Front. At least five of the fifteen members of the executive committee were members of the Indochinese Communist Party. At the end of the year Alliance missionaries reported that "conditions in large areas of the field are extremely unsettled and dangerous."[13] Unquestionably the dissidents were on the move.

The Americans were cheered, however, by several developments, most notably the return of Son Ngoc Thanh from France at the end of October 1951. He told an American diplomat that the "first problem of Cambodia" was to end the rebellion.[14] Over 100,000 Cambodians turned out to greet Thanh, a public display of affection that irritated Sihanouk. Now back in Cambodia Thanh enjoyed great prestige as an elder statesman. Thus at the end of 1951 the American perception of Cambodia was of a country that was making political progress. The security situation was worrisome but by no means hopeless. American assistance was beginning to flow. Son Ngoc Thanh had come home. All in all the United States felt vindicated in its policy of assisting Cambodia and urging other countries to recognize Sihanouk's government.

Indicative of the good relations between the two countries and in appreciation for American aid, Sihanouk decided to send Truman a white elephant. After an article about the matter appeared in the *Junior Scholastic*, school children wrote to the president imploring him to accept the gift, despite Truman's alleged preference for a tiger. Animal trainers and circuses offered to care for the animal. The Southeast Asia director of the Isthmian Steamship Company in Singapore, which was transporting the elephant, sent the president pictures of the animal, which the crew had named "Harry," and arrangements were made to house the elephant in the Washington zoo. But unfortunately "Harry" died in Cape Town, South Africa, while en route.

The optimistic reports about calm in Cambodia were quickly dashed in 1952, as the resistance became more formidable. French security now estimated that more than 60 percent of the country was insecure, meaning that it was too dangerous to enter even with armed escorts. Particularly disheartening was Son Ngoc Thanh's defection. Convinced that the French did not intend to move toward real independence, he joined the resistance. Although Thanh denied being a Communist or having ties with the Viet Minh, American officials in the region quickly concluded that he was playing ball with Ho Chi Minh and was not to be trusted. Only later would the Central Intelligence Agency (CIA) work with him.

Hoping to forestall a Communist victory in Cambodia, the United States was now even more reluctant than ever to urge the French to make concessions to the Cambodians. Concern with Communism also meant that the United States was less committed to democratic rule in Cambodia and made no objections when Sihanouk virtually ended democratic pluralism in the country.

While Sihanouk was moving away from democratic rule in Cambodia, in Washington Dwight Eisenhower and John Foster Dulles assumed power. As the new administration was deciding what course to adopt, things began to unravel in Cambodia itself. In March 1953, a company from the Royal Khmer Army in Battambang defected to Son Ngoc Thanh, a particularly embarrassing development since in a major concession the French had recently transferred control of that region to the Cambodians. But more troubling were reports that Sihanouk, who was himself becoming increasingly irritated with the French, was planning an uprising against them if his demands for independence were not met.

Sihanouk had recently traveled to France to try and get an agreement. He was not well treated in Paris, and when there was no progress he abruptly left France and flew to the United States. He consulted with American officials, including Dulles, who urged him to cooperate with the French lest the Communists win. Angered at such lectures, Sihanouk arranged an interview with the *New York Times* in which he recounted the limitations France still imposed on Cambodian sovereignty and asserted that if independence was not forthcoming soon, his people, who did "not want to die for the French and help them stay," might "become part of the Communist-led Viet Minh." The story appeared on the front page of the Sunday edition.[15]

Whether because of, or in spite of, Sihanouk, there is no doubt that by 1953 most Cambodians desired complete independence. As Francis Valeo, Secretary of the U.S. Senate who was in Phnom Penh in the spring of 1953 with Senator Mike Mansfield (D-MT), recalled, "the passion in Cambodia in terms of independence at that time was extraordinary. I remember getting up in the very early morning and seeing hundreds of men walking around with wooden rifles, parading and drilling with obvious enthusiasm."[16] Sihanouk was ready to lead an all-out crusade to get the French to grant his country complete independence.

Sihanouk's moves made the Americans very nervous and forced the new administration to review its options. But in the end the king was able to force negotiations. When a preliminary agreement was initialed on 9 May, the Americans were pleased because, as the State Department told the Cambodian ambassador, Sihanouk could then "resume the leadership of the struggle of his people against Communist aggression."[17] But within days Sihanouk decided that the tentative agreement was unacceptable. In a bold move, he left Phnom Penh for what American Chargé Joseph Montllor described as a

"rebel tour" of the northwestern provinces where he sought to secure Issarak support and perhaps make contact with Son Ngoc Thanh. Then he
went into voluntary exile in Bangkok.[18]

Sihanouk's rejection of the accord was a dangerous gamble because it
could have led to the reimposition of direct French rule. Many in the
French government thought Sihanouk irrational, even crazy, and racial
stereotypes colored their reports. But both Jean Risterucci, the French High
Commissioner in Cambodia, and General Pierre de Langlade, the French
military commander, admitted that there was a certain method to the
king's madness and concluded that the only solution was to grant Cambodia's demand for independence. Then, Langlade stated, the French could
negotiate a treaty giving them all they wanted. After all, Sihanouk himself
had said, "give me complete independence, and I will lease Cambodia to
you for 99 years."[19]

By September General de Langlade was completely demoralized. He had
come to Cambodia a good friend of Sihanouk. This final assignment was to
be the capstone of his career. Now all lay in tatters. He told an American official that "he despised this country and its people." The Cambodian Army,
he said, was sympathetic to Son Ngoc Thanh, and the Viet Minh would
probably come to power soon. The time had come, thought Montllor, for a
new French general.[20] For his part, Risterucci saw anarchy coming and de-
spaired. The king was in mystic communion with the Khmer gods at
Angkor, and no one in the government dared to advise him. The economy
was collapsing before their eyes. The Thais were intriguing. It simply made
no rational sense. If negotiations broke down, he saw no other course than
to withdraw completely from Cambodia.

The Americans found all of this very troubling, particularly when Sihanouk publicly announced that Cambodia was a neutral country and invited the Viet Minh and Issaraks "to join in a popular front government."[21]
Senators William F. Knowland (R-CA) and Mike Mansfield lectured Prime
Minister Penn Nouth about his country's obligation to battle Communism,
lectures that only angered the king.

But within weeks Cambodia was independent in significant respects. The
Cambodian government had negotiated control of the police, the judiciary,
and important aspects of the military. The French still retained military
control over operations against the Viet Minh in certain districts, and some
French Union troops, which included Cambodians, were stationed in
Cambodia. On 8 November Sihanouk made a triumphal return to Phnom
Penh. When French colonial troops departed from Phnom Penh the next
day, Sihanouk (though not major Issarak leaders) considered the country
independent. (Only with the conclusion of the Geneva Conference in
July 1954 did the major Issarak groups agree that independence had finally been achieved.)

"Members of the Cambodian [military] mission confer with U. S. Army officers during their visit to Taegu, Korea." Army Signal Corps photo by Master Sergeant Kaye, 15 July 1954. Courtesy of the National Archives and Records Administration.

By 1954 it was a commonplace American position that stopping Communism in Indochina was vital to the Free World's security. One consequence of this kind of thinking was that the United States had provided France with increasing amounts of military aid to keep it in the war in Vietnam. The war had not gone well, however, and long before 1954 it had become apparent to the American government that there was no longer much support in France for its continuation. While American officials were not unappreciative of French domestic political constraints, they feared the consequences of adding Indochina to the agenda of the forthcoming Geneva Conference. Given the military realities (Defense Department maps indicated that the Viet Minh was in control of large parts of Vietnam and that "Communist" forces also controlled substantial portions of Laos and Cambodia), they particularly feared that any negotiations would result in a divided Indochina, which would "be a victory for international communism." There was, however, no choice but to go to Geneva. "We have a difficult negotiation ahead of us," Dulles lamented.[22]

Initially, the French resisted inviting any of the Associated States, including Cambodia, to take part in the Geneva Conference, fearing that if Vietnam participated it would be very difficult not to invite the Viet Minh as well. But the American government insisted that the states receive invitations, and France relented. But what about the resistance movements? Although there was some discussion of keeping the Viet Minh away from Geneva, even the United States had to admit that the revolutionary organization controlled a substantial portion of Vietnam and could not realistically be denied a place at the conference. But no one in the Western camp was prepared to admit representatives of the resistance movements in Cambodia and Laos.

From the beginning the United States held that the Cambodian and Laotian resistance movements were negligible (although there were private—and justified—doubts to the contrary). The Communist side did not easily concede that the Khmer resistance was insignificant. But in the end, Sihanouk's government (which negotiated fiercely at Geneva on its own behalf) and the Western powers prevailed. The Cambodian resistance was ignored: no rebel group was even present at the peace negotiations, Cambodia was not divided, and there would be no coalition government. The final agreements reached at Geneva provided for a ceasefire and a withdrawal of all French Union military combatants, as well as those "from other countries or regions of the peninsula" (a veiled reference to the Viet Minh). The forces of the Khmer resistance were to be demobilized, and some limitations were put on Cambodia's ability to join military alliances and to allow foreign military bases on its territory. Cambodia was, however, allowed to solicit foreign military aid and technical assistance "for the purpose of the effective defence of the territory." An International Commission for Supervision and Control (ICC) was established, consisting of representatives from Canada, India, and Poland, to supervise the cessation of hostilities. Finally, a Joint Commission of the military commands of Cambodia and the Viet Minh was to help implement the withdrawal of foreign forces from Cambodia.[23]

While the United States viewed the results of the Geneva Conference regarding Vietnam as decidedly mixed, it was pleased with provisions affecting Cambodia. The country remained undivided, and now with complete independence the Americans hoped there would be more incentive to resist Communism. Long-time American missionaries on the ground in Phnom Penh found the new developments very much to their liking, and their statements reflected general American optimism that a new day had dawned. Although not so long ago they had been skeptical of Cambodian abilities, they found they welcomed independence. Attitudes toward Americans were "very favorable," they reported. The new constitution guaranteed religious liberty, and, unlike the French, the government was favorable to their work. "We sometimes feel we must pinch ourselves to make sure we are still in the same country where preaching the gospel has been severely hampered by the authorities and circumstances in the past," wrote one.[24]

But it would take a deft diplomacy to maintain American influence in Cambodia, which had opted for nonalignment, while at the same time the United States supported Cambodia's antagonistic and staunchly anti-Communist neighbor, South Vietnam. Whether the United States would be able to do this remained to be seen.

From Optimism to the
Year of Troubles, 1954–1960

"There is a general failure in Cambodia to recognize the nature and extent of the communist threat."—Charles A. Sullivan, 24 August 1954

"CINCPAC [Commander in Chief, Pacific] considered Cambodia as the hub of the wheel in Southeast Asia."—MAAG Chief Brigadier General Edwin S. Hartshorn Jr., 5 August 1958

A MAJOR COMPLICATION with respect to efforts to increase American influence in Cambodia was the continuing French presence in the country. Having lost influence in Vietnam, the French wanted to sustain and even increase their influence in Laos and Cambodia. They particularly wanted to retain their role in training the Cambodian military and reportedly tried to prevent the Cambodians from even talking with the Americans about military training.

While the Americans could understand and even sympathize with French psychological needs, they considered the French advisers incompetent and wanted them to withdraw, if not immediately, then eventually. The Americans badly wanted to supply and train the Cambodian military because they thought the Cambodian Army and police were unprepared to cope with Communist subversion and infiltration. Most fundamental of all, the Americans believed that the Cambodians themselves were naive about the Communist threat. "There is a general failure in Cambodia to recognize the nature and extent of the communist threat," read one representative—and by no means the most alarmist—American analysis.[1]

Furthermore, while the Cambodians wanted American aid, they were hesitant to ask the French to leave, much to the annoyance of Ambassador Robert McClintock. However, given Cambodian reluctance to request the withdrawal of French advisers, McClintock agreed that the advisers could be gradually phased out, rather than being replaced prior to the signing of a military assistance agreement with the United States. Indeed, he argued, it was only sensible to retain French instructors until such time as the United States could provide replacements. Dulles concurred. But the Defense department was not yet persuaded, and that, along with French pressure on the Cambodians, delayed an agreement. President Eisenhower himself ultimately had to resolve the dispute between the State and Defense Departments. On 19 February 1955 he approved Dulles's plan, which would allow the French to continue their training mission, provided the Americans retained control over how American funds and equipment were used by having the chief American military officer in Cambodia become the king's military adviser; his advice would be channeled through the king to the French training mission. The secretary was now free to negotiate with the French and the Cambodians.

The first discussions took place two weeks later in Phnom Penh, when Dulles himself traveled to Cambodia, the first visit ever by an American secretary of state to that country. Dulles presented the formula to Sihanouk, as well as to other officials, who thought it might work. Nevertheless, the Cambodians were not enthusiastic about the American proposal. They feared that a strong American presence in their country would compromise their sovereignty and have too much influence on their independent foreign policy. Sihanouk's trip to India in March, during which Prime Minister Jawaharlal Nehru presumably encouraged a neutralist course, reinforced Cambodian uneasiness about an agreement. Further encouraging caution, the opposition Democratic Party began to argue that the current caretaker government was not competent to negotiate any international agreements. Strongly anti-American articles began to appear in the opposition press. McClintock even suspected, perhaps correctly, that the Democrats were secretly doing Sihanouk's bidding. In sum, it would be a mistake to blame Cambodian procrastination entirely on the French.

Nevertheless, on 16 May 1955 the United States and Cambodia signed a Military Defense Agreement (MDA) that provided for an American Military Assistance Advisory Group (MAAG)—Cambodia was the only professedly neutral country in the world where the United States established a MAAG. It is not yet clear how all of the obstacles were removed so quickly. But it appears that Dulles took the matter directly to the president, who again overruled the Defense Department. The MDA was consistent with a course Dulles had suggested the previous January: the United States agreed to establish a "logistics MAAG" whose sole responsibility would be to bring in supplies for the Cambodian Army. The issue of who would train the Cambodian Army remained to be settled; for the moment the French were left in charge.

Reaction to the agreement was initially muted, but hostility to it surfaced soon enough. To varying degrees France, India, the People's Republic of China (PRC), the Democratic Republic of Vietnam, some Cambodians, and the ICC opposed the agreement. The French, of course, had long argued that any arrangement that replaced them as military trainers would violate at least the spirit of the Geneva Accords, and even though the U.S.–Cambodian agreement did not provide for American training, the French knew that the Americans wanted to take over. As the Australian legation pointed out, thirty American military officers were to be assigned to Phnom Penh, when six or seven could carry out the logistics tasks outlined in the agreement. The suspicions that a training role for MAAG was envisioned in the near future were accurate. As an NSC paper put it, the MAAG was to be "prepared after 1 July 1955 to assume increased responsibilities for training."[2]

The criticism of the agreement from the French and others forced Sihanouk to defend the agreement more vigorously and publicly than he wanted to. At a rally organized by Sihanouk's political organization, the Sangkum Reastr Niyum (People's Socialist Community), the prince (Sihanouk had abdicated as king so that he could play a more active political role) "raved against opposition and sweepingly defended American aid." The Americans took heart that the former king was so adamant in his support of the agreement and "seems to discover new reasons for saying nice things about US."[3] In an election on 11 September 1955 the Sangkum swept to victory, gaining (according to the official count) 83 percent of the vote and winning every seat in the national legislature. Although, as historian David Chandler writes, the results were "obviously cooked," the opposition was routed.[4] The elections in effect ratified the MDA and discredited those who opposed it.

Just how the agreement was to be implemented, what the relationship with the French would be, and whether the Americans would ever take over the training of Cambodia's troops remained to be addressed. The relationship with the French continued to be difficult. "Our French friends under cover are doing their utmost to sabotage our effort here," Ambassador McClintock wrote, although he thought the difficulties could eventually be overcome.[5] The American military continued to trumpet its constant refrain: it must have sole control of military training.

Meanwhile, Sihanouk's general attitude cheered the United States. With the overwhelming (if suspect) victory of the Sangkum in the September elections, Sihanouk was more willing to take pro-Western positions in public, and McClintock optimistically thought that the prince was "ready to slough off much of ambiguity surrounding previous pro-Indian type of neutrality, [and] align ideologically more closely with West." Nevertheless, the ambassador argued that the time had not arrived to approach Sihanouk about having the Americans take over the training of the Cambodian armed forces. But the military would not easily desist. At the end of the year the secretary of defense ordered that planning begin for MAAG to "take over all training of Cambodian Armed Forces."[6]

The year 1956 began on a good note when the Cambodian prime minister stated that Cambodia was deeply grateful for American assistance. But tensions soon reemerged as Sihanouk moved increasingly toward a neutralist position. Hints of the prince's orientation emerged in remarks he made while in France. On 10 January he publicly complained that American assistance to his country had caused him "terrible troubles" *("ennuis terribles")* because the Americans were not happy with Cambodia's international posture. France by contrast provided aid without strings, he stated.[7]

Sihanouk's more outspoken neutralism produced a vigorous debate among American officials. Some argued that the time had come to cut back support for a country that refused to toe the American line. Why, they argued, should the United States support Cambodia when it was hard pressed to give adequate aid to reliable allies, such as the Philippines or Thailand? Others, however, contended that Cambodia was still staunchly anti-Communist at home. Its neutralism might be irritating, but the main thing was to keep it out of Communist hands and thus prevent the spread of Communism in Southeast Asia. From this perspective it remained important to continue assistance to Cambodia.

Deepening this debate was Sihanouk's decision in 1956 to visit Peking (Beijing). Although the Americans did not try to stop the trip, they were determined to try to prevent Cambodia from recognizing the Chinese government. The Cambodians almost certainly concluded that American irritation at their actions went beyond verbal harangues. From their perspective, a Thai decision to give aid to Son Ngoc Thanh, as well as South Vietnam's imposition of an economic embargo on the kingdom, was due to American influence, the result of vexation at Sihanouk's proposed visit to China. The American ambassador termed these fears "fantasies" but admitted that they worsened the political atmosphere.[8]

American irritation did not change Sihanouk's plans. He proceeded to visit Peking, was photographed in friendly poses with Chinese leaders, and made a number of comments that could not have been reassuring to the Americans. He explicitly rejected the protection of the Southeast Asia Treaty Organization (SEATO), although American intelligence reports insisted that his privately expressed views were different. He said that commercial relations between Cambodia and China would begin soon and expressed the hope that cultural exchanges would be established before long as well. Of most concern to the United States, the prince reportedly said that the "time is ripe" to establish diplomatic relations between the two countries.[9] He then returned to a tumultuous (though perhaps rehearsed) welcome in Phnom Penh. On hand to greet him at the airport were local pro-Communist Chinese. Shortly thereafter in a speech to the National Assembly the prince contrasted the American approach to foreign assistance with the unconditional aid China had offered.

Some Americans concluded that Sihanouk was not only not pro-American but was actually "promoting pro-Communist policies," as Admiral Felix B. Stump put it. "I think it is about time for the US to make some reaction other than turning the other cheek when neutralists and others spit in our face," he wrote colorfully. American taxpayers were tired of providing "aid for pussyfooters."[10] But others took a less panicky view. Although Sihanouk was often trying and Cambodian foreign policy naive, they thought the Cambodians ultimately understood the dangers of moving too close to the Communist powers. McClintock reminded Stump that the country was "still without Communist taint." If the United States stopped military assistance, however, the Communists would soon win, he concluded.[11]

McClintock appeared to have the correct analysis, for Sihanouk soon began to speak favorably of the United States again, referring several times to the American ambassador as "Mon Ami."[12] Important causes of Sihanouk's rhetorical change included the transfer on 14 March 1956 of eight American L-19 aircraft to the Cambodian Air Force and, more importantly, the American decision to inform him of an approach from his nemesis, Son Ngoc Thanh, who had urged the United States to intervene against the prince. But within a few weeks Sihanouk had reversed himself and once again began to accuse the United States of instigating Thai and South Vietnamese actions against Cambodia as a way of forcing Cambodia to join SEATO.

As a result, political pressure grew in the United States for a cutback, perhaps even an elimination, of American aid to Cambodia—particularly when in June Cambodia and China signed an aid agreement giving Cambodia $22.8 million over two years in economic assistance primarily to build factories, irrigation systems, and other kinds of infrastructure. By the end of the year Sihanouk would also travel to Moscow and several other Communist countries, including Poland, Yugoslavia, and Czechoslovakia. Sihanouk also suggested that Cambodia should accept a representative from North Vietnam equal in status to the South Vietnamese representative in Phnom Penh.

McClintock put much of the blame for Cambodia's continuing neutralism on India, especially the nefarious influence of "a psychotic young [Indian] Chargé d'Affaires, warmly seconded in Delhi by the equally psychotic Krishna Menon." But he continued to argue that Cambodia's neutralism deserved American support. Over time, he was convinced that Sihanouk would see the advantages of allowing the United States to train the Cambodian armed forces. In sum, the ambassador did not seem to want a basic change in policy, and for the moment he was reassured. "There will be no radical change in our policy," Assistant Secretary of State Walter S. Robertson assured McClintock.[13]

However, at just that moment there was talk of adopting a new policy that would permit an effort to replace Sihanouk. Late in August the National Security Council took up the issue, as part of a larger review of policy toward Southeast Asia generally. Eisenhower was present for the lengthy discussion and took an active part. There was considerable debate about how to approach the issue of military and economic aid to countries that were not part of regional security arrangements, versus those that were. Arthur W. Radford, representing the Joint Chiefs, took a hard line, whereas Dulles insisted that what mattered was what was in the best interests of the United States. Under certain circumstances, that might mean favoring a neutral country over an American ally. In a surprising statement, given his public rhetoric about neutrality, Dulles said that "he would rather see us lose Thailand, an ally, than to lose India, a neutral." Eisenhower sided with Dulles.[14]

Most of the debate about assisting neutrals focused on Burma, however. Opinion on Cambodia was less divided—and more negative. In preparation for the meeting Eisenhower was informed that efforts to strengthen Cambodia's ties to the West had "lost ground" and that the recommendations being proposed took "into account the recently increased trends towards pro-Communist neutralism" in Cambodia.[15] In the end the NSC sanctioned support to anti-government forces in Cambodia. It would be American policy (outlined in NSC 5612/1) to "encourage individuals and groups in Cambodia who oppose dealing with the Communist bloc and who would serve to broaden the political power base in Cambodia." The United States would also provide "modest military aid for indigenous armed forces capable of assuring internal security." This ambiguous language left open the possibility that the United States would support dissident armed movements deemed to be anti-Communist in orientation.[16]

By early October 1956 the Americans were considering replacing Sihanouk. McClintock now believed that Sihanouk was "a bad influence and the time might come when a Palace revolution might have to be arranged to remove him." According to Australian sources, McClintock's thoughts about eventually removing Sihanouk "came out much more clearly in private conversation." Among possible candidates to replace Sihanouk were Dap Chhuon, a former Issarak rebel who had surrendered to Sihanouk in 1949; Nhiek Tioulong, a man with a military background who was then ambassador to Japan; and Prince Sisowath Monireth, the minister of defense.[17] All three wanted to improve relations with the West.

It is doubtful that the Americans had decided unequivocally that Sihanouk must be replaced. It would all depend on what policies the prince adopted. Basically, the Americans were creating options for the future. For the moment Sihanouk's popularity within the country was recognized, and if he could be persuaded to be less open to the Communist powers, so much the better. But the United States also wanted to court the Cambodian military and potential dissidents who could implement pro-American policies and might serve as possible alternatives to Sihanouk somewhere down the road. To accomplish this, it now became explicit American policy to replace the French military training mission with an American one. But for the near term Sihanouk's cooperation would be essential.

One gesture designed to improve relations with Sihanouk was the departure of McClintock, for whom Sihanouk had developed a profound contempt. Despite his recommendations in support of Sihanouk's government at crucial times, the ambassador privately belittled the prince; it was McClintock who first referred to him as "Snooky." "McClintock was a martinet," recalled Frank Valeo, a staffer on the Senate Foreign Relations Committee and a close associate of Senator Mike Mansfield. "He carried a riding crop and he walked with two poodles wherever he went . . . ," Valeo added. "I'm surprised that Sihanouk never asked for his removal, but he should have at some point," Valeo said. "It would have done him some good and it would have certainly done us some good." McClintock's behavior, which Valeo personally witnessed while in Cambodia, made him "almost sick to my stomach. I'm sure that many of our problems in Cambodia had nothing more to them than this kind of personal clash with Sihanouk that started with McClintock."[18]

In addition to McClintock's leaving Phnom Penh, Cambodia's agreement to a substantial increase in MAAG personnel, and even to acceptance of two temporary mobile military training missions, improved relations. Also, Cambodia agreed to American training of some police technicians (the training to be done in Thailand), while twenty-five police officials, including Phnom Penh's police chief, came to the United States for four months of study. Soon Cambodia would send some military personnel to the United States for specialized training. By December, then, relations with Cambodia were once again on the upswing.

But relations became tense again as the year concluded. Perhaps Sihanouk's well-tuned antennae had picked up secret American attempts to forge relations with segments of Cambodian society that might in the future be encouraged to move against him. The overall international political situation in Cambodia was also more complicated by this time. Early in 1957 some of the promised aid from Communist countries began to arrive. In addition, Communist influence among the local Vietnamese population in Cambodia seemed to increase—or at least so the Americans thought. But more worrisome to the Americans were fears of growing Communist influence among the local Chinese. Sometimes American concern reached the level of farce. There were rumors that Chinese stevedores and barbers in Phnom Penh would soon demonstrate against the Americans because they had been told that the United States had given Cambodia aid on the condition that the stevedores and barbers not be allowed to carry on their normal employment.

Brigadier General Clyde Box greets Cambodia's Minister of Defense Lon Nol on his arrival at Ft. Bragg, 15 November 1960 and illustrates the growing American commitment to training Cambodian forces, despite bitter French objections. Army Signal Corps photo by Sergeant Betty Farmer. Lon Nol would later be instrumental in ousting Prince Sihanouk. Courtesy of the National Archives and Records Administration.

Thereafter Sihanouk moved back toward the United States for a time. He expressed gratitude for American assistance and brutally castigated the Cambodian opposition party for its allegedly pro-Communist views. Though the prince continued to accept assistance from Communist countries, few Americans charged with making policy thought it rational to eliminate American military assistance. The American purpose was "to deny Cambodia to Communism," even though the Cambodians could be expected to show little gratitude for assistance and would probably not even cooperate fully with American officials.[19]

Whether the Americans always got what they paid for was a matter of some debate. There was little question that MAAG had transformed the Cambodian military, particularly in terms of equipment. But the U.S. Army attaché in Cambodia detailed serious problems of graft and corruption, especially in the Cambodian Army. Military commanders reportedly stole

equipment and supplies, took bribes and kickbacks, lent money at exorbi-
tant rates to soldiers, and maintained false payrolls (what in later years
would be termed ghost soldiers).

In sum, with the advent of Communist assistance to Cambodia and the
prince's proclivity to visit Communist countries, the situation had become
more complex. The Americans nevertheless thought most trends were favorable. Sihanouk seemed to be aware of the Communist menace and had
taken steps to curb it, and there was little evidence that the Communists
had made headway in influencing the government directly. The decision
was made to continue American economic and military assistance, and the
Cambodians sent an increasing number of military and police personnel
for specialized American training. But there was also concern that the overall internal security situation had deteriorated "as a result of more vigorous
communist activity," activity made possible by Cambodia's increasing ac-
commodation with Communist countries.[20]

Overall, however, the United States was increasingly pleased with conditions in the country. Sihanouk's decision on 7 January 1958 to dissolve the
National Assembly demonstrated his concern with Communist influence,
the Americans thought. By calling for quick new elections, the prince could
preclude the Communists from preparing well for them. Therefore, although officials continued to feel that Sihanouk and other Cambodian officials remained naive about the dangers Communists posed to their country, the American embassy's year-end examination of American policy
toward Cambodia was optimistic and called for no basic changes. Above all,
embassy officials recommended continued support for Cambodian neutrality as the best available way to preserve the country's independence. For
the next several months American officials felt that events justified their
optimism. In mid-January, for the first time ever, there was a public demonstration against the "Khmer Viet Minh."[21] And on numerous occasions embassy officials reported that Sihanouk attacked Communist subversion,
sometimes viciously. Pierre Mathivet de la Ville de Mirmont, the counselor
of the French embassy, told an American official that Sihanouk "has had a
real change of heart with regard to Communism," an assessment that Thai
and Filipino officials shared.[22]

However, at the highest level it still remained official American policy
under certain circumstances to assist Cambodian dissidents against Sihanouk, a policy reaffirmed on 2 April 1958 in NSC5809. Some Americans
might have been tempted to look to alternatives to Sihanouk because almost immediately after new elections in March there were signs that the
Cambodian leader was again beginning to rethink his strong anti-Communist position. He remained "unconvinced of the sincerity of the United
States' acceptance of Cambodia's neutrality policy," reported the ambassador.[23] Cambodian concerns were doubtless not assuaged when in May the

Americans in Phnom Penh celebrated Cambodian Armed Forces day with a party in the government guest house, which they decorated with photographs of new American aircraft, rockets, and atomic submarines. In an adjoining room they showed continuously a film of Vanguard rockets taking off. The Australians found it a distasteful "Boy, Look what we've got" show. "And would anyone but the Americans have thought of giving a film show of their rocket devices in the Cambodian government's state guest house?" the Australian minister wrote in his diary.[24]

A particularly dangerous problem was the increasing number of disputes and armed clashes along the Cambodian-Vietnamese border. Many Cambodians, including Sihanouk, reportedly believed that the United States had incited the Vietnamese attacks.

Sihanouk's suspicions led to a debate among the Americans. Ambassador to Cambodia Carl W. Strom argued that Cambodia was "at a crossroads," that Sihanouk genuinely wanted a settlement with Vietnam, and that the prince felt "put upon and abandoned." He believed that his "Western friends have been indifferent in his time of trouble." It was vital to settle the problem, Strom thought, and the United States should take the lead. In Saigon, Ambassador Elbridge Durbrow emphatically disagreed. Cambodia was not at a crossroads, he wrote, "but rather somewhat past that point along road to left." Sihanouk, he charged, had "deliberately elected to exacerbate Cambodian-Vietnamese relations." The time had come "to call his bluff."[25]

The State Department sided with Durbrow. Sihanouk had no grounds for believing that the United States had incited the Vietnamese, wrote Under Secretary of State Christian Herter, and in any event the United States was not in a position to control Vietnam's actions. There was nothing dramatic that the United States could do, Herter concluded. Eleven days later Sihanouk announced that he would recognize the Communist government in Beijing. This constituted a grievous political setback for the United States, thought the Americans, and the State Department recalled Strom for consultations.

Never were the conflicting perspectives of Cambodia and the United States more clearly evident. The United States viewed Cambodia only as a part of the larger worldwide struggle against the Communist menace. Sihanouk, on the other hand, saw events much more in their regional context. It mattered little to him that the South Vietnamese government was anti-Communist, for example. What was important was that Vietnam represented a potentially mortal threat to Cambodia, a much more immediate peril than any posed by the Communist Chinese. Vietnamese actions had been the final straw in his decision to recognize the Beijing government. "No Cambodian would ever believe Chinese were more dangerous than Vietnamese," he told Ambassador Strom.[26] Traditional anti-Vietnamese sentiment was clearly in the ascendant and much more important than an abstract anti-Communism.

Two weeks later American officials gathered at the State Department to reassess American policy in light of Sihanouk's decision to recognize China. Despite their anger at his actions, there was little the Americans could do to punish him, tempting as it was to contemplate. Keeping Cambodia independent remained the paramount objective. As CINCPAC once put it, Cambodia was "the hub of the wheel in Southeast Asia," a view informally endorsed by the Joint Chiefs of Staff. Thus, there could be little change in American policy. Robertson summed up the frustration American officials felt: "Sihanouk would not live forever," he stated.[27]

The Vietnamese (and perhaps the Thais as well) were not inclined to let nature take its course. Instead, they actively considered attempting to remove Sihanouk from power through an internal coup d'etat, a possibility they discussed with American officials. The Americans devoted considerable time to assessing a coup's prospects. After all, the Americans had themselves envisaged such a possibility.

The idea of a coup first surfaced in August 1958 and continued to be discussed for the rest of the year. Ngo Dinh Nhu, brother of South Vietnam's President Ngo Dinh Diem, was an especially persistent advocate. Although there may have been some American interest in helping to organize a coup (this was, after all, only a few years after the United States had succeeded in covertly helping to overthrow what were thought to be pro-Communist governments in Guatemala and Iran and in stamping out a Communist threat in the Philippines, and it was currently supporting dissident military rebellions in Indonesia), the evidence currently available indicates that the Americans believed that there were simply no creditable alternatives to Sihanouk. Therefore the United States discouraged Vietnamese coup plotting. It did not, however, inform Sihanouk of the plotting.

As for Sihanouk himself, having recognized Beijing, he now "made an obvious effort to mend his bridges with the West."[28] While in New York, where he led his country's delegation to the United Nations, he visited with Dulles, whom he thanked for American friendship and aid, and presented an Angkor statue to President Eisenhower. Sihanouk enjoyed his trip to the United States. He spoke to the Asia Foundation and the Council of World Affairs, and in Hawaii was taken for a ride and a dive in an atomic submarine. He arranged for a reception on his return to Phnom Penh, one even more elaborate than on his return from China, thus giving the impression that his trip to the United States had been a great personal and national success. All in all, Sihanouk's trip gave the deliberate impression that he had "come back to a central position."[29]

Sihanouk's moderation did not impress the Vietnamese, whose desire to overthrow the prince reached a fever pitch in November 1958. On at least two occasions Ngo Dinh Nhu spoke with American officials, including the ambassador, outlining in detail how Sihanouk might be replaced. President Diem himself told an American official that Sihanouk ought to be removed.

The Americans ultimately rejected the Vietnamese advice, angering Nhu. Strom strongly opposed talk of a coup and argued that removal of Sihanouk would only increase Communist influence. Durbrow, too, saw many problems with a Vietnamese-initiated coup. But what is interesting is how tempted the ambassador actually was by the prospect of overthrowing Sihanouk. Durbrow told Nhu that "we had been thinking about the matter quite seriously."[30] In the end the United States rejected the idea of a coup and, from the available evidence, used its influence to discourage one. But it is apparent that the idea of American support to overthrow the prince was at the very least the subject of serious discussion and analysis. It was rejected mostly because it appeared unworkable, not because (Strom's comments aside) there was much objection in principle. In any event the plotting continued.

Early in 1959 the Soviet Union, China, and France informed Sihanouk that there was a plot against him. The conspiracy involved simultaneously the establishment of an opposition party, an armed insurrection near the borders, efforts to produce insecurity in the countryside, and an uprising in Phnom Penh itself. Cambodian authorities saw this as one in a long line of established, ongoing plots by Vietnam and Thailand aimed at settling accounts with Cambodia. When Sihanouk's government was brought down, a new Cambodian Republic would supposedly emerge that would be pro-Western and under the protection of SEATO. According to Sihanouk himself, the conspirators were "armed and paid from sources which were ultimately those of [a] . . . great western power."[31]

The plot was real, and its leader was Sam Sary, a prominent Cambodian politician, one of the founders of the Sangkum and, until recently, a close adviser to Sihanouk. In 1957 the prince appointed Sary, who had pronouncedly pro-Western views, as Cambodian ambassador to the United Kingdom where in 1958 he severely beat a Cambodian woman who had been his mistress, later explaining that this was a typical Cambodian practice. As a result of this personal scandal Sary was immediately recalled. Feelings against him in Cambodia were so strong (primarily because he had given the impression that Cambodians were "savages in the eyes of the civilized world") that one Cambodian observed that he would be lynched if he dared to appear at the forthcoming National Assembly meeting.[32] Sary's decision to go into opposition after his return to Phnom Penh could not have been a great surprise to Sihanouk.

Unquestionably the South Vietnamese and the Thais were involved in the plot, which very likely also involved Son Ngoc Thanh. But from the beginning there were allegations that implicated the United States in the "Bangkok plot," as it was now termed. The Cambodians (and the French) suspected that the legendary intelligence agent, Edward Lansdale, was involved. As Charles Meyer, a shadowy but well-informed and reliable French adviser to Sihanouk, told an American embassy official, Lansdale "was the key to the whole story."[33] The Americans argued vehemently that the United States was not involved in the plot. But few believed American denials, and Sihanouk once again expressed his suspicions of American complicity or at least of "individual Americans acting independently of USG [United States Government]," notably Lansdale.[34]

Whether or not Lansdale was involved, it seems likely that some American intelligence operatives were. The Australian minister reported in a personal letter that he thought it probable. "We have no doubt that the ambassador would have quashed any such activity at once," he wrote, "but when the Counsellor, [Edmund] Kellogg, was questioned to-day by the French Counsellor, Mathivet (who came to see him with the plea to avoid involvement at all costs, if rumours of involvement were in fact well founded)[,] Kellogg behaved as though he knew CIA had been engaged in something of the sort. The U.K. Chargé d'Affaires had a similar interview with Kellogg and got the same impression."[35] Two weeks later the Australians reported that French officials in Vietnam were convinced of American involvement.

While Cambodian suspicions about American involvement in the Sam Sary affair were still strong, Dap Chhuon, the governor of Siem Reap Province, decided to break with the prince and join the rebels. Chhuon had grown disenchanted with the prince's courting of Communist China, and in July 1957 he was dropped from the cabinet and relegated to Siem Reap. He sent his brother to tell Strom that "his determination to see Cambodia remain independent could prove superior to his loyalty to the Prince."[36]

In the month or so before his break, Chhuon had become increasingly defiant toward Sihanouk's government. He refused to let army officers inspect Siem Reap's military establishment, nor did he attend the wedding of Sihanouk's daughter, Bopha Devi, and the aircraft sent to fetch him came back empty. Finally, he sent a letter to the queen saying that he was going into rebellion to save the monarchy from Communism.

Chhuon initially managed to elude General Lon Nol's troops, who went to Siem Reap to capture him. (He was later killed.) But the troops did search Chhuon's house, in which they found evidence that demonstrated "beyond doubt" that the governor was "engaged in treasonable activities and was in regular communication with foreign countries." Soon Sihanouk triumphantly summoned the diplomatic corps to Siem Reap, where he laid out the impressive evidence. For Western representatives the event was one of "great discomforture" since Sihanouk explained that Chhuon wanted to overthrow the monarchy because he disagreed with its neutralist posture; he was a partisan of the West who supported SEATO.[37]

The evidence of Vietnamese involvement was overwhelming. And, although Sihanouk doubtless suspected that the United States was involved in the Dap Chuuon rebellion, he did not immediately make such a charge. Instead, even before he took the foreign representatives to Siem Reap he wrote directly to President Eisenhower asking him to rein in the Thais and the South Vietnamese. Could the United States not intervene with them, he pleaded, particularly since they received such significant amounts of American assistance? Could the United States at least insist that they not provide American arms to the rebels, something which was against American policy? The prince insisted that Communism had no attraction for him personally nor for his people.

The various conspiracies led to a major debate within the American diplomatic community and among the country's allies that, in important respects, would not be resolved for several months. From the beginning Strom argued, as he had before, that the United States must condemn plots against Sihanouk and take strong action against South Vietnam and Thailand. That Vietnam was an ally did not exempt it from criticism, he thought. If it failed to do so, thought Strom, all of the ingredients were there for a major debacle.

"Sihanouk is not a Communist and I am convinced he will not willingly allow his country [to] come under Communist control," Strom wrote on 3 March 1958. "I am equally certain that more incidents . . . will drive him irretrievably into Communists' arms." The United States must stand up to Diem. Once the problems with Vietnam were ameliorated, Cambodia's "natural resistance to Communism will come into effect," he predicted.[38] Ambassadors U. Alexis Johnson in Bangkok and Elbridge Durbrow in Saigon, on the other hand, were more equivocal. Eventually the Strom approach would win out, but not for many months.

While the State Department procrastinated, a new and potentially serious wrinkle developed in mid-March 1959 when, under interrogation, the Vietnamese technicians revealed that the radios found in Chuuon's home were delivered by Victor Matsui, a second secretary (but actually an intelligence agent) in the American embassy in Saigon. Sihanouk told the British ambassador, quite accurately, that the involvement of Matsui and another American (whom he did not name) constituted definite proof of American complicity in the Dap Chhuon plot. But for the moment he took no action, although he may discreetly have let the Americans know that he knew about Matsui.

A recently released document adds to the evidence that Sihanouk's suspicions about American foreknowledge of, and involvement in, the Dap Chhuon plot were well founded. In September 1959, several months after the events, Ambassador Strom, by then transferred to La Paz, Bolivia, wrote a personal letter to his successor in Phnom Penh, William C. Trimble. It is worth quoting the letter at length:

There was a good deal about the fracas last January and February that I did not understand. On January 20 Alex Johnson received the most precise instructions for representations of an emphatic nature to the Thais. He carried out his instructions to the letter and the Thais withdrew from the plot. Durby [Durbrow] did not get instructions until February 3 or 4 and they were discretionary rather than peremptory as in Alex's case. Durby reported that in his estimation the plot was tapering off and he did not carry out his instructions until February 14. In the meantime, on February 7, Diem sent his radio equipment, gold, technicians, etc., to Siemreap and was irremediably committed at the time representations were made to him. It was recognized from the start that the mainspring of the plot was in Saigon. What I cannot understand is that Alex should have got such firm instructions immediately, while Durby got only discretionary ones, two weeks later. I tried to run this question down while I was in the Department but had no success at all.[39]

Strom's letter makes it clear that the United States knew about the Dap Chhuon rebellion in advance, interceded strongly with the Thais (which the Americans thought had resulted in the Thais withdrawing from the conspiracy) but made only belated and weak representations to the South Vietnamese, who were more central to the plot. Strom did not overtly address the possibility of direct American involvement, but the failure to take strong action with the Vietnamese almost surely resulted from the participation of Victor Matsui and other intelligence agents, who were unquestionably a part of the plot.

Evidence of CIA involvement in the plot emerges even more clearly from Trimble's recently declassified oral history. American involvement appears to have begun in 1958 when Dap Chhuon's brother, Slat Peau, came to the United States on a U.S. government Leader Grant. While he was there intelligence agents contacted him, almost surely as a way of communicating with his brother. After the rebellion began, Sihanouk's forces captured Slat Peau and discovered the connection to the CIA. At that time Trimble was in Washington receiving briefings about his Cambodian posting when someone, presumably from the CIA (the name and affiliation have been redacted), told him that "an awful thing had happened." Sihanouk had discovered written messages, apparently from a CIA agent, to Slat Peau. Strom had denied to Sihanouk any knowledge of American involvement in the Dap Chhuon matter, and the prince not unnaturally concluded that the ambassador was lying—although he may not have been. (Trimble claims that Strom had not been informed of the connection.) Trimble recalled "hit[ting] the ceiling" when he learned of this and saying he would not go to Cambodia "without assurances that this type of thing would never happen again." Trimble claimed that the messages sent to Slat Peau by American agents warned Dap Chhuon not to rebel. But even if true, the messages clearly proved an American connection. Sihanouk had every right to be upset.[40]

Ambassador William C. Trimble with the Queen Mother Sisowath Kossamak Nearireath. From the Private Collection of Ambassador Julio A. Jeldres.

In any event, Eisenhower's response to Sihanouk, which was sent on 29 March 1959, over a month after Sihanouk's letter was received (a cordial interim reply had gone out earlier) reflected State Department reservations about being too sympathetic to the Cambodian case. The response reportedly disappointed the Cambodian leader. Even though the United States knew that Cambodia's neighbors were responsible for the plots against the prince, Eisenhower's letter made no such acknowledgment. Nor did the United States admit that its own intelligence agents had been involved, even though Sihanouk knew this, and the Americans probably knew that Sihanouk knew.

Helping to assuage Cambodian anger for the moment, however, was Eisenhower's decision to send former Ambassador to Laos J. Graham Parsons on a special mission to the region to see what might be done. Parsons's visit improved relations with Cambodia, largely because Cambodia wanted a change. Despite being allowed to use only unconvincing denials to allay Cambodian suspicions of American involvement in the plots, Parsons concluded that the visit "went as well as we could have hoped for."[41] The visit turned Parsons into a strong advocate of forceful diplomatic action against South Vietnam. He was impressed that Foreign Minister Son Sann documented his case against the Vietnamese "exhaustively and impressively," while the latter were entirely unresponsive to suggestions about opening negotiations. Indeed, they were in all probability still plotting the prince's overthrow. Parsons's final report amounted to a slashing attack on the South Vietnamese government whose plotting was, he wrote, jeopardizing "free world position in SEA." It was time for the United States to use the leverage it possessed against Vietnam, and he proposed reducing aid if needed.[42]

Parsons's strong recommendations altered American policy. The change was evident in a second Eisenhower letter to Sihanouk, in which the president personally assured the prince that the United States did not support any efforts to overthrow his government and would use its influence to encourage better relations between Cambodia and its neighbors.

Relations improved further when Secretary of the Interior Fred A. Seaton visited Phnom Penh in May to inaugurate the new American-built highway linking the capital city with the new port of Kompong Som, a project that had cost $33 million. By all accounts the visit was a huge success. Although Trimble found Seaton to be a "rather cold politician" who was nervous when he called at the royal palace, he could also be charming when need be. At a press conference Seaton emphasized American support for Cambodian neutrality and referred to Sihanouk as "one of the really great men of the world," a sincere sentiment.[43] Sihanouk in turn entertained the American in royal fashion, including hosting a performance of the magnificent Royal Ballet. In the aftermath of the visit, Sihanouk offered free land with no tax obligations for a new American embassy building, an offer that saved the United States at least $100,000. This did not mean that Sihanouk had changed his mind about American involvement in the plotting. But in light of Eisenhower's assurances, the Seaton trip, and evidence that the United States was intent on improving relations, Sihanouk was content to let these matters lie.

However, it was not an easy task for the United States to make strides toward a better long-term relationship because that required improving relations between Cambodia and its neighbors. Given the views of the South Vietnamese government in particular, this was a difficult, if not impossible, task. Ngo Dinh Nhu was the most important obstacle to peace. Nhu, who was in charge of the regime's covert operations, had little patience with those who counseled restraint. The Vietnamese continued to support Son Ngoc Thanh's clandestine operations.

Any prospect of a Cambodian–South Vietnamese rapprochement ended abruptly on 31 August when a bomb exploded at the Royal Palace in Phnom Penh, killing Prince Norodom Vakravan and a servant and narrowly missing the king and queen who had just left the room. It is now generally agreed that Nhu sent the bomb, apparently reasoning that with Sihanouk dead he could put Son Ngoc Thanh in as his replacement. Trimble was disheartened, fearing that the Communists would find a way to associate the Americans with the outrage. And in fact leftist newspapers in Phnom Penh were soon blaming the United States. Privately Sihanouk believed that there was an American connection with the bombing; American popularity hit a new low.

This time the United States did respond quickly to Sihanouk's request that it intervene with Vietnam. But Cambodian suspicions of the United States grew when on 30 September 1959—a month after the palace bombing—Slat Peau was tried and sentenced to death for his involvement in the Dap Chhuon plot. In his testimony Slat Peau confessed that he was the intermediary between Dap Chhuon and intelligence officials from South Vietnam and the United States, and he named names, in particular Victor Matsui. He also claimed that Chhuon's "radio circuit was [connected?] internally with the American Embassy and the Vietnamese representative at Phnom Penh, externally with a central station in Vietnam."[44] Although Sihanouk had known of Matsui's involvement early on, this was the first time that the information had been made public. The Americans, in other words, were now publicly and directly implicated in the rebellion, something they had repeatedly denied. The fact that American agents had some connection with the Dap Chhuon plot had profoundly negative consequences. As a State Department official put it a few months later, "the importance of this development in shaking Cambodian confidence in US motives cannot be overemphasized."[45] The official was right. Sihanouk never forgot the Matsui case and regularly mentioned it in future years. In 1964, for example, he told Ambassador Charles Bohlen about it. Despite the State Department's confidential admission that "Sihanouk had physical evidence" of Matsui's involvement, it continued to deny any involvement in the affair. Bohlen was told to disclaim any knowledge of the matter.[46]

Despite the strains, by the end of the "Year of Troubles" the United States was committed to move quickly whenever tensions developed. While the Americans were not willing to allow Sihanouk to call for them on a whim, they did, as Under Secretary of State C. Douglas Dillon put it, "promptly protest any support by Thailand and Viet-Nam to anti-Sihanouk dissidents."[47]

But a few weeks into the new year, 1960, an incident occurred that nearly destroyed the slowly improving relationship. In January a news magazine in India, *Blitz,* published a letter dated the previous September allegedly from Sam Sary to Edmund H. Kellogg, the former counselor and deputy chief of mission of the American embassy in Phnom Penh. The letter implied not only that Kellogg and Sam Sary were on close terms but also that the United States was aiding Sary, and it implicated Trimble personally.

Kellogg, who had left Phnom Penh the previous August, had at one time been a CIA officer and was not on good terms with Sihanouk. Trimble asked Sihanouk to suppress publication of the article in Cambodian newspapers, but the prince refused, saying he would be accused of yielding to American pressure. Angered, Trimble asked (unsuccessfully) to be recalled.

The Americans went to unusual lengths to discredit the letter, arguing that it was a forgery. But most Cambodians were certain that Sary had written the letter, and they gamely held their ground against strong American pressure. They received support from French handwriting experts, who concluded that Sary was the author. The Americans countered with U.S. Post Office experts, who concluded that the letter was a forgery, and not even a very good one.

The *Blitz* affair exasperated Trimble. "I am getting a little fed up with having a 'crisis' every three or four months," he wrote in a personal letter to Durbrow.[48] The next crisis, however, worked out to Trimble's liking. On 10 February (the very day Trimble wrote his letter to Durbrow) a young Cambodian, Reath Vath (or perhaps Reath Suong), entered the American embassy and requested assistance in his plan to assassinate Sihanouk (because of his foreign policy) during the prince's forthcoming visit to Svay Rieng. The Americans turned him over to the Cambodian police. Whether the man was a Communist agent, someone sent by Sihanouk to test the Americans or even to distract attention from the *Blitz* affair, or simply a deranged individual, was the subject of much debate. In a thorough review of the case John C. Monjo, the third secretary of the embassy, concluded that most likely Sihanouk had sent Reath Vath to test the Americans. Later the embassy concluded that he had been sent by local Communists. Whatever the truth, the Cambodian government blamed the deed on the Communists and praised the Americans for acting responsibly. As for Vath, he was initially reported shot by the police while allegedly trying to escape, although this seems not to have been the case, since in 1961 Sihanouk commuted his death sentence to life at hard labor. The following year it was commuted further to twenty years.

These various extraordinary developments—the Bangkok plot, the Dap Chhuon rebellion, the *Blitz* letter, and the Svay Rieng conspiracy—resulted in a review of the basic American policy toward Cambodia adopted in April 1958 (NSC 5809). The stated policy was that the United States should assist groups and individuals, including dissidents, who would work to stop Cambodia's drift toward a pro-Communist neutralism. But it was now clear that support for anyone other than Sihanouk was almost certain to fail. Therefore the Operations Control Board (OCB) recommended the NSC 5809 be modified. Containing Communism in Southeast Asia remained, of course, the objective, but the methods had to change. The United States should be more sensitive toward Cambodia's brand of neutrality, and it should accept "the urgent need" to "exert a moderating influence" on Cambodia's neighbors.[49] Trimble agreed that for the foreseeable future there was no one remotely as powerful and popular as Sihanouk, and therefore any policy that failed to take this into account was unrealistic.

Trimble was under no illusions that a change in approach would produce quick results, however. Sihanouk's "temperament does not make for an easy relationship," he wrote. Trimble's forecast was soon realized, for while Sihanouk praised the United States for its handling of the Svay Rieng conspiracy and again turned against the leftist press, his relations with South Vietnam continued to be poor. Consequently Sihanouk once again shifted leftward. In April 1960 he appointed the strongly anti-American Chau Seng to be Minister of Information, a move the Americans strongly disliked. (Trimble privately characterized Chau Seng as a "cryptocommie.")[50] Later the same month Sihanouk turned again to China as a potential protector and invited Zhou Enlai to visit Cambodia.

Trimble concluded that China had now established its influence in the heart of Southeast Asia, and he questioned whether Sihanouk's policy could be called neutral at all. The effort to revise American policy to one of accommodating Sihanouk was already in trouble. The State Department was less alarmist, however. A "residual, intuitive pro-West orientation probably continues to exist," concluded the director of the Office of Southeast Asian Affairs. Nevertheless, the United States made known to Sihanouk its unhappiness with the Zhou visit, representations one British Foreign Office official privately characterized as "rather clumsy," while noting pointedly that neither Great Britain nor France had joined the Americans.[51]

Sihanouk's anger at the United States seemed only to grow in the next few weeks, however. A recent history of Cambodia, written by Martin Herz, a foreign service officer who had been stationed in Phnom Penh in the mid-1950s, contributed to the prince's sour mood. Herz's book, Sihanouk surmised, was "written with the sole aim of besmirching me." An American official was physically roughed up, and "public attacks" on the United States "mounted to a level of bitterness, unusual even in comparison with periodic Cambodian tactics of this nature in the past."[52] In June State Department officials privately acknowledged that the United States had "no diplomatic influence in Cambodia whatever."[53]

Sihanouk's suspicions about the United States may also account for difficulties that American missionaries and their converts faced in Cambodia at this time. All of their publications were now subjected to "complete censorship." Evangelism and the distribution of their literature became "almost impossible," as Christian workers were detained and sometimes jailed temporarily. In Battambang the pastor and several members of the Chinese church were arrested. The authorities, read the organization's annual report for 1960, were "committed to a course that give little or no recognition of the Gospel."[54]

Despite the prince's actions, the United States decided on a cautious response. At the highest levels the United States continued to move away from its stated policy, which allowed support for dissident Cambodian groups. After several weeks of internal discussion, the NSC changed the official policy on 21 July 1960. No longer was it American policy to support dissidents in Cambodia.

The administration's new cautionary approach was soon rewarded. Official and semiofficial Cambodian publications continued to attack the West, but late in July they also began to attack the Cambodian left. When the left criticized Sihanouk's plans for introducing French and English instruction into the public schools, Sihanouk's fury knew no bounds. Khieu Samphan (who would later gain notoriety as one of the Khmer Rouge's leading intellectuals, then the editor of a Communist journal, *Observateur*) was attacked in broad daylight when Sihanouk stated that he could not expect police protection because he was so hated in the country. The anti-Communist campaign, with numerous demonstrations, marches, and speeches, continued for many weeks.

Meanwhile, the United States stepped up efforts to court the prince. When Sihanouk traveled to New York at the end of September to address the United Nations, for example, Eisenhower met with him at the Waldorf Astoria Hotel. One American official, who was present, described Sihanouk as "extremely amiable,"[55] although there were subsequent indications that he was upset—even "bitterly critical"—of some aspects of the treatment he received in the United States.[56] Among other things, he was accorded the shortest interview of any head of state.

The most difficult matter to be decided affecting American relations with Sihanouk at this time involved the question of supplying jet aircraft to the Cambodian government. The first rumors that Cambodia wanted to obtain a few jet fighters surfaced in June 1960. This put the United States in a potentially awkward position. The aircraft would add little to Cambodia's defensive capability, and providing them would only antagonize Vietnam and Thailand, which would also want American jets. On the other hand, to refuse them ran the serious risk that Cambodia would turn to China or the Soviet Union, which would probably provide them for the asking. Consequently, the United States did not dismiss the request for jets out of hand.

One difficulty was that the Military Security Act allowed assistance only to resist "Communist subversion." Since the jets, if provided, would be mostly for prestige and would bolster internal security only in a general sense, the policy would have to be modified. By mid-October a tentative American consensus was emerging around offering pilot training—but not the jets—while at the same time posing no objections if Cambodia purchased jets from "some free world country."[57] Cambodia's minister of defense Lon Nol forced the issue early in November when he visited Washing-

President Dwight D. Eisenhower meets with Prince Norodom Sihanouk at the Waldorf Astoria Hotel in New York, 1959. Courtesy of the Dwight D. Eisenhower Library.

ton and specifically requested two jets and training for eight pilots. Both the Air Force and the State Department supported the request, but the Defense Department was opposed.

Ultimately Eisenhower had to decide. In mid-November 1960 he offered immediate training for ten Cambodian pilots, along with other forms of military aid. Jet planes were not mentioned. The issue was left for the incoming John F. Kennedy administration. Eisenhower did, however, authorize the sale of 10,000 carbines for paramilitary forces and reduced planned cuts in other areas of military assistance. The prince thanked the president for his "very generous aid."[58]

Very shortly thereafter Sihanouk toured Czechoslovakia, the Soviet Union, Mongolia, and China, where he acquired a number of other assets including complete factories, dams, treaties of friendship, and, from Moscow, a technological institute. In Beijing Sihanouk signed a treaty of friendship and nonaggression with the PRC, implied support of China's position on Taiwan, accepted more economic assistance, and spoke in favor of the PRC's admission to the United Nations (not a new stand). But there was no indication that China had agreed to support Cambodia militarily in defense of its borders, and most important of all, there was no indication that Cambodia had accepted Chinese military assistance. Despite American anger at the trip, the United States could at least take some comfort in still being the sole supplier of military aid to Cambodia.

By the time Eisenhower left office, then, the United States had modified its policy toward Cambodia. Although it continued to see events from a bipolar worldview and was concerned about Sihanouk's increasing involvement with Communist nations, it had come to accept his leadership and his neutralism. As long as he did not lean too far toward the Communist countries, the United States intended to support him. In 1960 the NSC dropped its policy that permitted American support for Cambodian dissidents, and the United States was formally committed to trying to bring about better relations between Sihanouk and his neighbors. Whether the new policy meant that there were now absolutely no American covert activities of a contrary nature is difficult to determine. The Cambodians themselves thought that the United States had discarded Sam Sary but suspected that it was working with Son Ngoc Thanh. But for the moment the official American position was that actions aimed at undermining Sihanouk's government were counterproductive.

The prince, of course, saw events in Southeast Asia from a regional—rather than from a global—perspective. He worked assiduously to maintain his freedom of action and for the time being continued to maneuver successfully between the two superpowers.

A Casualty of War

"In what he has achieved in Cambodia Prince Sihanouk is an object lesson for Southeast Asia."—Marquis Child, *Washington Post,* 15 June 1962

"We have consistently underestimated Sihanouk's astuteness and ability and overrated his naivete and instability. In my judgment he and his principal advisors are exceptionally able and are playing their cards totally in terms of Cambodia's independent survival and other interests."—Mike Mansfield
to Lyndon Johnson, 9 December 1964

WHILE THE EISENHOWER ADMINISTRATION had reluctantly come to accept Sihanouk's neutralism, Kennedy was more positive about Cambodia's stance. This could be seen in his reactions to Sihanouk's calls for an international conference to address the war in neighboring Laos. The Eisenhower administration, while not rejecting the idea, had been decidedly cool. But Kennedy engaged Sihanouk in a lengthy and detailed correspondence about how the situation might be resolved. (Ironically, though, Sihanouk thought that U.S. delays in accepting his ideas—the result, he felt, of pernicious CIA influence—meant that the Communists would ultimately control Laos. The chance for a truly neutral Laos had been lost. The West, he believed, had already been defeated in Laos.)

The Kennedy administration also moved beyond the Eisenhower administration when it decided to provide jets for Cambodia, though admittedly it acted under pressure from a Czech offer to give Cambodia twenty MIGs. The United States hoped to supply four T-37 jets in time for the independence day celebrations on 9 November, by which time the Cambodian pilots would have completed their training. Sihanouk was pleased. In general, then, the Cambodian-American relationship appeared to be unusually healthy in the spring of 1961.

Late in May, however, an incident threatened to unravel the growing rapprochement. Sihanouk ordered the arrest of Kou Roun, the former minister of national security, in part because he was allegedly working for the Americans. This incident had the potential to poison relations between the two countries, since Cambodians still distrusted American intentions in their country and suspected that the CIA continued to operate covertly in ways detrimental to Sihanouk. They may have had good reason to suspect the CIA, for the Australian embassy in Phnom Penh commented at this time about "the still apparently independent activities of the CIA." But the prince, who was then deeply involved in international diplomacy of the Geneva Conference on Laos, declined to make the Kou Roun matter public. In July Trimble informed President Kennedy that in spite of Sihanouk's "cyclothymic temperament," relations were good.[1]

Sihanouk's experience at the Geneva Conference on Laos in July provided an additional opening for the United States—or at least so the Americans thought. He came back "disabused about the Communists," Walt Rostow advised Kennedy.[2] With Laos no longer a secure buffer to the north, Sihanouk might be unable to maintain a completely independent posture, American officials thought, and might have to accommodate himself to one bloc or the other. When Sihanouk visited the United States in September 1961 Kennedy engaged him in a serious discussion of current issues affecting Southeast Asia. He sought Sihanouk's views about Laos and spent considerable time discussing Vietnam with him. (Asked what was wrong with Vietnam, Sihanouk stated frankly that Vietnam could never become stable as long as Diem was in charge, for he was "not in touch with his people.")[3] At the end of the meeting Kennedy invited Sihanouk to return on a state visit the following year. Sihanouk appreciated that Kennedy had taken him seriously. Within days of the prince's visit the United States had airlifted earth-moving equipment to Cambodia to assist with flood protection for which Sihanouk, then in Hawaii, expressed his appreciation.

But while Sihanouk undoubtedly felt that he had received better treatment than on his previous visit to the United States, his private reaction was less enthusiastic than the Americans thought. He objected to his accommodations at the Waldorf Astoria Hotel, complained (apparently with justification) about his treatment in Los Angeles, and (more substantively) contended that Kennedy had pressed him insistently to join the anti-Communist camp. His discomfort probably accounts for his frank comments to the Asia Society in New York the day following his visit with the president, where he criticized American policy and recalled with some bitterness that in 1958 "several western agents and diplomats" were involved in the Dap Chhuon

President John F. Kennedy meets with Prince Norodom Sihanouk in New York on 25 September 1961. Courtesy of the John F. Kennedy Library.

plot. "I refrain from giving more details," he stated. The Communists, he noted, were much more subtle and effective in former colonial areas than the West.[4]

It was therefore not all that surprising that just as the U.S.–Cambodia relationship seemed about to reach a new level of friendship, it was stretched almost to the point of a break. On 23 October, shortly after Thai Prime Minister Sarit Thanarat had compared Sihanouk to a pig, the prince delivered a "highly emotional two hour speech" accusing Thailand of planning to invade his country, announced a total break in relations with his neighbor to the west, and complained about the United States.[5] In 1958 he had heard Eisenhower's sweet words, he said, only to find out that the CIA was simultaneously supporting Dap Chhuon and other dissidents. He implied that the same thing had happened this time as well.

The bilateral relationship nearly unraveled. Sihanouk quickly severed all air links to Thailand and ordered the MAAG not to work with the Cambodian military. Following criticism by the *New York Times*, Sihanouk lashed out at the United States, calling American leaders "the most stupid people in the world." The United States, he added, was now "my enemy." Trimble believed Sihanouk was "at least temporarily mentally deranged." A break in relations with the United States seemed possible.[6]

Alliance missionaries also noticed the cooling relations, despite the fact that they went out of their way to avoid criticizing the government. Their written materials now required clearance by three separate Cambodian ministries before they could be published, and they were having trouble getting visas and other necessary documents. "Compared with the previous decade, when we had great freedom to carry on our work," one of them reported, "restrictions of the past few years give cause for some discouragement."[7]

Cambodia's ambassador Nong Kimny tried to calm the waters, telling Assistant Secretary of State for Far Eastern Affairs Walter P. McConaughy that Sihanouk's speech was improvised, and much was lost in the translation. For example, while he did say that the Americans were stupid, he meant it in the French sense of "someone who is too generous or too indulgent." McConaughy replied that the Americans did not like to be called stupid even in the French sense but that he was glad to hear that Sihanouk meant no affront. (Privately McConaughy considered Sihanouk "a psychopath.")[8] Kennedy postponed sending Sihanouk an autographed picture. What particularly worried the United States was the fear that Sihanouk's remarks might signal a fundamental change in foreign policy away from nonalignment. Kimny promised to inquire. Much would clearly depend on the answer.

On 3 November Kimny reported back to the State Department. Instead of providing a direct reply from Sihanouk as to whether there had been a basic change of policy, Kimny called the department's attention to certain passages of Sihanouk's strong speech of 28 October which indicated that very small changes in the Western perspective would assuage the prince, in particular an admission that Cambodia's neutrality was not a problem for the United States. After some internal debate, the administration decided that this provided a sufficient base on which to rebuild the relationship, and a presidential message soon went to Sihanouk.

Just as a slight thaw was beginning to take place, on 12 November 1961 *New York Times* correspondent Robert Trumbell reported that South Vietnamese intelligence and American military authorities in Vietnam were certain that there were Viet Cong bases in Cambodia. Such allegations were not new. But they infuriated Sihanouk, who tended to believe that American press accounts were officially inspired. As they had in the past, Trimble and U.S. military officials in Cambodia came to Sihanouk's defense. Trimble said that the photographic evidence showed *Cambodian* military installations, not Viet Cong bases, and he urged Trumbell to take Cambodia up on its offer to visit the locations in question. Even more compelling was the testimony of General Edward H. ("Pony") Scherrer, chief of the MAAG in Cambodia, who insisted that he and other Americans had investigated reports of Viet Cong bases and had found none. "We believe there are none," he wrote.[9] Although some intelligence operatives, including Lansdale, believed that such views were naive, prevailing opinion within the State Department supported the American officials in Cambodia. "It is doubtful," wrote Roger Hilsman, director of the department's intelligence bureau, "that the Cambodian frontier has been of more than marginal importance to the Viet Cong effort in Vietnam during the past two years or so."[10]

In the end this issue, which had threatened to destroy the fragile rapprochement, actually helped to improve relations. Trumbell went to Cambodia and after a thorough investigation concluded that there were no Viet Cong bases there. (Privately Trumbell told American officials that South Vietnamese intelligence officials had duped him.) Thereafter Sihanouk praised Trumbell and the *Times* and was in much better spirits. Indeed Trimble found him positively euphoric at a party thrown for the departing Australian ambassador. Sihanouk played the saxophone and the clarinet, danced with the guests, and sang. The party ended so late in fact that it made the drive back to Phnom Penh difficult. The crisis seemed nearly resolved.

Early in December the United States turned over to Cambodia four T-37 jet trainers and two other airplanes at a ceremony at Pochentong Airport. Cambodian flyers, trained at an Air Force base in Arizona, did aerial acrobatics, much to the delight of the crowd. On 19 January 1962 the American embassy reported that a "phased return to normality" was taking place.[11]

But in 1962 the pace of hostilities in Vietnam escalated, complicating the U.S.–Cambodia relationship. Cambodia wanted to improve its police and armed forces to maintain better security in border areas, and it hoped for American support. The Kennedy administration was supportive, with Chester Bowles complimenting Cambodian accomplishments in the area of civil action and the fact that the peasants actually liked the army. But on one important issue the United States was unwilling to accommodate Sihanouk's requests: his desire to neutralize Vietnam. To this end he wanted to call an international conference, similar to the recent Geneva Conference on Laos. Unfortunately the prince found no support. Neither the British, the French, nor the Americans wanted a conference. Indeed, the United States considered it dangerous.

More immediately threatening to the improved Cambodian-American relationship were credible reports that Cambodian dissidents, sustained and encouraged by Thailand and South Vietnam, were again about to enter Cambodia to try and overthrow Sihanouk. A few years earlier such reports might not have disturbed the American government. But now the State Department moved quickly to inform Sihanouk of the information it had and pledged to support him; secondly, it tried (though without success) to discourage the Thai and Vietnamese governments from supporting the dissidents.

Another issue potentially affecting U.S.–Cambodian relations was cross-border attacks on Cambodian villages. Such raids were not new even in 1962, but as the pace of fighting increased in South Vietnam, there was more danger of serious incidents. One very serious attack took place on

21 January 1962 when planes strafed the Cambodian village of Bathu. The attack was almost surely deliberate, since the South Vietnamese suspected the village of harboring Viet Cong. Of great potential harm to American relations with Cambodia was the fact that American advisers and observers were present. If this became public, Trimble warned, it "could well do us as much damage as alleged US involvement [in the] Dap Chhuon affair [of] February 1959."[12] Fortunately for the United States, South Vietnam quickly accepted responsibility for the "mistake in navigation" and agreed to pay compensation to the victims. American involvement remained secret. The Bathu and other incidents, along with the various plots emanating from Thailand and South Vietnam, might have seriously damaged U.S. relations with Sihanouk. But Sihanouk, who was then attacking domestic Communists, chose not to use these matters to create a crisis in relations. Sihanouk later told Trimble that the Bathu incident was "just one of those things."[13]

Overshadowing these events, and ultimately contributing to the growing rapprochement, was a serious crisis involving an ancient temple. Preah Vihear (or Kha Phra Wiharn) was located in disputed territory between Thailand and Cambodia. Since 1954 Thailand had controlled the area, but both sides agreed to submit the case to the International Court of Justice. Each country had hired distinguished American lawyers: Dean Acheson presented the Cambodian case, while Thailand retained Philip Jessup. (When Jessup himself was named to the court, he had to give up his role as Thailand's attorney.) The case was heard early in 1962.

The Thais were confident of victory, and Sihanouk thought the decision would go against Cambodia. But on 15 June 1962 the court voted 9–3 in favor of Cambodia. Cambodia celebrated with four hours of festivity at the palace. Sihanouk's speech, according to an American diplomat, "resembled football rally following upset victory." The prince proclaimed a seven-day holiday and said he would shave his head in gratitude.[14] In contrast, the Thais were stunned and bitter. They resented Dean Acheson's role and surmised that he was working for the U.S. government. They saw a conspiracy to get Jessup off the case. There was a real possibility that they would not carry out the court's decision. And there were threats to shoot any Cambodians who crossed the border.

Washington feared the consequences. Secretary of State Dean Rusk stated that the Thais were "on the verge [of a] colossal international blunder" by rejecting the decision, and he feared they might even attack Cambodia.[15] The United Stated worked frantically to calm the waters. President Kennedy himself sent messages to the Thai king and prime minister. The United States also urged the Cambodians not to gloat over their victory— though without much success.

Fortunately for the United States Thai King Bhumibol Adulyadej insisted on caution, and in the end the Thais, while not accepting the decision, complied with it. Yet another crisis had come to an end, one in which the United States played a calming and constructive role. In mid-July Thailand surrendered sovereignty over the temple. Cambodian euphoria over the decision was doubtless a contributing reason that the Cambodian government did not make a serious issue of four more South Vietnamese incursions into Cambodia on 16 June, including another attack on Bathu involving fatalities. As before, Americans were present during the incidents.

With the potentially disastrous temple issue resolved, the United States hoped for a period of relative calm. But it was not to be. Even before the new ambassador to Cambodia, Philip D. Sprouse (who had replaced Trimble just as the temple case was being settled) was able to present his credentials to the Cambodian government, he found it necessary to confront Cambodian officials over the detention of an American official, Kwang P. Chu, charged with espionage. The Cambodians insisted that they had conclusive proof that Chu, a low-ranking official with the U.S. Agency for International Development (AID) mission in Phnom Penh (who was in reality a CIA employee) and another AID official, Samuel H. B. Hopler, were guilty. When Sprouse said that it was unbelievable that any American official would conduct espionage in Cambodia, Cambodian officials, no doubt recalling Victor Matsui in the Dap Chhuon case, "rejoined in almost inaudible tone that such had happened in [the] past."[16]

In the end, the Cambodians released Chu (who was badly treated in police custody where he was reportedly "subjected [to] inhuman imprisonment and painful, although not crippling or dangerous, torture"),[17] and Chu and Hopler were quickly, and very quietly, flown out of the country. The United States filed a stiff protest against the treatment accorded Chu. Fortunately for the United States, Sihanouk chose not to pursue the matter publicly, which would have had a seriously negative impact on Cambodian-American relations.

Frustrated with the apparent CIA meddling in Cambodia, irritated at insufficient military assistance, and angered at American unwillingness (as he saw it) to rein in the Thais and Vietnamese, Sihanouk announced on 20 August 1962 that he was calling an international conference to guarantee Cambodia's neutrality and its territorial integrity. Invitations went out to all of the powers that had participated in the recent Geneva Conference on Laos.

Most American policy makers did not like the idea of an international conference, which they feared would result in unrealistic international guarantees that would be cumbersome and potentially embarrassing. At the same time, the administration wanted to find some way to meet Sihanouk's legitimate desires to preserve his country's neutrality and territorial integrity. Therefore for the next several weeks the United States engaged in high-level, and at times frantic, diplomacy toward this end. At times the issue demanded the personal attention of the president. Eventually the United States proposed, as an alternative to a conference, country-by-country notes pledging to respect Cambodia's neutrality and territorial integrity. In response Cambodia proposed a protocol to be signed by all fourteen signatories of the Geneva Agreement on Laos guaranteeing Cambodia's neutrality, independence, and territorial integrity. The United States disliked certain aspects of the Cambodian proposal (including one that would have required the dismantling of the MAAG) and, while not rejecting it out of hand, suggested the establishment of a border commission and a declaration signed by Cambodia, Thailand, and South Vietnam pledging to respect each other's sovereignty.

Sihanouk was doubtless pleased that his proposals were the subject of intensive discussions in foreign offices around the world, and when in January 1963 correspondents for *Time-Life* interviewed him they found the prince in "one of his sunniest and more expansive moods." This, thought an American official, indicated a relaxation of "Princely tensions."[18] But in the end it proved impossible to find a formula acceptable to all sides. Some Americans, including Ambassador to South Vietnam Frederick Nolting, objected to any efforts to respect Cambodian neutrality, and predictably neither the Thais nor the South Vietnamese were receptive to any multilateral agreement with Sihanouk. The French objected to those portions of the American draft that seemed to call into question Cambodia's boundaries, which had been firmly established in 1946, and they preferred multilateral agreements to bilateral ones.

The possibility of an agreement also suffered a significant setback when Sihanouk, then visiting Beijing (where he received what can only be described as spectacular treatment), announced that he was no longer bound by a previous pledge to avoid public discussion of his differences with Thailand. This was because the Chinese (perhaps Mao Zedong himself) informed him of an alleged new plot by Son Ngoc Thanh supported by South Vietnam, Thailand, Taiwan, and an unnamed imperialist power. Sihanouk lashed out at his enemies and indicated that he would have no dealings with the present Thai or Vietnamese governments. The United States concluded that it could now only approach Sihanouk one step at a time, with Sihanouk's reaction and mood determining what if anything more might be attempted. Although desultory discussions continued with Sihanouk and other interested parties about a possible neutrality agreement, the United States never did present a complete draft agreement to the Cambodian government. The neutrality proposals continued to fester and proved to be a problem in American relations with Cambodia for several years to come.

If by late spring 1963 the neutrality issue had strained relations, the United States could take some comfort in other developments. Despite Sihanouk's red carpet treatment in Beijing, the prince did not get the economic or military aid he had hoped to receive from China. Thus the United States retained important leverage with its aid, which it thought was vital to

Cambodia's military and the civilian economy. In addition, Sihanouk continued his campaign against domestic leftists, which to a certain extent counter-
balanced his concern over the alleged Son Ngoc Thanh plot. On the other
hand, Cambodia accepted six MIG-17 aircraft and two antiaircraft batteries
from the Soviet Union. This was the first breach in the Western monopoly of
military aid to Cambodia, and it deeply troubled the United States. The Americans acknowledged Cambodia's right to acquire such weapons but pointed
out that the expenses involved in training pilots and maintenance made the
continuing provision of American aid to Cambodia problematic.

Over the next few months Cambodian-American relations slowly deteriorated. Sihanouk had more contact with Soviet bloc countries than with
the West, strongly criticized Diem's attacks on South Vietnam's Buddhists,
expressed outrage over air raids on a Cambodian village, and finally broke
diplomatic relations with South Vietnam, all the while blaming the United
States for losing sight of its own ideals. The relationship threatened to deteriorate further when early in September 1963 the United States declined to
support a Cambodian request to station United Nations observers along the
Cambodian-Vietnamese frontier. The drift toward a serious breach in the
U.S.–Cambodian relationship was beginning to accelerate.

The tragedy was that Sihanouk had no sympathy with Communism and
no illusions about the result of a Communist victory in Southeast Asia. An
independent Cambodia would not long survive such an event, he believed,
and he welcomed Western influence as a necessary counterweight to
Communism. But *his* method of resisting Communism, he contended with
considerable evidence, was superior to that of the West. He had defeated the
threat of internal subversion, and Cambodia constituted a much more certain
barrier to Communist expansion than, say, South Vietnam, where the United
States had made major miscalculations and errors over the years, making the
triumph of Communism more certain. The West seemed to feel that only
"blind, brutal and heavy-handed" methods would suffice, he stated.[19]

In October Sihanouk once again began to accuse the United States of
supporting Son Ngoc Thanh and Sam Sary. Indeed, secret Khmer Serei radio
broadcasts from Vietnam, after two years of silence, had started up again.
On 5 November, in what appeared to be a dramatic shift in his previously
expressed view that a Western presence in Southeast Asia was needed to
balance the Communist bloc, Sihanouk in a highly emotional broadcast declared that if Khmer Serei broadcasts were not stopped by the end of the
year, he would end all Western aid, turn to China for economic and military assistance, and even turn the country into a People's Republic. The fact
that the speech was subsequently published by the official Cambodian
press office indicated that it was to be taken seriously.

Among the more plausible explanations for the prince's statement was
his reaction to the recent overthrow of Ngo Dinh Diem in South Vietnam.

While Sihanouk deeply disliked and distrusted Diem, he suspected that the Americans were behind his ouster and surmised that they wanted to replace Diem with someone they could more easily control, someone who would pursue the Viet Cong more effectively and vigorously. This, Sihanouk may have reasoned, would end any possibility of neutralizing Vietnam, which the prince believed was the best solution. He also believed that the CIA might have the same fate in store for him as it had for Diem.

The American response was restrained. On Cambodian independence day (9 November) Kennedy sent a longer and warmer message to the prince than was customary, in which he indicated full American support for Cambodia's nonalignment policy. But on 12 November Sihanouk stated that it was not just the Khmer Serei that troubled him; American aid to the Khmer Serei, he said, "irritates me and Cambodians of all persuasions more and more." Should the aid end, he said, it would be an "immense relief to us." Sihanouk also responded angrily a few days later to President Kennedy's remarks at a news conference that urged Sihanouk not to surrender the independence of his country. No one needed to give him lessons about devotion to independence, he stated. A State Department official later observed that Kennedy's message to Sihanouk on Independence Day "made no impression whatsoever."[20]

Khmer Serei broadcasts resumed on 16 November, and Sihanouk asserted that the Cambodians knew precisely where in South Vietnam the transmitter was located (he even provided specific coordinates). The broadcasts, the prince said, bothered him so much that he was sick, could not sleep, and would "not have the strength to go on if they do not stop."[21] Rumors also circulated that a coup against Sihanouk was imminent and that the prince had named one of his sons to take over if he were killed. South Vietnamese Army units were put on alert. Sihanouk was clearly addled.

On 19 November, riled by the broadcasts, irritated at continual American denials of involvement with the Khmer Serei, and fearing that he might be assassinated, Sihanouk convened a special meeting of the National Assembly where he called for the immediate termination of all American aid. Given the seriousness of the situation, the State Department prepared a letter for Kennedy to sign, in which he categorically denied American involvement with the Khmer Serei and offered to send Dean Acheson as his personal representative to Cambodia to discuss problems. But it was not sent since it was overtaken by events. The next day the Cambodians informed the United States that they wanted an end to all American aid. They claimed to have specific proof, provided by a Khmer Serei agent, that "American agents were in fact the direct suppliers of arms, propaganda material and money" to the Khmer Serei.[22]

Although Kennedy's letter was not sent, the president, through Roger Hilsman, informed Cambodia's Ambassador Nong Kimny that there was no American involvement with the Khmer Serei. Kennedy may have been sin-

cere. He had to ask Hilsman what the Khmer Serei was. Kennedy administration officials bemoaned the fact that they were paying the price for the
Eisenhower administration's support of Cambodian dissidents. Sprouse had
told this to Hilsman, who passed it along to Kennedy. "Is it true?" Kennedy
asked. "Yes," replied Hilsman, "there was money involved. We are paying
for it all over Asia. . . . They did things we did not know about."[23] The next
day Hilsman discussed with Averell Harriman the alleged difficulties that
CIA activities during the previous administration were continuing to cause.
Harriman confirmed the allegations. "They were doing things against Sihanouk. They were doing things that looked suspicious," he stated, adding
that "it was crudely handled."[24] Whatever the degree of American involvement with the Khmer Serei in 1963 (which remains murky to this day), the
Cambodians were not alone in thinking that the United States could have
done more to stop the broadcasts. As Sprouse put it in January 1964, the
United States had not been willing in the past to mount an all-out effort to
stop Khmer Serei activities because of the Americans' "evaluation of com-
parative US policy interests in this area."[25]

Kennedy still hoped that there could be a resolution of the issues dividing the
United States and Cambodia. He told Hilsman that in three or four weeks he
wanted to send Dean Acheson to Phnom Penh. But Hilsman, fearing a leak,
thought it best to wait a couple of days before Kennedy contacted Acheson. Two
days later Kennedy was assassinated, and Acheson did not go to Cambodia.

Michael Forrestal, who was in Asia when President Kennedy was killed
and who wanted to return to Washington, was ordered instead to go to
Cambodia. In Phnom Penh, Forrestal told Sihanouk that both Presidents
Kennedy and Lyndon B. Johnson had personally looked into the charges of
American complicity with the Khmer Serei, and both had concluded that
there was none. Perhaps indelicately, Forrestal also told the prince that the
United States had tried very hard to pressure South Vietnam to stop broadcasts by Khmer Serei, which seemed to be emanating from Vietnam. The
prince was not convinced. He did not believe that the Khmer Serei could
operate in Thailand and South Vietnam without, at the very least, American approval. Given Sihanouk's obsession with the broadcasts, there was no
hope of restoring friendly relations with the West until they ended. (The
United States did put more pressure on Thailand and especially Vietnam to
rein in the Khmer Serei. It may have had some success this time with the
new Vietnamese government, but the American pressure only angered Thai
leaders. Foreign Minister Thanat Khoman claimed not to know anything
about the broadcasts, "but if he were asked, he would strongly recommend
that the broadcasts should continue.")[26]

Having determined that American military aid was not sufficient to safe-
guard his country's very survival, Sihanouk revived his neutrality proposal
and this time formally asked the co-chairs of the Geneva Conference of

1954 (Britain and the USSR) to reconvene the conference with a view to increasing the powers of the ICC to ensure Cambodia's neutrality.

While the Americans pondered how to respond, unexpected developments increased tensions. On 7 December Sarit Thanarat died. Sihanouk had particularly detested Sarit, and the prince called for a national celebration on learning of the prime minister's death. For two weeks civil servants were allowed to come to work two hours later than normal. Averell Harriman privately called the celebration "barbaric."[27]

The crisis was further exacerbated when Sihanouk delivered a speech in Khmer (which was broadcast the next day) in which he suggested that the deaths of Ngo Dinh Diem, Sarit Thanarat, and John F. Kennedy resulted from divine intervention to save Cambodia. "We had only three enemies, and the leaders of these three countries all died and went to hell, all three, in a period of a month and a half," he was reported as saying. "They are meeting there in a conference of the Free World's SEATO." Sihanouk also referred to the "great boss of the aggressors" who had met the same fate, an obvious reference to Kennedy.[28] Although Sihanouk's comments were in the Cambodian language to a local audience and did not appear in an official translation, the State Department protested in the strongest possible terms.

The Cambodia government disavowed any intention on its part to associate Kennedy's death with those of Sarit and Diem. Kennedy, the statement read, "was unanimously respected by all Cambodians." But Sihanouk was reportedly "incensed" at the American protest. Quite correctly he reminded the Americans that he had declared three days of national mourning when Kennedy was assassinated.[29]

Sihanouk now ceased negotiations on the modalities of ending American aid, ordered all economic, military, and cultural teams to leave by 15 January 1964, and recalled Ambassador Nong Kimny (who was reported privately distressed at the decision). Indeed, after initially deciding to leave the cultural attaché in charge, Sihanouk decided to close the embassy altogether after he learned that the Americans had used the term "barbaric" when they summoned Nong Kimny in to protest the Cambodian reaction to the deaths of the three leaders. This was, Sihanouk said, "contemptuous and gratuitous."[30] The United States began to reduce its staff in Cambodia to a bare minimum, and, after Kimny was recalled, Ambassador Sprouse was ordered to return to Washington. The United States was ready to close down and wait for better days.

Later, in justifying his decision to terminate American aid, Sihanouk recalled all of his problems with the Americans in the 1950s and early 1960s: American support for various Cambodian opposition movements, the failure of the United States to prevent raids by South Vietnamese forces into Cambodia, the American refusal to allow him to use American equipment to repulse the Vietnamese and Thai incursions, the huge amounts of aid given to Laos (when compared with what was given to Cambodia), the interminable time it took to get four *"avions à réaction"* (and then they came incompletely equipped), and in general the humiliating way he felt Cambodia had been treated. Although diplomatic relations were not broken, the Cambodian-American relationship lay in tatters. For the next seventeen months, until relations were severed in May 1965, "dealings between the two countries became a dialogue of the deaf."[31]

Initially, however, both the United States and Cambodia held out some hope that the breach could be repaired. Despite the fact that both ambassadors had been formally recalled, each country allowed its ambassador to remain for several weeks. The Cambodians wanted the United States to withdraw its "barbaric" comment and stop the Khmer Serei broadcasts. A positive response to Sihanouk's proposal for a neutrality conference would also have done much to restore the relationship. The Americans for their part hoped that the Cambodians would accept their contention that they were not involved with the Khmer Serei and had attempted to influence the Vietnamese and the Thais to stop the broadcasts. They also thought that the cost of ending American aid would begin to sink in and that the armed forces and other internal Cambodian influences might moderate Sihanouk's position.

The visit early in January of the French minister of armed forces, Pierre Messmer, did much to calm Sihanouk. Messmer offered arms and economic aid and reopened a friendly Western channel to the prince. Soon thereafter both sides accepted Philippine president Diosdado Macapagal's good offices to try and arrange a settlement. Considerable effort went into the attempt, but after some initial optimism the effort came to naught. As Sihanouk said in a news conference at Siem Reap on 11 February 1964, "there were too many 'things' between USA and Cambodia" to be optimistic about the mediation's success.[32]

Cambodian assertions that the United States was collaborating with Thailand, South Vietnam, and Son Ngoc Thanh to destabilize their country constituted a particularly important irritant at this time in the relationship. In February Cambodia accused the United States of helping the Khmer Serei form commando units to infiltrate Cambodia. The charges were accurate. John Shaw, *Time* magazine's Hong Kong correspondent, who had managed to arrange a special interview with Son Ngoc Thanh, reported that about half of the 1,000 Khmer Serei troops served in the Civilian Irregular Defense Groups (CIDG) funded by the CIA and led by American and Vietnamese Special Forces teams. They operated along the Cambodian border, Shaw wrote. The other 500 Khmer Serei operated independently.

At about the same time Military Assistance Command, Vietnam (MACV, which had replaced the MAAG-Vietnam) conducted its own investigation and identified even more Khmer Serei forces than the journalist. Of the

1,677 soldiers of Cambodian descent in "strike force companies," about 1,000 were believed to be Khmer Serei. Americans trained them. In sum, there is little doubt that Khmer Serei forces were integrated into the CIDG units, which the United States funded, trained, and commanded. Sihanouk's charges that the Khmer Serei served with the American Special Forces were entirely accurate. Equally, if not more, damaging were allegations that the United States had sanctioned military raids on Cambodian border villages. Sihanouk was infuriated when on 5 February 1964 South Vietnamese aircraft attacked the village of Mong (or Muong) two kilometers inside Cambodia, killing five and wounding six.

Contributing to Sihanouk's annoyance with the United States was the unfavorable American reaction to his renewed interest in an international conference to guarantee his country's neutrality and borders. This ultimately required a very unilateralist American approach, however, since the British and the French wanted a conference. By January 1964 the British were ready to present to the Cambodians a draft statement that all of the parties at the international conference would sign respecting the independence, neutrality, and territorial integrity of Cambodia. Sihanouk accepted their draft proposals for consideration at the conference and announced that he expected American acceptance soon. But the Americans said they would attend a conference only if all parties had agreed to a text in advance of the meeting. The Americans wanted the British to inform the Soviet Union about Cambodia's acceptance of their proposal, expecting that the USSR would reject the British proposal. Ultimately the tactic worked. The British, under pressure from the Americans, adopted the position that the parties should agree to their draft ahead of time, but the Russians were willing only to discuss the British draft at the conference. In the end, this difference stymied the calling of a conference, to the relief of the Americans.

Sihanouk then moved quite close to the American position when he offered to negotiate a quadripartite agreement with the United States, Thailand, and South Vietnam, setting a deadline of the end of March. But the Americans miscalculated when in response they circulated their own draft agreement, which, in the words of an Australian analysis, was "rather derogatory in tone" and which, by suggesting the establishment of boundary commissions to determine border questions, "appeared to ignore the various treaties" that dealt with the border.[33] Sihanouk condemned the American draft as a rejection of his own ideas.

The Americans later admitted that it would have been better to have simply gone to the conference. This was surely a correct assessment, for a day after the Cambodians rejected the American draft, a large mob, most likely organized by the Ministry of Information on Sihanouk's instruction and led in part by the leftist former Minister of Information (and current Minister of Agriculture) Chau Seng, stormed the American embassy.

Sacking of the American embassy chancery in Phnom Penh, 11 March 1964. This photo was found in a Khmer Rouge stronghold in Kampot province in 1971. Ambassador Emory C. Swank identifies "the individual in long sleeved shirt, tie and wearing sunglasses, apparently helping to direct the efforts of the mob," as Chau Seng, former minister and Sihanouk adviser who later went into exile in France. When the Khmer Rouge came to power in 1975, Chau Seng, a Communist, returned to Cambodia. Like most exiles who returned from Western European countries, he was arrested in 1977, imprisoned in the notorious Toul Sleng prison, and executed. Courtesy of the National Archives and Records Administration.

Demonstrators threw rocks and bricks at the embassy, broke windows, tore down and burned the American flag, broke into the embassy building itself, and wrecked the first floor. The mob, urged on by speakers, trumpets, drums, and a youth band playing stirring music, also stormed the nearby United States Information Services library, wrecking the interior and burning books. They inflicted similar damage on the British embassy and other British offices.

An Australian Landrover, parked at the British embassy, was also destroyed. The damage to American property was estimated at $160,000.

Some, including Donald Lancaster, Sihanouk's English language secretary at the time, have asserted that Sihanouk himself gave the order to trash the buildings. However, Australia's Ambassador Noël St. Clair Deschamps, who knew Sihanouk better than any Western diplomat, believed the damage shocked the prince. "He was furious that there was actual damage done and that they had actually broken into the [embassies]," Deschamps recalled. ". . . He did not authorize the trashing of the embassies. No way, no way. That's not the way he does things."[34] In any event Sihanouk promptly apologized and agreed to pay for the damage, and he now saw no reason to break relations with the United States, even if no Geneva Conference was called. Recognizing that Sihanouk had in fact moved close to the American position of bilateral diplomacy, the United States had made a good-faith effort to respond positively to Sihanouk's proposed quadrilateral conference. But in the end the Americans could not convince Sihanouk that they seriously wanted a solution that would preserve his nation's territorial integrity in the face of challenges from his regional enemies who were America's allies. Although the quadripartite conference did not take place, in a sense the United States won the larger diplomatic game because the Geneva Conference it did not want was not held. But its "victory" was at considerable cost in its relations with Sihanouk.

The Americans believed that nothing they could reasonably have done would have improved the relationship. Sihanouk's actions, they believed, resulted from his conviction that China's strength was growing and that the National Liberation Front (NLF) would prevail in Vietnam. Consequently, they concluded, he had decided he must cut the best deal with them that he could. Offers of reasonable American concessions, therefore, would be futile. There was, in sum, little the United States could do to influence events. It could only keep a low profile and be patient—or so American officials believed.

But the American position was also heavily influenced by the perceived need to remain on good terms with Sihanouk's disruptive neighbors. And faced with a choice, there was little question as to whom the United States would support. The Australian ambassador in Phnom Penh caught the American perspective well. In a personal note to a colleague about "the complete bankruptcy of American policy in Cambodia," he asserted that the Americans had never considered Cambodia or its problems important. Rather, they always viewed the country as part of some larger issue. Even the current American chargé, Herbert Spivack, regularly reminded his staff that in the larger framework of American objectives, Cambodia was unimportant. "If the man on the spot thinks so," Deschamps wrote, "the attitude of the State Department becomes more comprehensible."[35] Deschamps' insight was accurate. As Hilsman put it in a telegram to Henry Cabot Lodge, "our fundamental objective is to cope with problem of Cambodia in such a way as to meet security interests of Free World in Southeast Asia."[36]

Even as the parties were adjusting to the new situation and trying to determine what to do next, on 19 March—only nine days after the violent demonstrations at the embassies—aircraft from South Vietnam attacked the Cambodian village of Chantrea. The attack lasted over two hours. Seventeen Cambodians died, and at least thirteen more were wounded. South Vietnamese troops on the ground with American advisers also participated. In an unusual move, the ICC commissioners went immediately to the scene (almost becoming casualties themselves when their helicopter crash-landed). The Canadian commissioner described the chilling devastation:

> We first saw fresh traces of numerous track vehicles (reported to have been twelve) which had obviously just gone through village. We saw at least twenty of reported 40 killed bulls and buffalos [sic]; some were still dying. We were being prepared slowly to see on actual spot where they had just died thirteen villagers including pregnant women and children, death was so recent blood had not rpt not yet dried. Some had died from bullet wounds other from shells and three at least had been run over by very heavy vehicles. [Cambodians claimed that wounded people had been deliberately run over.] Later in hospital we saw two children who had died half hour earlier as result of burns when incendiary bombs had completed destroyed their huts. In fact cinders were still smoldering when we looked at site of huts and picked up pieces of napalm bombs which French M[ilitary] A[ttaché] identified. We found tank caps which read twenty USA gallons. We saw numerous bullet holes and later spent cartridges with inscription 20mm Nessco which French M[ilitary] A[ttaché] said were used on Sky Raiders planes which SVN army uses. . . . [Back in Svay Rieng] we saw 14 wounded two of whom were children reaching delirious stage. . . . Violence of attack has shocked Cambodians and I admit Commissioners who saw results.[37]

The American military attaché, who went to Chantrea the next day, confirmed the devastation and reported that Americans had been seen in the armored personnel carriers (M-113s) and that one American reportedly piloted a plane that was shot down and landed in South Vietnam. The report was true. Michael Forrestal informed President Lyndon Johnson that American personnel had penetrated Cambodian territory; they were, in the language of official military doublespeak, allegedly "deficient in determination of their geographical position."[38] Henry Cabot Lodge was cold and unsympathetic, blaming the incident on Viet Cong use of Cambodian territory. South Vietnam nevertheless immediately apologized for the incident. Johnson was also inclined to apologize but was persuaded that to do so would play into Sihanouk's long-standing contention that the United States controlled South Vietnam.

The seriousness of the Chantrea attack led some to question if the raid had deliberate political implications. It occurred just as a high-level team from Saigon, led by General Cao Van Vien, was arriving in Phnom Penh to conduct negotiations. Deschamps reported that the "synchronization of action with the arrival of General Cao's mission to Cambodia is incomprehensible, unless it was a deliberate attempt to sabotage negotiations." Cao Van Vien himself said that he had "been stabbed in the back."[39] Whether deliberate or not, the incident illustrated the unimportance of Cambodia to the Johnson administration. American policy toward Cambodia, wrote Deschamps, was characterized by "unimaginativeness, rigidity, indifference and plain stupidity. How, otherwise," he wrote, "in the present tense and potentially dangerous situation, could American officers have been involved in the worst and most blatant and inexcusable Vietnamese aggression against Cambodia on record?"[40]

There was understandable concern that the situation in Phnom Penh could turn violently against the Americans. But fortunately for the United States, Sihanouk's venture to strike a bargain with North Vietnam on border guarantees went sour at precisely this time, and General Lon Nol had little success in getting military equipment from China. Sihanouk accused the North Vietnamese of acting just like the Thais. Consequently the danger of a complete break with the United States faded. For the time being Sihanouk decided not to pursue either the quadripartite meeting or the Geneva Conference and ignored previously issued ultimatums. He would now, he said, devote himself to his family and internal matters and visit France. The immediate crisis had passed. Sihanouk's various gambles had failed, and the prince was prepared for the time being to watch and wait—though he also railed against the United States. "Wherever you go," Sihanouk asserted, referring to the Americans, "you spread war, revolution and misery."[41]

Late in July after several weeks in France for rest and medical care Sihanouk returned to Phnom Penh. He was relaxed, jovial, and in good humor and went out of his way to be friendly to the American chargé. The very next day, reports arrived that seventy-seven villagers (a number later raised to 107) in Ratanakiri Province had died from "yellow powder" dropped, it was said, by South Vietnamese planes. (A similar incident occurred in Svay Rieng Province shortly thereafter.) Both the United States and South Vietnam denied any involvement, but the incident immediately returned relations to their previous hostile state, as Sihanouk soon accused the Americans of responsibility for the deaths.

In late August and early September another important series of border incidents occurred, in which South Vietnamese planes strafed the village of Koh Rokor and Cambodian boats on the Mekong River; ground troops also attacked. These raids, along with renewed reports of chemical attacks and the first American bombing of North Vietnam in response to the Gulf of

Tonkin incident, deeply angered Sihanouk. In October yet another major border incident occurred, this time at Anlong Kres in Kompong Cham province, which was attacked twice. Fire from South Vietnamese aircraft killed eight villagers (including two women and four children). In another incident the Cambodians shot down a C-123 American transport plane over Dak Dam. Eight crew members died. The Cambodians removed the wrecked plane to Phnom Penh where they put it on display. By the end of the month there had been at least eight cross-border raids, for which an angry Cambodian government held the United States jointly responsible with South Vietnam. Sihanouk threatened to break relations with the United States and recognize North Vietnam and the NLF if any more violations of Cambodian territory occurred. The United States quietly evacuated more dependents from Cambodia.

By this point Alf Bergesen, the new American chargé in Phnom Penh (who, in the opinion of one Australian official, was "much more helpful and cooperative than Spivack"),[42] had become convinced that American policy was becoming counterproductive. Detecting a "distinct hardening" in American policy since the C-123 incident, Bergesen wrote to Thomas J. Hirschfeld, the State Department's officer in charge of Cambodian affairs, that "after 12 years of trying, American policy in Cambodia has failed." Sihanouk was "simply *sui generis,* a fact which we are apparently unable to accept. For this reason many of our finest and most polished three cushion shots wind up on the floor as far as achieving the effect here that was sought." Anything resembling threats must be avoided, Bergeson advised, for they were only counterproductive.[43]

Whether Bergesen's letter had any direct impact on American policy is not clear, but soon thereafter Rusk asked the French if they thought a discreet meeting of American and Cambodian representatives would be fruitful. Rusk probably intended his comments to be a gesture only. But the Cambodians unexpectedly accepted the American offer quickly and suggested New Delhi as the venue. The proposal for talks in New Delhi was the one constructive effort made to confront the issues during this entire period. The Cambodians hoped that the talks would end attacks on Cambodian villages, stop accusations that Cambodia harbored the Viet Cong, and get South Vietnam to withdraw claims to certain coastal islands. Secondary concerns included indemnities for those killed or injured in the border raids, an ending to the Khmer Serei broadcasts, and the freeing of Cambodians whom the South Vietnamese had arrested.

American expectations from the talks were modest. Bergeson hoped that they might result in a restoration of normal diplomatic relations, with Ambassador-designate Randolph Kidder returning to Phnom Penh (Sihanouk had earlier refused to accept him) and the Cambodian embassy in Washington being reopened. Possibly also the Americans might be able to get an understanding with the Cambodians to tone down the rhetoric in the press and not publish obviously false stories (such as, they thought, the "yellow powder" allegations). The talks might also have some value in convincing Cambodia that the Viet Cong were not going to take over South Vietnam and that it would be more difficult to restrain South Vietnam if Cambodia recognized the NLF.

On the other hand, some influential Americans who followed Cambodian developments thought the talks might produce a significant agreement, if only the United States would take Cambodia seriously. "We have consistently underestimated Sihanouk's astuteness and ability and overrated his naivete and instability," Senator Manfield told the president. "In my judgment," he continued, "he and his principal advisors are exceptionally able and are playing their cards totally in terms of Cambodia's independent survival and other interests."[44] But Mansfield's advice had little impact. Cambodia's demands only irritated Dean Rusk, who told a high-ranking Australian official that Sihanouk's mind was "poisoned against the United States" because he thought the Americans wanted a wider war in Southeast Asia (which, as it turned out, was an accurate projection).[45]

The New Delhi talks began 8 December 1964. All of the issues were explored. But the State Department concluded that the Cambodians were not willing to offer sufficient concessions and ordered its negotiator, veteran diplomat Philip Bonsal, to adjourn the talks. The negotiations had succeeded in preventing a break in diplomatic relations. But none of the issues was resolved. In the end the two sides could not even agree on a joint communiqué, as each side issued its own final statement to the press. On a personal level, however, the talks did not end in acrimony, as both sides jointly hosted a dinner honoring their Indian hosts.

There was certainly some blame on both sides for the inability to reach any agreements. Some of Sihanouk's statements were provocative, and his efforts to undertake simultaneous negotiations with the Chinese and North Vietnamese irritated the Americans. But the Johnson administration bears considerable responsibility for the breakdown. Although the Americans had first suggested the talks, they did not anticipate that Sihanouk would respond positively to them. When he did, the Americans did not appoint a diplomat with the authority to arrive at a settlement and then forbade Bonsal from concluding a compromise settlement when one was possible. Indeed the American delegation felt, as NSC official James C. Thomson Jr. told Harriman in 1966, that "our participants felt at the time that they came within a day or so of success but were undercut by Washington."[46]

American officials feared that the collapse of the talks might result in violent demonstrations at the American embassy or perhaps in a diplomatic break. Relations were so poor that, at about this time when the Polish representative on the ICC was gravely injured in an automobile accident near the Phnom Penh airport, local people at first refused to assist him, thinking he was an American.

(The diplomat later died.) By the end of the year the U.S. presence in Cambodia numbered only twelve individuals, down from over 300 a year earlier.

A very basic problem facing those who wanted to improve relations with Cambodia was (as Sihanouk suggested) that at this very moment the United States was in the process of choosing war in Vietnam, and the idea of improving relations with Cambodia was increasingly a very secondary concern. There were, therefore, almost no significant steps in the first months of 1965 to improve the relationship. Sihanouk continued to criticize the United States, often in angry tones, for any number of lapses: providing aid with strings, criticizing his nonaligned posture, allowing American journals to publish unflattering stories about him and Cambodia, and the new sustained bombing of North Vietnam. In February Sihanouk told an Indian journalist that the United States "was today hated more than the French were in the worst phase of the colonial war."[47]

Continuing cross-border raids were particularly dangerous to the U.S.–Cambodian relationship. In January Son Sann had pleaded with the United States to avoid any border incidents. If one Cambodian were killed, it was likely that Sihanouk would break relations with the Americans, he said. But the incidents did not stop. From Phnom Penh, Bergesen continued to argue that the raids, as well as continued Khmer Serei operations, were counterproductive. He believed that the prince was "unquestionably the most effective Khmer leader," despite his erratic behavior and anti-American outbursts, and that Cambodia had prospered under his leadership. Therefore the United States should try to "keep the wild men in Bangkok and Saigon from getting out of control and attempting to 'liberate' Cambodia. We do not believe that in the long run the best interests of the Free World would be served by an attempt to unseat him."[48] But every week there were more raids on Cambodian villages. After an attack on Kompong Trach, a village in Kampot province, Sihanouk threatened to break diplomatic relations if there was one more attack. But the raids did not let up.

If there was no progress on resolving these matters, there was some movement on Sihanouk's long-standing demand for a Geneva conference on Cambodia. A new call for a conference emerged from Sihanouk's Conference of Indochinese People, which met from 1 to 9 March 1965. The serious possibility that a conference would be convened deeply divided the American diplomatic community. From the American embassies in Saigon and Bangkok came the usual dire warnings that American participation would be seen as a sign of weakness. In Phnom Penh, on the other hand, Bergesen thought that a favorable American response would likely improve U.S.–Cambodian relations. In Washington William Bundy twice presented a negative recommendation to Rusk, but George Ball and Harriman weighed in on the other side, and in the end the secretary seemed inclined to give the conference his blessing. Particularly important in this respect was President Johnson's televised address on 7

April at Johns Hopkins University in which he offered to engage in "unconditional discussions" on Vietnam. Could the United States now refuse to discuss the less difficult Cambodian situation?

Still, as in the past the United States hoped that agreement on the major issues could be reached informally ahead of time; the conference itself would be only ceremonial. However, the momentum for a conference was strong, in part the result of a mission to Southeast Asia by former British foreign secretary Patrick Gordon Walker, who helped persuade Thailand and even South Vietnam to support a conference. The Americans stalled, but then on 25 April 1965 Secretary of State Dean Rusk suddenly announced that the United States would gladly participate.

Why, after weeks of foot-dragging, had the United States suddenly moved at this particular time to fully support the conference? The reason lay with Sihanouk. On 23 April in a speech dedicating USSR Avenue in Phnom Penh, the prince asserted that the United States was considering attending a conference only because it might lead to progress on Vietnam. Any conference, he insisted, must deal only with Cambodia. Even more troubling, the next day at a ceremony opening a new grocery store, Sihanouk indicated that he now did not want Thailand, South Vietnam, or the United States to attend. He appeared to be fed up with American stalling. The United States, he stated accurately, "without saying 'no', do not say 'yes' either." Sihanouk even appeared to be saying that he no longer wanted a conference at all. "This conference interests us today much less than at [the] time when we were demanding [it] and when [the] Anglo-Saxons were obstructing it," Sihanouk told his audience.[49]

Sihanouk's remarkable about-face forced the American action. As Rusk explained to American diplomats in Bangkok and Vientiane:

> By Sunday we were confronted with the fact that Sihanouk's remarks at grocery store opening had been published. . . . Gordon Walker was on point of leaving Saigon for Phnom Penh. There seemed some reason to hope that, by announcing US and GVN [Government of Vietnam] agreement beforehand, we could forestall official Cambodian response to Gordon Walker that US and GVN attendance at conference unacceptable. It was thought that announcement might equally forestall RKG [Cambodian Government] demand for Liberation Front representation. These factors seemed to us to warrant risks that announcement might, on the contrary, get Sihanouk's back up, and precipitate official confirmation as well as disadvantage seeming to be unduly anxious about conference.[50]

Why, at a time when the British and the Americans were finally willing to support a conference, when Thailand and South Vietnam had fallen in line, and when China, the Soviet Union, North Vietnam, and the NLF had also voiced support, did Sihanouk throw a fatal wrench into the works? He may have been convinced, as he stated, that the Americans had stalled too long; and in any event if they were finally interested, it was only to speak with their opponents about Vietnam. But Sihanouk also acted for reasons not directly related to American stalling. We now know that China's Premier Zhou Enlai personally asked Sihanouk not to go ahead with the conference he had so long championed because it might work to the disadvantage of China's Vietnamese allies. Chinese support for the conference had always been a façade because they feared it would increase Soviet influence in Hanoi. Thus they engaged in "intensive efforts . . . to sabotage the conference by convincing the Cambodian premier that negotiations are unnecessary."[51]

The day after Rusk's announcement that the United States intended to send a delegation to the conference, a "flash" telegram arrived at the State Department from the American embassy in Phnom Penh reporting that several hundred demonstrators were converging on the embassy, the crowd was growing steadily, and "rocks have begun to fly." All local employees were sent home, embassy automobiles removed from the vicinity, and American dependents sent to the Hotel Royal. In another hour most of the windows had been broken and the embassy's American flag burned. A few placards were seen calling on the United States to go home. The police, who had arrived late, made only perfunctory efforts to control the demonstrators and instead were reportedly "standing around watching the festivities."[52]

For another hour "rocks of assorted sizes" barraged the embassy, and then police in riot gear began to push back the crowd, which by then amounted to several thousand people. Bergesen characterized the participants as predominantly "riffraff." Cyclo (bicycle rickshaw) drivers were reputedly the chief rock throwers. By the end of the demonstration (it lasted from about 4:00 p.m. to 7:00 p.m.), the building was a mess "with rocks, tomatoes and broken glass in every room." Graffiti covered the exterior walls. However, unlike in March 1964 the crowd did not penetrate the embassy itself, and damage to the building was a relatively modest $4,878.06.[53]

On the day following the demonstration, for the first time in memory anti-American demonstrations took place in several provincial cities, demanding that Cambodia end relations with the United States. On 3 May Bergesen learned that Sihanouk was breaking diplomatic relations. By the end of May no official Americans remained in the Khmer kingdom. About the same time Cambodian authorities ordered the last American missionary, Carl E. Thompson, out of the country. He and his wife left Phnom Penh in June; most others had had to leave by the end of 1964 when their visas expired. The Cambodians told Thompson that all other Americans would soon be forced out as well, including even the American spouses of Cambodian citizens. Only after Sihanouk's overthrow in 1970 were American missionaries allowed to return to Cambodia.

The ostensible reason for the demonstration was outrage over Bernard Krisher's article in the 5 April edition of *Newsweek* magazine that alleged that Queen Sisowath Kossamak (Sihanouk's mother) was greedy and kept a string of bordellos on the outskirts of the capital. But in fact no single factor caused the demonstration. Rather it was the cumulative effect of the various issues that increasingly strained the relationship. The war in Vietnam was of central importance. The demonstration came shortly after the United States had begun bombing North Vietnam in a sustained way and had sent its first combat units to South Vietnam. The war was on the verge of escalating out of control, and Sihanouk feared that the hostilities would engulf his own country. Sihanouk allowed the demonstration to take place because of his long-standing anger at American support for the Khmer Serei, continuing cross-border military operations, American stalling on the conference, and his general irritation at what he regarded as a patronizing attitude toward himself and Cambodia, as well as internal political pressures. He used the Krisher article as the excuse.

However important these issues were in forming Sihanouk's general anti-Americanism or in bringing about the demonstration, they were not the most important cause of the break in diplomatic relations. That resulted primarily from yet another border incident. On 28 April, two days after the demonstration, four planes, thought to be South Vietnamese Skyraiders, bombed the villages of Phum Chantatep (or Cheam Tatep) and Moream Tiek in Kompong Cham province. The villages were about four kilometers from the Vietnamese border. One thirteen-year-old boy was killed, and others were seriously injured. American military attachés who went to the scene the same day confirmed the death and counted thirty-five bomb and rocket craters. As a last-ditch attempt to salvage the situation, Bergesen suggested an immediate South Vietnamese apology and compensation to the victims.

The situation was actually worse than Bergesen thought. An investigation quickly determined that the planes in question were *American,* not South Vietnamese. Consequently, Bergesen urged his government to apologize immediately and offer compensation. A note along these lines was prepared and delivered to the White House on 1 May, but it was never sent to Cambodia. Had it been, it might have prevented a break in relations. Any initial confusion about the primacy of the border attacks as the cause of the break soon disappeared, for Cambodian officials made it clear that an end to the cross-border actions was the only condition for restoring relations. Sihanouk himself told French officials that the break resulted from "repeated border incursions," and "he would be happy to restore relations if US put [a] stop to" them.[54]

In sum, the American bombs and rockets that hit Phum Chantatep and Moream Tiek were the immediate cause for the break in relations. The hundreds of such incidents involving South Vietnamese and/or American personnel were the most important underlying cause as well. American support for Sihanouk's bitter enemies, the Khmer Serei, also contributed to the break, as did American stalling on a Geneva conference. Less tangible factors, such as patronizing American attitudes toward Cambodia and unflattering stories in the American press, helped produce a general anti-American atmosphere in Cambodia. Sihanouk's own assessment of the future of Indochina, as well as his concern with domestic politics, also affected his decision. At the heart of it was the war in Vietnam, which seriously exacerbated preexisting tensions between Cambodia and its neighbors and consequently with their ally, the United States. Even more fundamental was the Cold War thinking that deeply affected American policy makers. Though not unaware of the regional character of Cambodia's problems, they generally viewed developments through a Cold War lens. Even when regional factors were recognized, the United States almost always subordinated them to Cold War considerations. It was too bad that Sihanouk would be angered, but opposing the spread of international Communism took first place.

Prelude to Tragedy

THE UNITED STATES' NONRELATIONSHIP

WITH CAMBODIA, 1965–1969

"Americans attract Communists like sugar attracts ants."—Norodom Sihanouk, February 1967

AFTER THE BREAK IN RELATIONS, the United States quickly explored its options as to which country would represent it in Phnom Penh. Britain and Japan were considered, but only two days after relations were broken, the Americans asked Australia to undertake the task. It was not a request that was accepted with alacrity. The Australians feared that the Cambodians would inevitably associate them with the U.S. position, and Australia would then lose its ability to be useful to all sides. But there were few viable alternatives, so Australia had to do it.

Since 1962 Noël St. Clair Deschamps had represented Australia in the Cambodian capital. Deschamps had already enjoyed a long and distinguished career with the Department of External Affairs, which he had joined in 1937. He had served four years as counsellor of the Australian embassy in Paris, three years as head of the military mission in Berlin, three years as chargé at Bonn, and three years in a similar role in Dublin. And he was not very happy at the prospect of being the protector of American interests, sharing the view of his compatriots in Canberra that Cambodia would identify Australia with the United States.

The decision having been made, Deschamps had no choice but to go along, and Sihanouk posed no objection to Australia representing the United States in Phnom Penh. France, meanwhile, represented Cambodian interests in Washington. In what turned out to be a period of four years, Deschamps represented the United States ably and well. Among other matters, he helped arrange Jacqueline Kennedy's visit to Cambodia in 1967, assisted with the occasional release of American POWs, and helped secure the release of the son of an AID official in Bangkok who had tried to

Australia's Ambassador to Cambodia Noël St. Clair Deschamps presents his credentials to Prince Sihanouk in 1962. From the Private Collection of Ambassador Julio A. Jeldres.

smuggle some Angkor treasures out of the country. (The young man's mother sold smuggled Cambodian antiquities in an antiques store in New York.) In this case Deschamps talked the Americans out of bringing in the "heavy artillery," such as a letter from Mike Mansfield to Sihanouk. Instead the ambassador arranged for the young man's father to purchase a tractor from Singapore in exchange for his son's release (after a trial in which he was found guilty). The Cambodians were disappointed that the tractor had no attachments but kept their word and released the young man the next day. Dean Rusk wrote a personal note of appreciation to the Australian Minister of Foreign Affairs thanking Deschamps for his efforts. "Without doubt the Ambassador's fine efforts and excellent judgment were the crucial factors in obtaining [the young man's] . . . release and restoring him to his family," Rusk wrote.[1] In these, and other similar instances, the United States was most grateful for Deschamps' services.

The Americans also relied on Deschamps' advice in sensitive political matters. But valuable as Deschamps' counsel was, the Americans privately considered the Australian too pro-Sihanouk. As a consequence there were sometimes tensions between Australia and the United States. Yet overall Deschamps' close relationship with Sihanouk was an asset. In the end, as journalist Robert Shaplen wrote in 1966, Deschamps probably did "a better job for the United States than it could have done for itself."[2]

Deschamps had plenty to do, and representing the United States put a considerable strain on the small Australian embassy staff in Phnom Penh. Although the Americans had left Phnom Penh, the issues separating the two countries remained and kept the relationship from healing. These included differences over recognition of Cambodia's territorial boundaries; continued American allegations that the Vietnamese Communists were abusing Cambodian territory, using it as a refuge and sanctuary, getting supplies through and inside Cambodia (perhaps with the support of the Cambodian government), and even establishing base camps in the country; continuing border raids on Cambodian villages and outposts, and other violations of Cambodian sovereignty that seemed to intensify whenever prospects for improved relations seemed possible; continuing Cambodian allegations of American support for the Khmer Serei; and the American belief that Sihanouk could no longer be considered neutral at all but had firmly allied himself with the Communists, particularly the Chinese Communists.

With respect to the boundary question, now that the Geneva Conference approach was on hold, Sihanouk tried get unilateral pledges from as many countries as possible to respect Cambodian neutrality and its territorial integrity within its present borders. Having the Americans make such a pledge became a major condition for reestablishing relations.

Deschamps saw no reason why the United States should not accede to the Cambodian request. Sihanouk's position as to what constituted the boundary was clear: treaties between Siam and France in 1904 and 1907 had spelled out the Thai-Cambodian boundary with clarity, modified only by an International Court decision in 1962 favorable to Cambodia in the Preah Vihear temple case. As for Vietnam and Laos, Sihanouk accepted the boundaries imposed by the French administration of Indochina, even though the boundary with Cochin China was unfavorable to Cambodia. In sum, in Sihanouk's view the Cambodian frontier corresponded "to the regions at present under Cambodian administrative control, no more and no less."[3] Deschamps always thought this was a perfectly reasonable position. But the United States, under pressure from the Thais and especially the South Vietnamese, refused to recognize specific boundaries and was only willing to make a general pledge to respect Cambodia's sovereignty and territorial integrity. Indeed the Americans kept referring to the "ill-defined" border, which angered Sihanouk. All told, the unwillingness of the United States to meet this Cambodian demand was the most important reason why diplomatic relations were not restored.

The border question remained always in the background. But for the rest of 1965 the question of Vietnamese Communist use of Cambodian territory attracted more immediate attention. Sihanouk always denied that there was serious abuse of his territory by the Viet Cong or the North Vietnamese and feared that American reports to the contrary were intended to justify military incursions into Cambodia. After one such report, Sihanouk invited prominent American journalists to investigate, and the *New York Times* sent Seymour Topping. After an investigation Topping concluded that it was probable that the Viet Cong used the area to some extent, but he was convinced that no headquarters or base camp existed. In this case, and in a number of others, the American military made embarrassing errors. But American officials remained convinced that the enemy nevertheless was making substantial use of Cambodian territory and that some army elements did from time to time move their headquarters into Cambodia.

When late in November 1965 Secretary of Defense Robert McNamara and Deputy Ambassador to Vietnam U. Alexis Johnson made statements that implied enemy use of Cambodian territory, Sihanouk again urged a respected American journalist to investigate, and shortly thereafter the well-known foreign correspondent of the *Washington Post,* Stanley Karnow, arrived in Phnom Penh, where Cambodian authorities promised to take him wherever he desired to go. After five days of intensive travels to various border areas, Karnow concluded that, while there was doubtless some smuggling and commerce with the Viet Cong, he was "inclined to doubt any significant Viet Cong presence or activity in Cambodia, with or without Cambodian knowledge."[4]

By some accounts, the American military had good reason to be suspicious of Sihanouk's relationship with the Vietnamese Communists. The prince may have negotiated an agreement with China that allowed arms and supplies to be sent to them, while also permitting NLF forces to pass through Cambodia and take refuge there. The accounts assert that as early as 1964 Hanoi and Beijing agreed to give Sihanouk's armed forces 10 percent of the Chinese weapons that were shipped through the port of Sihanoukville. Perhaps enough weapons to support 50,000 soldiers arrived in this manner between 1965 and 1967. However, the evidence for these agreements is not entirely conclusive.[5] Sihanouk denied any but the most minimal Viet Cong activity in his country because he feared that the Americans would use their alleged presence to justify military action against Cambodia—as in fact the Joint Chiefs did.

The most serious border incident in the months after the break in relations came in October 1965 when at least five South Vietnamese and American planes bombed, napalmed, and machine-gunned the Cambodian village of Ba Thu in Svay Rieng Province. In three separate waves of attacks seven persons died, six were wounded, nineteen houses were destroyed and thirty-two more damaged, and fifty-three water buffalo were killed and thirty-six wounded. The incident came (as all of the most serious incidents seemed to come) at an especially bad time. The Soviet Union had just snubbed Sihanouk by canceling an invitation to him to visit Moscow. The prince described the Soviet behavior as being even worse than that of the United States. Never, he said, had the Americans sought to humiliate him in this manner. The attack on Ba Thu presumably prevented any rapprochement that might have emerged in the wake of the Russian snub.

In addition to citing the border incidents, the prince continued to charge that American intelligence agencies controlled the Khmer Serei. By and large the State Department was convinced that support for the Khmer Serei was counterproductive and urged Thailand and South Vietnam to cut their ties with the dissidents. The State Department appeared to be serious about this. South Vietnam's new Prime Minister Nguyen Cao Ky promised to end such aid, and indeed in 1965 most of the independent Khmer Serei activity (as opposed to Khmer Serei units integrated into the CIDG) appears to have shifted to Thailand. But there was always a temptation to work with the Khmer Serei, particularly now that diplomatic relations had been broken and it seemed even less important to keep Sihanouk happy. Although the United States continued to deny categorically that it supported the Khmer Serei in any way, in fact the American military continued to help pay for and train Khmer Serei forces in the Vietnamese CIDG units and probably trained others in Thailand. It is certain that there were CIA contacts with Son Ngoc Thanh.

Despite the increase in Khmer Serei activity and the continuing violations of Cambodian air space and territory, by late 1965 there was some movement toward a better relationship. Senator Mansfield's unofficial visit to Cambodia late in November 1965 provided a symbolic beginning. Sihanouk indicated to Mansfield his desire to improve the bilateral relationship but reiterated the three conditions that would mark Cambodian policy toward the United States for two more years: the United States must recognize Cambodia's present boundaries, pay an indemnity for Cambodian lives lost in the border incursions (here he softened his previous insistence on one bulldozer for each dead Cambodia and said just a token amount would be acceptable), and stop bombing Cambodia and launching incursions into its territory. However, the United States was not yet ready to accept any of Sihanouk's conditions for improved relations.

In June 1966, however, President Johnson ordered his aides to try to improve relations with Cambodia. NSC official James C. Thomson Jr. took the task to heart and after a vigorous investigation proposed a number of ways to improve the relationship. The military disliked all efforts to assuage Sihanouk, preferring instead military action against Viet Cong strongholds in Cambodia. The civilian bureaucracy was also unenthusiastic about some of

Thomson's ideas. But the president approved all of Thomson's recommendations with enthusiasm. "This is excellent," the president wrote with respect to Thomson's ideas. "I'm proud." He rejected calls for a military solution and instead directed the State Department and the CIA to "press the Thai and Vietnam Governments to cease all support for the Khmer Serei rebels." Shortly thereafter orders went out to the American military in Vietnam not to "penetrate a 200-meter-wide belt on the Vietnamese side of the Cambodian frontier." The principle of "hot pursuit," originally approved in December 1965, was for the moment discouraged.[6]

Coinciding with the American initiatives, Sihanouk made a conciliatory speech at the Royal Military Academy. He did not attack the United States and even offered some faint praise, while urging immediate expansion of the ICC (something the Americans favored). According to the Australian ambassador, "the Chinese Ambassador practically and the North Vietnamese representative failed to applaud the speech." Lest there be any doubt about the speech's significance, Cambodian General Nhiek Tioulong told Ambassador Deschamps, "that speech should clarify our position. We are relying on you to explain it to Canberra and Washington." The administration moved into high gear to take advantage of the improving relations. It pressured the Thais and Vietnamese to better their relations with their neighbor, asked for Japanese assistance, and attempted to reopen the Bowles-Kimny channel in New Delhi. Sihanouk responded by inviting Harriman to visit. "Averell has got a nibble on the Cambodian line," Rostow informed President Johnson, "and it looks as though he will be going there in September."[7] Sihanouk was circumspect in his public statements about the United States and dropped his second condition—compensation for Cambodian casualties—for restoring relations. In sum, for the first time in many months there was positive movement in the relationship.

But all of the momentum toward improved relations ended when on 31 July and twice on 2 August American planes attacked the adjoining villages of Thlok Trach and Anlong Trach, killing several Cambodians. What was particularly embarrassing about these attacks was that, by chance, the American civil rights leader Floyd McKissick and other members of the "Americans Want to Know" group, as well as a CBS journalist, arrived at Thlok Trach shortly after the first bombing and saw the casualties and damage. Furthermore, members of the ICC, military attachés from various embassies in Phnom Penh, and journalists who were on the scene investigating the attack of 31 July actually witnessed the later incidents. American planes bombed and strafed within two hundred yards of the international visitors, who, as Ambassador Lodge put it, "fled to the jungle and hid." The Canadian report was more graphic. The investigators "spent half [an] hour face down in mud, water and nettles" before beating a "hasty retreat." The Indian member, Bindra, "won 1200 metre dash in field of forty runners by good Aryan nose."[8]

The eyewitness report by the Canadian member of the ICC was scathing. There was "absolutely no . . . evidence" that American forces had come under fire from the Cambodian villages, and thus the attack violated current rules of engagement. Furthermore, even from the air Cambodian villages could not be mistaken for Vietnamese villages, since in Cambodian villages houses are built on stilts. He was further convinced that the spotter pilots saw the international observers, most of whom were white and wore white shirts (one even had a business suit on)—there were no villagers present since the survivors of the first raid had long since fled—and in an apparent effort to impress the group, the pilots "performed [a] remarkably neat surgical operation along edge of woods" where no Viet Cong could possibly have been hiding. "It seemed in the first place that men had been sent to do boys job and in second place that trigger happy spotters, finding nothing, laid on useless and wasteful show to impress Cambodians or foreign observers or both."[9] Coming from a man who almost always took the American point of view, this was strong criticism indeed.

The Americans immediately took the position that their maps showed the bombed villages to be in South Vietnam, even though they quickly acknowledged that the people living in them were Khmers. Rather quickly they conceded that the villages were administered by Cambodian authorities. But they continued to insist that all the maps, including one provided by Cambodian authorities, showed the villages to be in South Vietnam. Other observers disagreed. In addition to the Cambodians, the Canadians, the Australian services attaché, and the French military attaché all concluded (after a study of maps) that the villages were in Cambodia. Ambassador Deschamps himself was highly skeptical of the American version, finding parts of it "alarming and extraordinary."[10]

Had the United States not hidden behind legalities and responded with an immediate and sincere apology, the diplomatic damage might have been minimized and the improvement in the larger relationship might have proceeded after only a temporary disruption. But the Americans continued with their legalisms (only later did they admit that the villages were in fact in Cambodia), and the danger of long-term damage increased. After Sihanouk received the American note, which expressed only regrets, not apologies, and which stated that Thlock Trach was in Vietnam, he angrily postponed Harriman's trip indefinitely.

Sihanouk believed that the U.S. military and intelligence agencies deliberately targeted Thlok Thach to sabotage the improving atmosphere. "American 'hawks' did not want better relations with Cambodia," one Cambodian editorial stated. "The prospect of Mr Harriman's visit had given them sleepless nights so they had torpedoed it."[11]

It is not impossible that Sihanouk was right. Neutral observers in Phnom Penh at the time thought it might have been the case, and journalist Robert Shaplen wrote that "a week before the incidents took place, some well-informed Vietnamese in Saigon were privately predicting just such an attack." The American military was entirely anti-Sihanouk and even within the State Department there was precious little sympathy for Cambodia. "The Cambodia Desk was the first which seemed not to possess any basic sympathy for the point of view of the country for which it was responsible," an American diplomat commented in confidence to an Australian.[12]

The Thlok Thach incident set back a possible reconciliation, but since Sihanouk was clearly turning away from the Chinese Communists, there were hopes that improvement could resume after a few weeks. The prince said he hoped that Harriman could visit Cambodia soon, something McNamara enthusiastically endorsed.

Harriman's hopes to return soon to Cambodia unfortunately ran afoul of Sihanouk's renewed drive to have the various powers pledge to respect Cambodia's territorial integrity "within its present borders." In September 1966 France's President Charles DeGaulle had made this pledge on behalf of France, but the United States was not ready to do so. Consequently the Cambodians rebuffed suggestions that Harriman come in October. "We have nothing to say to him and no business to conduct with him so long as his country has not recognized the present frontiers of Cambodia as France has done," read an editorial in *Le Sangkum*.[13] Sihanouk remained bitterly critical of American policy in Southeast Asia. As he put it perceptively in February 1967, "The best way to create Communists is to bring in Americans where there aren't any [Communists]. Americans attract Communists like sugar attracts ants."[14] Sihanouk also continued to charge that the United States financed and assisted the Khmer Serei and that the CIA had resumed operations in Cambodia aimed at overthrowing him.

Despite the angry rhetoric, the relationship in 1967 did not reach the nadir of earlier years. For one thing, since the Thlok Trach fiasco the Americans had learned how to respond more constructively to border incidents. They also offered to share intelligence information about Viet Cong activity in Cambodia. This, plus Sihanouk's growing disenchantment with China, an incipient rebellion in Battambang, and perhaps the increasing dislike of Vietnamese Communist activities in his country, inclined him away from a serious confrontation with the United States.

On the positive side, Sihanouk engaged in negotiations with Pan American Airlines for air rights into Phnom Penh and the establishment of a Pan American hotel near Angkor. He graciously received Senator Edward Brooke (R-MA), who visited Phnom Penh in March. Perhaps the most important development that potentially tended toward a better relationship was

Sihanouk's warm response to Jacqueline Kennedy's inquiries about visiting Angkor. From the very beginning Sihanouk encouraged Mrs. Kennedy to come to Cambodia as his personal guest. Deschamps thought the proposed visit very important. Even though private, it would "bring a warmer tone to Cambodian/American relations. . . . It will be seen as a considerable mark of respect and a friendly gesture towards Cambodia."[15] When Mrs. Kennedy visited Cambodia in November, where Deschamps escorted her about Angkor, she struck a responsive chord. "Sihanouk went to extraordinary lengths not only to be gallant and courteous but also to ensure that every detail of the arrangements was personally supervised by him," Michael Forrestal informed the State Department.[16] Extensive coverage in *Life* magazine made many Americans aware of Cambodia for the first time. At the same time, however, the prince went out of his way to emphasize the private nature of the visit. And in fact the trip did not immediately result in any positive change in the relationship; frustration and enmity were more characteristic of the relationship for most of the rest of the year. Sihanouk again accused the United States of continuing to support the Khmer Serei and sending CIA operatives to destabilize his government.

For the Americans, the alleged growing use of Cambodian territory by the Viet Cong and the North Vietnamese People's Army of Vietnam (PAVN) produced frustration and even anger. American military leaders became increasingly outspoken on the subject, which only infuriated Sihanouk. As he had before, the prince invited journalists to come visit Cambodia and see if they could find any Vietnamese Communists. This time two journalists— George McArthur of the Associated Press and Ray Herndon of United Press International—took Sihanouk up on his offer and discovered what they claimed was a major, battalion-sized Viet Cong camp near Mimot. The Cambodians (all of them army personnel) accompanying the journalists were as surprised as the reporters. The United States insisted on independent verification of the discovery, and the ICC did eventually investigate. By that time the Cambodian government, which had initially charged that the report was a fabrication, was arguing that the camp was really a Cambodian government operation for training guerrilla fighters, and the ICC was unable to find clear evidence of Viet Cong involvement. The Americans, however, believed that the journalists had indeed found a Viet Cong base.

The McArthur-Herndon discovery had two results. On the one hand, it encouraged the U.S. government to follow through on its long term plan to present to the Cambodian government detailed, nonemotional reports documenting Viet Cong and PAVN abuse of Cambodian territory over many months. The first report was presented to Sihanouk's government on 4 December 1967. (The transfer of these dossiers was codenamed VESUVIUS.) The other effect of the journalists' report was to increase pressure—especially from the American military—to take strong military action against the sanctuaries in Cambodia.

The pressure for strong action peaked in December 1967 when General William Westmoreland, commander of American forces in Vietnam, formally requested sustained B-52 strikes for "at least 72 hours" in an area of Cambodia into which, he said, the entire 1st North Vietnamese Division had retreated after the recent battle of Dak To. Westmoreland acknowledged that the timing was difficult—the United States was just then attempting to present to Sihanouk its evidence of North Vietnamese activity in Cambodia, and a bombing strike would hardly have given Sihanouk a chance to respond. Furthermore, because the "B-52 strikes will leave a clear signature in Cambodian territory," it would be difficult to deny that the operation had taken place. Nevertheless, Westmoreland recommended that the strikes be carried out immediately "and if necessary explain our actions as hot pursuit by fire in an uninhabited area."[17]

Westmoreland's recommendation led to a major debate at the White House. Rusk, the first to offer an opinion, was flatly opposed. At first, however, the president appeared to support the plan. "We must tell Cambodia that we will not continue to permit them to house and protect these killers," he said. But Secretary of Defense Robert MacNamara supported Rusk, stating that he was "scared of a policy based on an assumption that by going somewhere else we can win the war." Supreme Court Justice and Johnson intimate Abe Fortas also objected strongly, as did the incoming Secretary of Defense Clark Clifford, who was "unalterably opposed to the action." In the face of such strong opposition, Johnson decided against precipitate moves.[18]

Perhaps the president was influenced by the wildly conflicting conclusions of the government's own reports about the extent of Vietnamese Communist use of Cambodia. In any event, instead of sending the B-52s against Cambodia, Johnson decided to press Cambodia to confront the Vietnamese Communists and put on a full court press to make the ICC more effective.

Crucial to defusing the situation were Sihanouk's actions at the end of December. In an important, rambling interview on 28 December 1967 Sihanouk seemed to indicate that, although he would protest if American and Viet Cong forces battled in remote areas of Cambodia, he would not necessarily intervene militarily. More importantly, he indirectly praised President Johnson for not giving in to the warmongers and offered to receive a presidential envoy, should Johnson want to send one.

Although the State Department wanted to avoid a quick response to Sihanouk, Johnson overruled the department and informed Sihanouk that Chester Bowles was immediately available (the State Department had preferred Harriman). Sihanouk said that he would be glad to receive Bowles. Thus a frustrating year in U.S.–Cambodian relations ended on a positive note.

Prince Norodom Sihanouk meets with special envoy Chester Bowles in Phnom Penh,
January 1968. From the Private Collection of Ambassador Julio A. Jeldres.

The United States saw the Bowles-Sihanouk meeting as a way to impress
upon the Cambodians its concerns about the Vietnamese Communists' use
of Cambodian territory, support the prince's desire to strengthen the ICC,
and try to learn with more specificity just what Sihanouk would accept in
terms of American actions against the Vietnamese Communists. For his part
Sihanouk entered the talks to try and keep the war from spreading to Cambodia and to encourage those in the American government who counseled restraint. He was increasingly irritated at actions of the North Vietnamese and
especially the Chinese but did not appear ready to countenance U.S. military
incursions into his country. As he put it on the eve of Bowles' arrival, the
"United States was the wolf and Cambodia the lamb, and [the] latter would
avoid discussing what sauce he would be eaten with."[19] He also remained firm
in his determination not to restore diplomatic relations with the United
States short of a satisfactory border declaration.

Bowles, with career diplomat Philip Habib "firmly chained to him to see
that he is not carried away by his own enthusiasm" (as a New Zealand

diplomat put it), arrived in Phnom Penh on 8 January 1968.[20] Bowles hoped for a major breakthrough in relations. He made a good impression in Cambodia and engaged in cordial talks with high-level Cambodian officials and twice with Sihanouk himself. In the end the United States got Sihanouk to reaffirm his proposal to strengthen the ICC and agree to receive VESUVIUS information. Sihanouk also seemed to accept limited American incursions into uninhabited areas of Cambodia under certain conditions, making comments that the Nixon administration later used to justify its bombing of Cambodia.

The Cambodians for their part pressed Bowles hard on recognition of borders (the subject "ran like a red thread throughout the talks," Bowles reported)[21] and on stopping the border incidents. But Bowles lacked authority to negotiate either and could only say that the United States would do all that it could to prevent border incidents and that he would bring Cambodia's concerns to President Johnson's attention. The Joint Communiqué issued at the end of the discussions on 12 January pledged the United States to respect Cambodia's "sovereignty, neutrality and territorial integrity" and to "do everything possible to avoid acts of aggression against Cambodia, as well as incidents and accidents which may cause losses and damage to the inhabitants of Cambodia."[22] On paper at least the United States came away from the discussions with more than did the Cambodians, but it is possible that the talks themselves prevented a large scale American air or ground attack on the sanctuaries.

The talks greatly encouraged Bowles, and when he returned to New Delhi he immediately sent an "eyes only" telegram to Rusk and the president, urging a strong effort to reestablish diplomatic relations with Cambodia. But the administration was not yet ready for such a move.

A number of developments slowed the momentum toward improved relations. Assistant Secretary of State William Bundy made an unfortunate comment about the right of the United States to fight on Cambodian territory in self-defense. Then on 18 January an American patrol penetrated into Cambodia. In an ensuing clash, three Cambodians and most of the Americans were killed. Finally, by coincidence, Martin Herz, whom Sihanouk detested, took over the State Department's Cambodia desk, fueling Cambodian suspicions about American intentions.

Meanwhile, in the period after the infamous Tet Offense in Vietnam (which began on 30 January 1968), the American and South Vietnamese militaries planned large operations in the border areas, acknowledging in advance that this would probably result in firing into Cambodia and in some instances maneuvering across the border. In Vietnam, the Southeast Asia Coordinating Committee (composed of ambassadors Ellsworth Bunker, Leonard Unger, and William H. Sullivan, along with General Westmoreland and Admiral U. S. Grant Sharp Jr.) recommended ending restrictions on intelligence forays into Cambodia; approving small military operations into Cambodia, which, depending on developments, could be gradually expanded; and making B-52 strikes. These planned operations surely contradicted Bowles' assurances to Sihanouk that the United States would do everything it could to avoid border incidents.

At the same time, however, the Americans were cheered to see that Sihanouk was becoming increasingly outspoken about Chinese, North Vietnamese, and Pathet Lao interference in his country—in particular their alleged responsibility for stirring up unrest and rebellion, especially in Battambang Province. Sihanouk moved his government rightward and cracked down hard on his leftist opponents, even executing some who were engaged in armed rebellion. By mid-March Sihanouk's strongly anti-Communist policies at home, plus the fact that he was complying with the Joint Communiqué by receiving the VESUVIUS reports (and even assuring the Americans that he would try to verify the information the Americans had provided), finally convinced the administration that the advantages of exploring a resumption of relations outweighed the disadvantages.

Exploratory talks were to begin at the end of March in New Delhi. But various unfavorable developments, including new border violations, shelved them. Then suddenly—and unexpectedly—in June Sihanouk, using the assassination of Robert Kennedy as a pretext, released Americans taken prisoner on a tugboat that had strayed into Cambodian waters. This, along with the prince's continued attacks on the Communists, led the State Department to renew the initiative to explore a possible resumption of relations. In spite of resistance from ambassadors Unger and Bunker, Rusk was prepared to move ahead. But a major border incident on 29 June near the Cambodian village of Svay A Ngong in Prey Veng Province threatened to postpone the effort. Sihanouk's account of the incident was chilling:

> Two United States military helicopters attacked with machine guns a group of Cambodian peasants, including women and children, who were working the village . . . about one kilometer from the Vietnam frontier. Fourteen people were killed and four seriously wounded. The thirteen survivors stated that the cigarette-smoking American pilots, flying a few meters from the ground, launched a veritable manhunt during half an hour, methodically shooting down all who tried to flee, including women and children.[23]

It was the bloodiest incursion into Cambodian territory since the infamous Chantrea incident in 1964. Prime Minister Penn Nouth remarked that the Cambodians had not expected to be thanked for releasing the tugboat crew but neither had they expected to be repaid with a bloody massacre of innocent civilians.

Three weeks after Svay A Ngong, Cambodian forces seized an American landing craft, the LCU 1577. On 17 July 1968 the ship was making its way up the Mekong River when it ventured into Cambodian waters, where it was captured and the crew arrested. The Americans insisted that the boat had missed a turn and ended up inadvertently in Cambodia. They immediately apologized and asked for the return of the vessel and the crew of eleven. Sihanouk professed to believe that the intrusion was deliberate. He treated the detainees well, but he would not return them or the boat.

The Americans then spent enormous energy trying to get the crew released. They provided a detailed report of the incident to the Cambodians, hoping to persuade them that the intrusion was inadvertent, enlisted the help of the Australians and then the British, and asked Bowles to see Nong Kimny in New Delhi. They secretly got a prominent Sri Lankan Buddhist leader to appeal to Sihanouk for the crew's release. They also considered coercive measures but ultimately rejected nineteenth-century gunboat diplomacy. The coercive idea that received the most serious consideration was to withhold needed American parts for a Cambodian ship that was being repaired in Hong Kong. At the end of August Bowles suggested that the United States propose to Sihanouk that if he would release the crew, the United States would, without final commitments, enter into discussions with him about a border declaration and the resumption of diplomatic relations.

In the meantime, the State Department had asked for Deschamps' advice on how best to improve Cambodian-American relations. Although Deschamps was not optimistic in the short run, he did think that Sihanouk was looking for ways to defuse the crisis and urged the Americans to be patient about the LCU crew (which the ambassador thought would be resolved before too long), to keep up with the presentations of the VESUVIUS dossiers (which Deschamps thought the Cambodians were taking seriously if quietly), and to avoid pressuring Sihanouk in any way because the result would be counterproductive. But the most important thing the United States could do, Deschamps thought, was to issue a border declaration, something which some forty other countries had already done.

Deschamps, therefore, fully approved of Eugene Black's mission to Phnom Penh, which began on 11 September and ended on the 14th, for the American arrived with more authority than Bowles had been given in January. Black was authorized to discuss a border declaration, even the specific language, and to say that the United States would consider issuing one when it was clear that this would result in significantly improved relations. The Cambodians may well have expected Black to produce a border declaration immediately. And when that did not happen, little overt progress was made. After Black left Phnom Penh, one American official thought the possibility of an American border declaration and the resumption of diplomatic relations was now "dead." Rostow, in an overly harsh assessment, informed President Johnson that the "results were nil." But Deschamps, who continually emphasized the need for patience, was probably more on the mark when he said that the mission, "despite the lack of specific results, had been successful. The important thing . . . is to keep the dialogue going with the Cambodians."[24] The visit also made clear to the Cambodians that the United States was now not opposed in principle to a border declaration.

Still, by the end of September the hopes that the Bowles mission had inspired in January had not been fulfilled. As Sihanouk himself put it in August, "the cooling-off period lasted only a short while."[25] The Americans were upset at Vietnamese Communist use of Cambodia. Yet ultimately both sides wanted a better relationship. One advantage the Americans had was that, even as Sihanouk bitterly attacked the Americans, he was growing ever more angry at Cambodian leftists and their Chinese and North Vietnamese supporters, whom he continued to blame for civil unrest in Battambang. Furthermore, though he admitted only to minor incursions by Viet Cong and North Vietnamese forces into Cambodia, by some accounts he privately acknowledged that they controlled as much as one-third of Cambodian territory. As long as Sihanouk felt so threatened by the left, there was always the possibility that he would turn back toward the United States. He apparently told one Indian journalist that if the United States would only recognize Cambodia's frontiers, it could reestablish an embassy with 100 persons and even assign CIA agents to Cambodia. Furthermore the prince continued to say that he did not want the United States to withdraw entirely from Southeast Asia.

On 7 November Sihanouk made an important concession: he now said that he would release the LCU crew if the United States would only do its best to stop the border incidents. It is very likely that Sihanouk would have released the LCU crew as a goodwill gesture during the independence day celebrations on 9 November, had it not been for yet more embarrassing border incidents. In the first, helicopters attacked a Cambodian Public Works truck in eastern Cambodia, killing three people and wounding two others. The United States admitted later that the Cambodian complaint was well founded. Prime Minister Penn Nouth complained bitterly to Deschamps that conciliatory gestures to the United States "were invariably followed by incidents of this nature."[26] In the second incident, three helicopters attacked the village of Prey Tuol in Svay Rieng Province, about two kilometers from the Vietnamese border. One Cambodian died and 24 were injured, 11 seriously. These incidents caused Sihanouk to change his intention to release the crew on independence day. Nor did it help when on 16 November twelve persons—mostly women and children—died in an attack on a sampan (the Giang Thanh River incident).

A satirical Cambodian view of American military actions along the Cambodian-Vietnamese border. By Huy Hem. From *Kambuja*, No. 44, 15 November 1968, p. 143. Courtesy of Dr. Judy Ledgerwood.

Even so, Sihanouk seemed determined to release the LCU crew as part of a larger strategy to improve relations with the United States. He told various people, including the French ambassador in Phnom Penh, that he would release the crew if only President Johnson would send him a personal message requesting him to do so. The United States had been considering a presidential letter since mid-November, only to have the various border incidents postpone it. By 12 December it had been decided to send a letter, only to have it further postponed because of American concern about an enemy buildup near Saigon. Then on 16 December Lois M. Price of Columbus, Ohio—the mother of one of the LCU crew members—sent to the White House a copy of a letter that Sihanouk had written to her that again stated that he would release the crew if only the president would ask him personally. Why, Price asked, would Johnson not cable the prince? The same day Johnson received Price's letter he wrote a cordial and respectful letter to the Cambodian leader.

As it happened, Johnson's letter was delayed for a few hours in transmission (through the French), and before it arrived Sihanouk had decided to release the crew without condition. Two hours later Johnson's letter arrived, at which point Sihanouk also released an injured American helicopter crewman who had been shot down over Cambodian territory, something he had not planned to do. The LCU crew, who had been treated extraordinarily well and had even been treated to a luncheon by Sihanouk himself, were all home by Christmas. The United States was grateful.

Sihanouk's decision to release the crew without getting anything in return indicated that he was now seriously interested in improving relations with the United States. In addition to his concern about the Vietnamese Communists' use of Cambodian territory and the dangerous long-term prospects that a Communist-dominated Vietnam would pose once peace had been attained, the deteriorating economic situation troubled Sihanouk. Finally, Sihanouk wanted to move toward a restoration of relations while Johnson was still president. In a speech to a Cambodian audience, Sihanouk said that President-elect Richard Nixon was a "wicked" man, though he hoped he might change once in office.[27] Despite his great anger at Johnson's escalation of the war in Vietnam and its spillover into Cambodia, Sihanouk realized that he had managed to keep the "hawks" in check. Better to make peace with him than with a "wicked" Nixon. "The door was thus open if there was a corresponding desire on the American side," Sihanouk said. Hearing this, Deschamps, who had previously been cautious about recommending that the United States restore relations with Cambodia, felt "more optimistic" about improved Cambodian-Western relations "than at any time in the past six years."[28]

Responding to the new situation, early in January 1969 the United States for the first time agreed to pay indemnities on its own (usually this was done through the South Vietnamese) to compensate the victims of American raids on Cambodian soil that had taken place the previous October and November. It also took responsibility for the deaths of eight to ten Cambodians killed on 16 December by a secret DANIEL BOONE mission (intelligence teams that penetrated into Cambodia) that, acting against its own rules of engagement, tried to stop a Cambodian truck to capture enemy forces. It was also evident that the State Department was not entirely convinced of American innocence in the notorious Giang Thanh River sampan incident, since Rusk asked for additional information even after the final report, which had exonerated American forces, had been completed. Some thought was given to issuing the border declaration and reestablishing diplomatic relations before Nixon took over. But in the end the Johnson administration decided to leave these issues to its successor.

Richard Nixon and Cambodia

DIPLOMATIC RELATIONS AND BOMBS

"We have reported over recent months the instances of military leaks, particularly from MACV in Saigon, which have apparently been designed to impede the process of resumption of diplomatic relations between the United States and Cambodia."—Report from the Australian Embassy in Washington, D.C., July 1969

"[American and South Vietnamese forces are entering Cambodia to destroy] the headquarters for the entire communist military operation in South Vietnam."—President Richard Nixon, speech to the nation, 30 April 1970

"It was never our plan to capture COSVN. We didn't expect it and it would be a stroke of luck if we did."—General John Vogt, Director of Operations, Organization of the Joint Chiefs of Staff, 12 May 1970

ON 21 JANUARY 1969 Richard Nixon became president, and Sihanouk quickly congratulated him. The new administration saw advantages in improving relations with Cambodia. This would indicate that Sihanouk now thought that the United States would prevail in Vietnam, and an American embassy in Phnom Penh would allow for better intelligence collection. The president immediately responded to Sihanouk that he hoped to resolve differences. Sihanouk let the Americans know that if they restored diplomatic relations, he would not use a border incident as an excuse to break them off again—one of the fears that the Americans had. The lack of an acceptable American declaration recognizing Cambodia's current borders, Sihanouk indicated, was the sole impediment to renewing relations.

Nixon determined to move ahead. Acting on instructions, Deschamps informed Sihanouk that the United States would issue a border declaration if this would contribute to a lasting improvement in relations. Cambodia would have to understand that border incidents might occur even after the resumption of relations, although the United States would try to avoid them and would consult on ways to resolve them. It is significant that Nixon set a course toward normalization without first getting concurrence from the Thais and South Vietnamese, whose hostility to any border declaration had not diminished.

When Sihanouk explained that he did not expect all border incidents to cease, nor did he expect the Americans actually to help demarcate the border, important obstacles were removed. As a goodwill gesture Sihanouk quickly released four Americans whose aircraft had recently been shot down. Also, Cambodian armed forces moved against the Viet Cong, especially in Prey Veng and Svay Rieng provinces. Along the border, South Vietnamese and Cambodian officials consulted in a friendly manner on how they might deal with the Viet Cong. Therefore, on 2 April Nixon approved the issuance of a border declaration that read: "In conformity with the United Nations Charter, the United States of America recognizes and respects the sovereignty, independence, neutrality, and territorial integrity of the Kingdom of Cambodia within its present frontiers." Sihanouk was delighted.

Relations were not immediately restored, in part because the United States wanted to test Sihanouk's actions and attitudes. And in fact Sihanouk began to back away from accepting the border declaration when some American officials suggested that the declaration actually meant very little. Sihanouk's hesitation probably resulted in part from domestic politics and international diplomatic pressures. But he *was* clearly irritated at the glosses certain Americans put on the declaration, as well as with general American press reporting about Cambodia. Leaks from American officials about the meaninglessness of the declaration were possibly deliberate, intended to derail the reconciliation. "It is a pattern which has occurred frequently in the past, whenever an improvement in U.S.–Cambodian relations has appeared as a possibility," Senator Mike Mansfield (D-MT) wrote to the president.[1]

Mansfield (and Sihanouk) had genuine cause for concern. Just when relations were improving, a major border incident or other disruption often occurred that threatened to (and sometimes did) thwart efforts at reconciliation. Deschamps also saw this pattern. There was, he recalled, a "hydra-headedness" to American policy. "You've got so many institutions involved in foreign affairs, and more or less in rivalry and not always in cooperation." Asked to respond to the observation that every time there was an important potential breakthrough in efforts to improve relations there was a major bombing incident, he responded, "Exactly. . . . That's exactly what I mean by hydra-headed. The different institutions were working against each other instead of as a team."[2]

Elements in the American military establishment—most likely military intelligence officers—disliked this incipient rapprochement, just as they had disliked similar efforts in the past, and it is probable that they tried to derail the improvement. The military's disagreement with efforts to improve relations may explain, at least in part, the several cross-border incursions and bombing raids that took place in March and April. These, as well as published reports that defoliants had been used in Cambodia and that small teams of Americans were covertly going into Cambodia and occasionally kidnapping villagers, would undoubtedly have angered Sihanouk.

Potentially the most damaging military leak came on 9 May when William Beecher's accurate story about secret B-52 raids on Cambodian territory appeared in the *New York Times*. Beecher, who had a reputation as a Pentagon ally, was later appointed Deputy Assistant Secretary of Defense for Public Affairs. By some accounts his disclosure of the bombing was intended to help the Nixon administration by showing that it was getting tough.[3] But at the time the Nixon administration was almost apoplectic about the leak, and it is at least equally plausible that military officials in Saigon leaked the story to derail improving relations with Phnom Penh. As a consequence of the leak, the State Department deliberately avoided informing American authorities in Saigon about its most recent effort to assuage Sihanouk.

The leaks, whether intended to disrupt the pending rapprochement or not, slowed the movement but did not derail it. Mansfield played an important role in convincing Sihanouk not to reject the border declaration by assuring him that the administration stood staunchly behind it. This satisfied Sihanouk, who was perhaps influenced as well by an increasing number of armed clashes between Cambodian and Vietnamese Communist forces, and on 11 June the Cambodian government informed the United States that it was now prepared to resume diplomatic relations.

There were some concerns that the arrangement might unravel when American military officials in Vietnam announced that American artillery and aircraft would attack Vietnamese targets in Cambodia. But Sihanouk overlooked this provocation, and Thay Sok, who was already in the United States where he was attached to the French embassy, immediately took over as Cambodian chargé d'affaires. On 21 July Lloyd M. Rives, who had served previously in Hanoi and Vientiane as well as in Africa, was named American chargé in Phnom Penh. On 15 August Rives reopened the American embassy. After a hiatus of over four years, diplomatic relations had been restored, causing one relieved Australian official to comment, "Amen."[4]

The Australians, and some in the State Department, still feared that provocative leaks from American military sources in Vietnam could derail the improving relations. In fact in July when a story appeared indicating that the United States was preparing claims against Cambodia for damages, the Australian embassy in Washington reported that it was "another MACV leak." "What else?" wrote an External Affairs official on the telegram.[5] But Sihanouk chose to ignore or minimize such provocations and indeed seemed more concerned at Vietnamese Communist activity in his country.

Less than a week after Rives arrived in Phnom Penh, Mansfield came to Cambodia. Sent by Nixon to symbolize the new relationship, Mansfield was received almost as a chief of state. The atmosphere, reported Rives, was "extremely cordial." In a toast Mansfield said that American military force would be used on the Asian mainland only in the most extreme situations.[6] The bilateral relationship, it appeared, had gotten off to a good start.

The United States' major hope in restoring diplomatic relations was that it could gain an advantage over its enemies in South Vietnam who used Cambodia as a sanctuary and as a transit point for supplies. In this sense, for the Nixon administration Cambodia truly was (initially) a "sideshow," a term journalist William Shawcross later made famous. Even so, to a certain extent there was a confluence of interests. Viet Cong and North Vietnamese use of Cambodian territory angered Sihanouk. The Cambodian government even published a map depicting Vietnamese inroads into the country, and armed clashes took place between the Cambodians and the Vietnamese. At the same time the Americans believed that Sihanouk had made a deal with the Viet Cong allowing them to import arms through the port of Sihanoukville, provided none of the weapons got to the Cambodian Communists, whom he called the Khmers Rouges.

All of this illustrates how Sihanouk had to maneuver carefully in a web of conflicting pressures. His larger goal was to ensure his country's survival, to try to keep it from becoming further enmeshed in the violence in neighboring Vietnam, and to gain international acceptance of Cambodia's boundaries. To the United States, these were not the primary concerns.

Even as Sihanouk and Nixon were seeking to improve their bilateral relationship, Nixon ordered B-52 strategic bombers to hit Cambodia in highly secret raids that continued for over a year. They were not officially acknowledged until 1973. Because the motives of the two countries in seeking to improve their relationship were only partially coincident, the secret bombing of Cambodia was not as anomalous as it appears at first glance.

Just how extensively the Vietnamese Communists used Cambodian territory had long been a matter of considerable dispute. Officials in Saigon almost invariably concluded that the enemy's use of Cambodia was extensive and growing, that Sihanoukville had become the enemy's major source of armaments, that Cambodian officials were involved in the arms trade, and that the United States ought to respond with military action. Generally speaking the State Department and the CIA were more skeptical of the military's claims, as were the Australians. Even within the Pentagon there was disagreement. The Johnson administration had tried to arrive at some degree of consensus on the issue at an important conference of intelligence experts and American and Australian military attachés in Bangkok in December 1968. The most important person at the Bangkok meeting was James Graham, a respected CIA expert on evaluating intelligence data. Just what Graham ultimately concluded remains classified. But it is probable that his final report differed from MACV's conclusions in important respects.

Not surprisingly, therefore, when the new administration took office Earle Wheeler, chairman of the Joint Chiefs of Staff (JCS), renewed his request to attack enemy bases in Cambodia. On 9 February 1969 General Creighton Abrams, who had replaced Westmoreland as commander of American forces in Vietnam, recommended a single, intensive attack lasting about one hour on what he asserted was the headquarters of the enemy's Central Office for South Vietnam (COSVN).

Unlike Johnson, Nixon was predisposed to believe MACV's assessments. He came into office wanting to wipe out the sanctuaries. When Kissinger told him that little had been done to destroy enemy concentrations in Cambodia, Nixon was angry and approved Abrams' request. Postponed twice, the initial secret B-52 raid took place on 18 March.

Abrams promised that the raid—OPERATION BREAKFAST—would completely destroy the target. A joint American–South Vietnamese reconnaissance team that went in immediately afterward soon found out that this was not the case. Enemy automatic weapons fire nearly wiped it out, and a second team refused orders to go in. Post-strike analysis concluded that the bombing had resulted in numerous secondary explosions, suggesting that many munitions had been destroyed. But military officials subsequently admitted that they had seen "no evidence of enemy attempts to evacuate the area since Operation BREAKFAST and there has been no significant change in the enemy order of battle."[7] Obviously the attacks had not destroyed COSVN.

The failure of the raid to accomplish its objectives did not stop the military from recommending additional strikes in new areas. On 9 April the JCS recommended that standing authority be granted to use B-52s to attack enemy forces retreating into Cambodia. Two days later they recommended intensive strikes on two more base areas: 609 and 353. No mention was made of possible COSVN headquarters in these areas. And while the chiefs did envisage only "minimum risk to Cambodian civilians," they did expect some casualties. They estimated that 196 Cambodians lived in Base Area 609, while 1,640 lived in Base Area 353. The areas were not heavily populated, but they were not, as Henry Kissinger stated in 1973, "unpopulated." Similarly, Nixon lied to the American people when he told journalists in August 1973 that "no Cambodians had been in it [the area bombed] for years. It was totally occupied by the North Vietnamese Communists."[8]

In fact, the Cambodians living in these "unpopulated areas" were terrified. The governor of Ratanakiri, interviewed in 1999, recalled that in his village during the bombing "a great number of villagers were seriously affected by the bomb fragments," that they "could not endure the tragedy," and that most of them therefore fled their homes. A Viet Cong defector put it more dramatically: "To the Cambodian villagers, these bombings brought an incomprehensible terror."[9]

For more than a year, the B-52s secretly bombed targets in Cambodia. Only a few sympathetic members of Congress were informed. As late as April 1973 administration officials testifying before congressional committees denied that there had been any bombing of Cambodia prior to May 1970. But in fact from 18 March 1969 through 26 May 1970, B-52s flew 3,875 sorties and dropped 108,823 tons of bombs on Cambodia.

The bombing had little lasting impact on the ability of the other side to wage war. COSVN was not destroyed, and the Vietnamese Communists moved deeper into Cambodia. By July French officials in Phnom Penh were reporting that the area of Cambodia under control of the North Vietnamese and the Viet Cong had actually increased; roads that had been traveled without difficulty only a few weeks earlier were now closed. In December 1969, ten months after the bombing began, the head of Cambodia's military intelligence approached the American military attaché to say that on a recent trip to Stung Treng and Ratanakiri "he had been shocked at extent of Vietnamese Communist/Pathet Lao infiltration in area."[10] Clearly the bombing had not diminished the presence of the enemy in Cambodia; on the contrary the Vietnamese Communists now controlled even more of Cambodia.

The bombing had little impact on the war in Vietnam, but it had ominous consequences for Cambodia. Many who fled the bombing joined the Khmer Rouge. As the governor of Ratanakiri recalled, they wanted "to establish a struggle movement to coincide with the propagation of top Khmer Rouge leaders," while Truong Nhu Tang, the Viet Cong defector, wrote that the bombing drove "the more militant into the ranks of the Khmer Rouge." All told, as journalist Arnold Isaacs put it, the bombing "was upsetting the delicate balance on which peace in Cambodia rested."[11]

But there were few protests from Phnom Penh, and the question arises whether Sihanouk acquiesced in, or even approved of, the bombing. Once it became public in 1973, administration officials—including Kissinger and Nixon—claimed on several occasions that the prince had approved the bombing, at least tacitly. In 1975 a paper produced by officials in the Gerald Ford administration stated the bombing was kept secret "at Sihanouk's insistence." These papers falsely implied that there had been consultation with the Cambodian leader.[12]

In contemporary papers, as well as in his memoirs, Kissinger cites three specific pieces of evidence to support his assertions of Sihanouk's complicity: (1) over a year before the strikes, Sihanouk privately told Chester Bowles that he would not object to "hot pursuit in uninhabited areas"; (2) on 13 May 1969, two months after the first strikes, Sihanouk said that he had not protested the bombing because he had not heard about it and that he would make no protest unless Cambodians were killed or their property destroyed; (3) in August 1969 Sihanouk commented to Mansfield (who was unaware of the B-52 raids) that he would not protest bombings that affected only the Viet Cong.

Kissinger's first point is correct: Sihanouk did tell Chester Bowles that he would "shut my eyes" to instances of hot pursuit in uninhabited areas of Cambodia.[13] But a willingness to look the other way if the Americans ventured temporarily into uninhabited areas of Cambodia while pursuing fleeing Vietnamese forces cannot reasonably be construed to mean that Sihanouk approved of the intensive, ongoing B-52 bombing raids—raids that had nothing to do with "hot pursuit" and that (despite retrospective administration claims) were not confined to uninhabited areas. Nor does Kissinger point out that in the same conversation with Bowles in which Sihanouk invited hot pursuit in certain situations, the prince stated that the root of the problem was American disregard of the Geneva Accords (in particular the failure to hold elections in 1956), which had led to the war in Vietnam. He blamed the United States for driving the Vietnamese Communists into Cambodia and urged the Americans to stop the war in Vietnam immediately. Furthermore, Sihanouk remained as committed as ever to demanding that all powers respect his territory, and the question of B-52 attacks was never discussed with him.

Although relations between the United States and Cambodia were not very warm, Sihanouk did become increasingly agitated at the presence of North Vietnamese and Viet Cong troops on Cambodian territory. In the first weeks of 1969, Sihanouk's verbal assaults on the Vietnamese Communists and the Chinese increased. He complained that he could not even visit parts of his own country because the Vietnamese occupied it. The Americans were encouraged.

For those Americans (and South Vietnamese) who wanted to take aggressive actions against enemy forces in Cambodia, Sihanouk's remarks at a press conference on 6 March—twelve days before the first B-52 attacks—provided, they thought, an invitation to bomb areas of Cambodia where the Viet Cong were present. South Vietnamese Foreign Minister Tran Chanh Thanh asked an American official later when the Americans were going to "take Prince Sihanouk up on his invitation."[14] Actually Sihanouk's statement was really a condemnation of American bombing of populated areas, not an invitation to bomb areas where there were Vietnamese Communists.

Then on 28 March Sihanouk explicitly rejected reports that he would allow the bombing of Cambodia. Kissinger does not mention Sihanouk's remarks on 28 March. He does, however, maintain that on 13 May Sihanouk for "all practical purposes invited us to continue" the bombing. At a press conference, Sihanouk said he had not protested the attacks "because I have not heard of the bombings." No Cambodian had informed him about them, he said, and the Vietnamese would not do so because that would prove that they were on Cambodian territory. He would protest only if Cambodians were injured.[15]

Sihanouk did indeed make the statements Kissinger cites, although the news conference, which took place in a provincial area and was broadcast in the Cambodian language, was intended for a domestic audience. His remarks reflected his anger at Vietnamese use of his territory (he had, after all, lost to them control over a section of northeastern Cambodia the size of a province), and the Americans could reasonably conclude that Sihanouk would not protest attacks on Vietnamese forces in remote areas of Cambodia, as long as no Cambodians were injured or their property damaged. But in the same statement Sihanouk "categorically" denied that "he has ever allowed U.S. bombing of his territory" and insisted (as Kissinger acknowledges) that he would not permit violations of his territory "by either side. Please note that."[16]

As for Kissinger's third point, Sihanouk did discuss the bombings with his friend Mike Mansfield, who arrived in Phnom Penh in August 1969, shortly after diplomatic relations had been restored. Sihanouk pointed out to Mansfield that Cambodia had not protested bombings that affected only the Viet Cong and did not injure Cambodians, and he strongly urged the United States to avoid injuries to Cambodians. At the same time, he urged the United States, once again, to leave Vietnam, which of course would have meant the bombing would end. Although Kissinger sees the comments to Mansfield as confirming his view that Sihanouk knew of and approved the bombings, when the bombing became public knowledge in 1973 Mansfield commented publicly, and then wrote to Sihanouk directly, that "any suggestion that you were in accord, tacit or otherwise, with the several thousand secret bombing raids on your country and had so informed me was completely incomprehensible to me."[17]

In sum, Sihanouk was never asked to approve the B-52 bombings, and he never gave his approval. He steadfastly insisted on respect for Cambodia's integrity and sovereignty. He strongly protested American and South Vietnamese border incidents that injured or killed Cambodians and damaged Cambodian property. He sought the American border declaration in part to limit border raids and attacks. Though he said that he did not expect that all border raids would end and that he would not use them as an excuse in the future to break relations, he hoped they would diminish.

Nixon's initial letter to him on 14 February encouraged him, for the president promised to "exercise the utmost restraint."[18] And in instructions to Ambassador Deschamps to be conveyed orally to Sihanouk, the United States pledged that its forces would "do their best . . . to avoid incidents which might cause casualties or damage in Cambodia."[19] Deschamps stated emphatically that the Cambodian leader did not know about the bombings in advance. "No, no, no, no, very definitely not," he said.[20]

Sihanouk did acknowledge that his army of 35,000 was unable to control the frontier, and those Americans who wanted to bomb Vietnamese forces in Cambodia could take comfort in some of his remarks that suggested he would look the other way. Given his anger at the Vietnamese abuse of his territory and his belief that they were also supporting his domestic opponents, Sihanouk shed few tears over their casualties. He did, after all, renew relations with the United States, even as the bombing was well under way and, as Nixon pointed out, invited the American president to visit Phnom Penh. But the retrospective defenses of the American bombing seize on Sihanouk's occasional remarks about looking the other way and generally ignore the larger context of his ultimate goals, which was to keep the violence away from Cambodia and retain his country's independence and neutrality. And while he did not want the United States to withdraw entirely from Southeast Asia, he saw nothing positive to be gained from continued American military involvement in Vietnam.

Although (with one exception) Sihanouk did not protest the B-52 bombings, he protested numerous other instances of American and South Vietnamese incursions. In the first four months of 1969, Cambodia formally protested 109 incidents—21 more than during the same period in 1968. Also complicating the relationship were the numerous clandestine operations. Reconnaissance patrols had existed for some years but were systematized in May 1967 and given the code named OPERATION SALEM HOUSE. Initially teams of six to eight Americans and South Vietnamese operating under strict limitations sought tactical intelligence in the northeastern tip of Cambodia. Subsequently, the operations (renamed DANIEL BOONE) expanded to encompass the entire Cambodian-Vietnamese border region, and the teams operated up to thirty kilometers inside Cambodia. The previous requirement that each mission have approval from Washington was dropped, and helicopters were authorized to infiltrate the teams.

Beginning in October 1968, the number of covert missions increased sharply. For the first time, the teams used antipersonnel mines, and the limitations on the number of Americans who could be included were eliminated. Increasingly there were casualties of Cambodian civilians and military personnel. Covert incursions increased even more after Nixon took charge. In the first four months of 1969 alone there were at least 188 missions, several of which the Cambodian government protested. During all of 1969 there were 454 missions; 558 took place the following year. This compared with 99 in 1967 and 387 in 1968. By the time they were ended in 1972, at least 1,885 missions had been undertaken; twenty-seven Americans died, and the families of those killed were not told that they had been in Cambodia.

Tensions between the United States and the Cambodians also resulted from defoliation of trees and crops. From time to time there had been complaints about the dropping of "yellow powder" over areas of Cambodia, and at times defoliation (RANCH HAND) operations in Vietnam had resulted in unintentional drift of herbicide into Cambodia. But the most dramatic incident occurred in April 1969 when herbicidal damage occurred over an area of approximately 700 square kilometers. According to the Cambodians there were additional defoliation operations on 9, 12, and 14 May that "nearly doubled over the area affected up to 8th May."[21] The Cambodian government was especially concerned with damage to about one-sixth of this area, where fruit and rubber trees were most affected.

In response to Cambodian protests, the United States offered to send a scientific team to investigate, and indicative of the generally improving relations, Cambodia for the first time accepted American investigators. In July four American scientists entered the field. Their findings confirmed Cambodian allegations. Damage near the border was the result of the drift of herbicidal Agents Orange and White, which had been sprayed on South Vietnam when the meteorological conditions were not good. But plantations much deeper inside Cambodia had been sprayed and had suffered severe, though not irreparable, damage. The defoliation was deliberate, almost surely the result of some secret American operation. In July 1971 Senator Frank Church (D-ID) charged that Air America, the CIA contract airline, had done it. His source, Church wrote, was "an individual who is in a position to know the facts." Queried about this, Ambassador to South Vietnam Ellsworth Bunker denied Air America's involvement, but he acknowledged that some American airplane, as yet unidentified, might have been involved.[22] If it was not a CIA operation, some other American intelligence agency was probably responsible. In 1973 the legal affairs branch of the State Department determined unequivocally that the United States was legally required to compensate Cambodia for all the defoliation damage.

The restoration of relations in July 1969 and Senator Mansfield's visit seemed to mark a chance for a new beginning. But unfortunately, such optimism was premature. American violation of Cambodian territory and airspace only increased, thus keeping the relationship cool. In October alone Cambodia protested a "rather staggering" eighty-three separate incidents. In view of this impressive total, wrote Rives, "it appears some credit should be given Cambodia for restraint." He hoped such incidents could be reduced.[23]

The most serious incident occurred on 16–19 November when American planes and artillery repeatedly attacked Dak Dam (located seven kilometers inside Cambodia), the Cambodian military post located there (which was destroyed), and neighboring villages, including Bu Chric, which was hit by B-52s. (This appears to be the only time the Cambodian government specifically protested the use of B-52s.) The American action was triggered when enemy artillery fire, located near the town, hit the Special Forces camp at Bu Prang in Vietnam some nine to ten kilometers from Dak Dam. When American planes tried to suppress the artillery fire, Cambodian forces responded with antiaircraft rounds. The American pilots then attacked the antiaircraft guns and, in so doing, inflicted substantial casualties on *Cambodian* military personnel. At least twenty-five Cambodians died, and a number of animals, civilian and military buildings (including a school house), and vehicles (including an ambulance) were damaged or destroyed. It was, as one important official reported, "the most serious border incident yet in number of Cambodian casualties, [and] it is among the few involving significant losses among Cambodian Army personnel."[24]

This was not the first time Dak Dam had been attacked, and this new incident resulted in protests within the American bureaucracy. Several months earlier Rives had privately expressed the fear that such incidents would occur—and that they might be part of a deliberate effort by American military forces to undercut improved relations. "Rives is obviously perturbed—as we here have been before him," reported the Australian ambassador at that time, "by the possibility that the United States military authorities in Viet Nam will follow a policy towards Cambodia which was different to that of the White House and the State Department."[25] Now Rives told the State Department that he did "not quite see what I am expected to say to the RKG [Cambodian Government] in justification Nov. 16 and Nov. 17 attacks" since the Americans' own photographic evidence showed that a Cambodian military post, along with a school and an ambulance, had been destroyed and numerous Cambodian soldiers killed.[26] Fearing that another break in relations was possible, he strongly suggested that the president send a personal message to Sihanouk expressing his distress over the incident. There was no presidential message, but the United States did express its official regrets and sent solatium (compensation) payments. But the border incidents continued, nevertheless, including another attack on Dak Dam.

In sum, by the end of 1969 the United States and Cambodia still maintained diplomatic relations. But the border incidents persisted; Cambodians continued to die in bombing raids and clandestine operations; and the B-52s continued to take their toll, helping to destabilize Cambodia, driving the enemy deeper into Cambodia, and giving aid and comfort to Sihanouk's most bitter enemies, the Khmer Rouge. And Sihanouk appeared to be reverting to his earlier view that the Vietnamese Communists would prevail in Vietnam and that China would be the dominant outside power. Relations between the United States and Cambodia had cooled. There was no significant warming of relations until Lon Nol and Sirik Matak ousted Sihanouk in March 1970 while the prince was out of the country.

Sihanouk's dismissal (which followed constitutional forms, rather than a blatant military coup d'état) immediately produced much speculation as to its causes. From the beginning, Sihanouk claimed that the CIA was responsible. Antiwar critics, the North Vietnamese, the Soviet Union, and the Chinese made similar claims. Nixon and Kissinger maintained that the Americans had nothing to do with it and were, in fact, caught completely by surprise. "We had no role in the change of Governments," Nixon informed Indonesia's President Suharto in May 1970.[27]

The degree of American involvement has divided those scholars who have investigated it and cannot yet be determined with certainty. But most think there was some American foreknowledge of the coup, and if the CIA was not involved, American military intelligence officials in Vietnam probably were. There were a number of factors that probably led certain Americans to push for a change of leadership in Cambodia. The military had chafed at Sihanouk's constant protests over border incidents, his acquiescence in the presence of Vietnamese soldiers who sought sanctuary, and his complicity (so they believed) in conveying supplies to the enemy. Military leaders had even drawn up plans for an invasion of Cambodia in 1967 and 1968 and were upset that Lyndon Johnson would not approve them. With Nixon's election, they pushed even harder and soon received approval for the B-52 strikes and stepped-up intelligence operations inside Cambodia.

For a time in 1969 as Sihanouk himself worried about the presence of Vietnamese Communist troops in Cambodia, he cut off their supplies. But there were reports, apparently accurate, that shipments resumed later in the year. On the political side, Sihanouk appeared to have moved back closer to the North Vietnamese; in September 1969 he had attended Ho Chi Minh's funeral in Hanoi, and North Vietnamese Premier Pham Van Dong was scheduled to visit Phnom Penh early in 1970.

For those looking for evidence of Sihanouk's move toward the Communist bloc, the publication in *Sangkum* in September 1969 of the names of 3,000 alleged CIA agents would have been convincing evidence. *Sangkum* helpfully pointed readers to the names of those agents who had served in Cambodia. Critics would also have noted Sihanouk's warm reception of antiwar American scientists early in January. They might also have pointed out that shortly thereafter, after Sihanouk left Phnom Penh in January 1970 for medical treatment in Paris, there were reports that he would return via Prague, Moscow, and Peking. Furthermore, Sihanouk was making it very difficult to publicize the American viewpoint inside Cambodia. The embassy was unable to place news stories in local publications, to show movies, or to encourage Cambodians to visit the U.S. Information Center. Thus those who were predisposed to think that the American military situation in Vietnam would improve if there were a change of leadership in Phnom Penh could find reasons to support their perspective. Furthermore, with Sihanouk's position in Cambodian politics unraveling at this time, and with his major opponents, especially Sirik Matak, being amenable to American influence and support, an opening was there for those who wished to push Sihanouk out. The presence of American-financed, anti-Sihanouk Khmer Serei forces available in South Vietnam to assist a new government provided an additional incentive to support a coup. In sum, as Nixon's chief of staff H. R. Haldeman put it retrospectively, Lon Nol's ouster of Sihanouk "was all right with us"—a comment that contradicts those who contended that there was no motive for replacing Sihanouk.[28]

For his part, the exiled prince never ceased to believe that he had been the victim of an American-sponsored coup. In 1979, Kissinger met Sihanouk in Beijing and assured him that the United States had had nothing to do with it:

"You must believe that we were favorable to your returning to power and that we did not like Lon Nol. We liked you."

"Thank you very much," Sihanouk responded.

"I want you to believe it," Kissinger pressed on.

"Excellency," Sihanouk replied, "let bygones be bygones."

"No. No. No. I want you to say that you believe me," Kissinger insisted.

To which Sihanouk replied, "I apologize. I cannot say I believe you."[29]

After the coup Sihanouk urged his countrymen to join his former enemy, the Khmer Rouge, and formed a government in exile, the Gouvernement Royal d'Union Nationale de Kampuchea (GRUNK), in Paris. The United States ignored this development and professed considerable faith in Lon Nol. But the new head of state was a problematic leader for modern times. A proud Khmer, Lon Nol identified with and accepted traditional folk beliefs, including astrology and the occult, associated with what he called the "Khmer-Mon" people. In September 1970 his government officially encouraged the use of a number of occult practices to achieve military victory. Lon Nol himself was thought to believe that he personally had the power of divination. According to an official American embassy assessment, as time passed Lon Nol's reliance on mystical sources embarrassed many educated Cambodians.

Nevertheless, from the outset the United States sought to bolster the Lon Nol–Sirik Matak regime. Secretary of Defense Melvin Laird wanted a CIA communications post established in Cambodia at once. Whether or not the United States had played a role in Sihanouk's ouster, it clearly approved of the new government and was going to throw its full weight behind it.

A major concern for both the United States and the new Khmer Republic was to get the Vietnamese Communist troops out of Cambodia. To this end the United States for a time sought to build support for various international solutions. An Indonesian proposal for a conference of Asian nations that would try and "prevent Cambodia from being turned into a second Vietnam," as one Indonesian newspaper put it, attracted considerable American attention.[30] Although the project also attracted great skepticism from France and several other countries, Indonesia's Foreign Minister Adam Malik forged ahead with considerable energy, engaging in what the Australian ambassador to Indonesia termed admiringly "excellent broken field running."[31] On 28 April invitations went out to nineteen Asian countries to attend a conference on 11–12 May 1970.

But an Asian conference could not promise success, partly because the North Vietnamese wanted no part of it, and some American officials felt that more was required, and at once, if the new government were going to survive. In particular, they looked for ways to send it arms and supplies. Rives and the State Department were initially opposed, arguing that France was a better choice as an arms supplier and that American assistance would lend credence to the view that Lon Nol was an American client. Congressional opposition to American aid quickly developed as well. But Nixon was determined to provide assistance, and the administration quickly offered the Cambodian government 1,500 AK-47s, presumably weapons captured in South Vietnam.

Angry when news about the arms leaked to the press, the administration established a new channel for correspondence about "U.S. involvement in military assistance to Cambodia." Only top level officials would see communications sent via this NODIS/KHMER channel.[32] Soon, unmarked airplanes landed at Pochentong airport delivering several thousand weapons, primarily captured AK-47s but also M-1 and M-2 carbines. These deliveries were explained as a South Vietnamese operation, but it was an American action. The United States also allowed Khmer Krom (ethnic Cambodians who lived in Vietnam) soldiers serving in U.S. Special Forces camps to go to Cambodia to fight on the side of the Cambodian government. Once in Cambodia they were to be integrated into Lon Nol's army as the 43rd, 45th, 47th, and 48th brigades. Ostensibly volunteers, some of the Khmer soldiers were surprised when they stepped off the plane and discovered that they were in Phnom Penh. As in the case of the weapons, the United States tried to make this appear to be a South Vietnamese operation. The South Vietnamese were involved, but U.S. Special Forces shipped at least the 43rd and 45th to Cambodia.

The use of the Khmer Krom troops embarrassed the United States. These soldiers had conducted clandestine operations in Cambodia and some, perhaps most, were Khmer Serei, a group that the United States had regularly denied supporting. Charges soon began to circulate that these were American mercenaries. In important respects, the critics were right. Government officials in Washington were embarrassed to discover that the Khmer soldiers were not part of the South Vietnamese military but were instead "advised, equipped, supported and paid by US Special Forces."[33]

The United States also wanted other countries to assist Lon Nol. Nixon appealed personally to Australian Prime Minister John Grey Gorton, for example. But the most interesting (and most secret) effort involved Indonesia. Within two weeks of Sihanouk's overthrow, the United States encouraged Indonesian officials to give strong support to the Cambodian government. In fact, President Suharto and the Indonesian military were following events in Cambodia with deep concern. After all, in 1965 Suharto came to power in much the same way Lon Nol had. Foreign Minister Malik, who was trying to organize the international conference, opposed providing aid, as did Indonesia's ambassador to the United States Sudjatmoko. But on 15 April Suharto stated that Indonesia would not only provide small arms but also would bring Cambodian troops to Indonesia for training—provided the United States would secretly replenish the arms. However, for the moment Suharto held back, not wanting to take action that might undercut Malik's conference on Cambodia.

Yet another option for assisting the new Cambodian government was to employ American and South Vietnamese troops directly. In mid-April a State Department intelligence analysis of possible Communist reactions to cross-border military operations provided a mixed picture. On the one hand, the Communists had attempted to pressure the new Cambodian government into allowing them to operate unmolested. They had done this in part by expanding and consolidating their "zones of influence." Expansion of the zones was likely to continue if South Vietnamese border operations were restricted. On the other hand, "extensive, intense and regular South Vietnamese operations into Cambodia" might provoke the Communists to move directly against the Cambodian regime. They would certainly expand their operational zones significantly, give full support to indigenous "liberation movements," and generate international pressure from the Soviet bloc against the Cambodian government. The report was, thus, prescient. Read retrospectively, in fact, the report vaguely predicted that large-scale cross-border operations would increase the chances of a Khmer Rouge victory in Cambodia.[34]

But Abrams and the JCS wanted military action. And on 20 April the president told Haldeman that he would personally "take over responsibility for the war in Cambodia." Two days later, concerned at reports that the North Vietnamese were about to take Phnom Penh, frustrated at the Senate's failure to confirm his two nominees for the Supreme Court, anxious to assert his personal authority, angry at various perceived enemies, and perhaps spurred on by repeated viewings of the movie *Patton,* Nixon approved final planning for a South Vietnamese attack into the Parrot's Beak area of Cambodia. Nixon's original plan called for an invasion on 25 April. But Kissinger thought Nixon was moving too precipitously (although in principle he supported an invasion), and there was a slight delay.

The president was also now thinking about committing American troops to the operation (now planned for 28 or 29 April) primarily to destroy the ever elusive COSVN. Laird and Secretary of State William Rogers had been frozen out of the planning and were livid when they found out. Concerted opposition delayed the invasion again. But Nixon was determined to go ahead with a two-pronged attack, one involving primarily American troops. According to Haldeman, Kissinger saw the matter largely as one of presidential authority. "I think [he] would go ahead even if plan is wrong," wrote Haldeman, "just to prove P. can't be challenged."[35] On 30 April at 9:00 p.m. (Washington time), Nixon told the nation that American and South Vietnamese troops were entering Cambodia and going after "the headquarters for the entire communist military operation in South Vietnam." Destruction of COSVN was the campaign's major immediate objective.[36] Soon 44,189 ARVN and American troops (a slight majority American) were fighting in the Parrot's Beak (primarily a South Vietnamese operation) and Fish Hook (primarily an American operation) areas along the Cambodian border.

White House officials went to extraordinary lengths to measure the public response to Nixon's speech. They compiled reports of newspaper editorials, carefully watched and evaluated television news broadcasts and commentaries, made note of congressional reactions, sought out the opinion of business and labor leaders, and kept track of the telephone calls, letters, and telegrams that poured into Washington. Much of the opinion was bitterly critical of the invasion. White House officials, including the president himself, went to unusual lengths to try and reverse the trend and generate support, including organizing a recall of Governor Edmund Brown of California if the governor called for Nixon's impeachment. It was time for Barry Goldwater, Ronald Reagan, and other "inflammatory types" to attack the Senate doves, Nixon said, charging the doves with "knife in the back, disloyalty, lack of patriotism." There were times, he stated in one of his periodic displays of masculinity, when you had "to step up hard sometimes—not flinch." Finally, he saw advantages in student rage: "never underest[imate] value of turning the student thing to our advantage esp[ecially] if they get rough."[37]

The administration attempted to mobilize right-wing groups such as the Young Americans for Freedom, to have supportive senators keep tabs on doves, to generate letters and telegrams of support from (among others) the Reverend Billy Graham's mailing list, and to get astronaut Frank Borman on the Ed Sullivan show. Ross Perot's help was sought. Haldeman plotted to

President Richard M. Nixon explaining the American invasion of Cambodia in April 1970 to the American people during a nationwide television address. Courtesy of the National Archives and Records Administration.

withdraw Department of Defense research monies from universities where dissent was strong. Nixon was particularly insistent that all cabinet secretaries, under secretaries and assistant secretaries speak out in support. (Getting cabinet support proved difficult. Nixon was angry that none of the cabinet secretaries had called him after the speech to offer him their support, and in a fit of pique he ordered that they not be allowed to use the White House tennis courts.)

The administration was also intensely interested in the foreign reaction. Every diplomatic post in the world was asked to report official and media reaction to Nixon's speech and the military action. As a result, voluminous reports were compiled, many of them not comforting to the administration. In all major European countries there was strong criticism of the American action. Foreign Secretary Michael Stewart was humiliated at Oxford University and not permitted to speak. In Germany, Chancellor Willie Brandt refused to establish diplomatic relations with the Lon Nol government. The French government was almost palpably hostile. The Scandinavian countries all distanced themselves from the United States. In Yugoslavia, a country favored by the United States because of its split with the Soviet Union, the reaction was especially bitter. Marshall Tito hurriedly recognized Sihanouk's government in exile, and demonstrators smashed the windows of the USIS building in Belgrade. Venezuelans were uncomfortable, as were

Mexicans. In Iran, where Vietnam had scarcely been discussed, Cambodia was the subject of much discussion, all of it unfavorable to the United States. Non-Communist countries of East and Southeast Asia were more supportive, as was Australia. But the Indians were critical.

Particularly important to the administration was the reaction of the Indonesian government because of the planned international conference. Publicly Indonesian officials "deplored" or "regretted" the action, and a number were strongly opposed in private as well. Malik, however, privately expressed understanding for the decision, and Suharto told Nixon personally that the U.S. action was "essential and important." If Cambodia went Communist, he said, it would become "the base for subversion and infiltration" in the region and would threaten Indonesia.[38]

But at home opposition among Americans to the administration's Cambodia action intensified. On the day of the invasion, Senator J. William Fulbright (D-AR) and the Senate Foreign Relations Committee demanded to know on what legal basis American forces were being sent into Cambodia and whether the administration planned to consult Congress. By 7 May at least fifty senators had come out in opposition to the president and only twenty-one had voiced support. New York Governor Nelson Rockefeller likened the move to "dropping a match into a powder keg."[39] There was also outrage in the House of Representatives, where John B. Anderson (R-IN) introduced a resolution reaffirming the constitutional requirement for the president to consult with the Congress on questions of war and peace.

The most visible dissent was seen on the nation's campuses, many of which exploded in anger. Nixon called student demonstrators "bums" (he claimed, without being entirely convincing, that he was quoted out of context). On 4 May National Guardsmen killed four student demonstrators at Kent State University, setting off an enormous negative reaction around the country and the world. American students in Israel, for example, demanded that the embassy fly the flag at half staff. There was "revulsion" on campus against the invasion, University of Hawaii President Harlan Cleveland, a foreign policy specialist himself, wrote to Nixon.[40]

The country seemed about to be torn apart. Demonstrators took over a portion of the Peace Corps offices in Washington and issued a manifesto calling for withdrawal from Southeast Asia. Two hundred fifty Foreign Service officers and State Department officials signed a letter of protest to Secretary Rogers. There was fear of a military coup in Washington. But Nixon was far from apologetic. "No defensiveness from W[hite]H[ouse] . . . Don't worry about divisiveness," he said. "We've created division, drawn the sword. Don't take it out, grind it hard."[41]

After Kent State some administration figures, including Rogers, urged Nixon to tone down the rhetoric. In response, Nixon was conciliatory during an important press conference in early May, and publicly the Nixon administration liked to give the impression that the president relished opposing views. But if the rhetoric was momentarily lowered, behind the scenes the administration retained its "enemies" mentality. It soon undertook a major campaign to discredit student leaders. Among other things, Haldeman ordered Lyn Nofziger to get a column written claiming that the student disturbances were the result of Cuban-trained outside agitators. "This project is to be given top priority," Haldeman stated.[42]

The most celebrated example of internal dissent was that of the Secretary of the Interior, Walter Hickel, who criticized the administration's response to the students. Asked about this in his press conference, Nixon spoke highly of Hickel. "He is courageous. That is one of the reasons I selected him for the Cabinet," he stated, "and one of the reasons I defended him very vigorously before this press corps when he was under attack." However, Hickel's dissent was actually viewed as traitorous. And the administration's private response was much the same as toward others it considered its enemy: he was to be discredited and driven out. "Be extremely cold— don't invite to anything. . . ," Nixon ordered Haldeman. "Start a quiet job chopping Hickel[:] screwed everything up—behind the scenes encourage his enemies—build as incompetent—build pressure on him."[43] A few weeks later Hickel was gone.

Meanwhile, administration spokespersons made every effort to publicize the invasion's achievements. They recited endlessly the number of arms and amount of ammunition captured (Haldeman ordered that the number of *rounds* of captured ammunition, rather than tonnage, be reported), tons of rice seized (which was ostentatiously given to refugees), number of structures destroyed, and so forth. The numbers were impressive and doubtless caused the enemy some hardship for a period of weeks or months. But the incursions had not destroyed COSVN nor the ability of the other side to continue the war.

The invasion also brought Cambodia itself directly into the war for the first time—and with devastating consequences. Prior to the invasion, the Vietnamese occupied limited, if perhaps growing, parts of Cambodia, especially along the frontier with Vietnam. Now they had driven deeply into Cambodia and were within a few miles of Phnom Penh. Some observers thought they could take the capital at any time. They threatened other major interior cities and in June temporarily took over the airport at Siem Reap. If they succeeded in keeping Siem Reap, the Cambodian government feared, they might make it the capital of Sihanouk's government in exile, a move that (given the symbolic significance of Angkor) might have debilitating psychological consequences.

Lon Nol's soldiers pass out weapons to Cambodian villagers shortly after the ouster of Norodom Sihanouk and the American invasion of Cambodia. This picture appeared on the back cover of the Cambodian government magazine, *Cambodge Nouveau,* July 1970. Courtesy of Dr. Judy Ledgerwood.

Administration officials always denied that the invasion was responsible for spreading the war into Cambodia's interior because, they said, the enemy had moved deeper into Cambodia *prior* to the invasion. But no less an authority than Lon Nol disagreed. Among the consequences of the invasion, he told visiting Americans, was that "the enemy was unfortunately forced deeper into Cambodia."[44] In any event the situation was so desperate that Lon Nol himself requested, and received, asylum in Singapore for his family, despite State Department efforts to talk him out of it.

On 9 June with the announced withdrawal of all American forces from Cambodia less than three weeks away, the American embassy prepared an estimate of what the situation in Cambodia would be like after the Americans withdrew. The overall tone was pessimistic. As a result of the invasion a very substantial part of the country was now subject to enemy control—a dramatic change from the pre-invasion situation. Nor was the embassy certain that the government could survive at all. Certainly without substantial foreign assistance, all was lost. "If other immediate assistance . . . is not forth-coming," the embassy concluded, "there will remain nothing for diplomacy to deal with."[45]

But reports of Cambodia's weakness infuriated President Nixon. "The line that 'Cambodia is doomed' must be stopped," he said on 15 June. Nixon insisted that all that could be done to save Cambodia be done, regardless of the consequences. In essence, Nixon had changed the American mission from one in which Cambodia was a "sideshow" to protect the American withdrawal from Vietnam and assist Vietnamization, to one in which the preservation of a non-Communist Cambodia was a goal in itself.[46]

Nixon ordered direct assistance to Cambodia even before the invasion and without clear legal authority to do so. He also urged South Vietnam to keep its troops in Cambodia after the Americans withdrew and, in certain situations, to provide support to Cambodian military operations—in the event, for example, that Phnom Penh was threatened. The United States was also willing to support South Vietnamese operations with American air power, if required. South Vietnam was cooperative, but the United States had less success in getting other countries to support the new government in Cambodia. Japan, the Philippines, Australia, New Zealand, Malaysia, and Taiwan all provided only small amounts of aid or training.

But the United States had high hopes that Indonesia and Thailand would provide more meaningful assistance. With respect to Indonesia, the United States continued to support Malik's efforts to arrange an international conference. The invasion momentarily stopped the momentum in that direction, and there remained considerable skepticism in any event. No Communist government accepted an invitation, nor did the major neutralist governments in the region, such as India and Burma. Hanoi's accusation that Indonesia was an American puppet and Malik a CIA agent added to the skepticism.

The United States did not expect the projected conference to bring peace to Cambodia immediately. But it saw two important benefits that might emerge from it: the creation of a neutral observer group to replace the defunct ICC in Cambodia, and a followup mechanism for continuing consultation among the conference participants. Not wanting to be seen as influencing this conference of Asian nations, the United States nevertheless made its views known behind the scenes.

In the end, the conference was held. It did not send a neutral observer group to Cambodia, but it did demand the withdrawal of all foreign forces in Cambodia, urged respect for Cambodia's territorial integrity and neutrality, and called for the reactivation of the ICC and the convening of a new international conference. The foreign ministers of Indonesia, Malaysia, and Japan were charged with working with the Geneva cochairs, other countries, and the United Nations to implement the conference's recommendations and work for the end of the war in Cambodia.

Although the conference did not accomplish as much as the United States had hoped, most observers nevertheless thought it was an important, if somewhat surprising, success. For the first time Asian countries had come together to deal with Asian problems and propose Asian solutions. "Malik's willingness to risk his own position domestically, as well as Indonesia's non-alignment, appears more than vindicated by the successful outcome," Ambassador Francis J. Galbraith concluded.[47]

Whatever the judgment about the Jakarta conference, international diplomacy did not offer a short-term solution, and with the very survival of the Lon Nol government in doubt the United States once again sought Indonesian military assistance. The Indonesian government remained split over this question, but the Americans were optimistic. If the Indonesians were not yet persuaded that arms were immediately required, they did go ahead with plans to train Cambodians in special warfare techniques (both in Indonesia and Cambodia) and to send advisers to Cambodia.

The Indonesians continued to hedge on weapons, though they seemed willing to supply them if the United States would commit itself to major military assistance to Indonesia, something the Americans were willing to do. But meanwhile attention turned to reconfiguring a factory in Bandung, Indonesia, to produce AK-47 ammunition for use in Cambodia. The Indonesians had apparently raised this possibility during Suharto's visit to Washington, and in June the Indonesians invited American technicians to visit the plant to determine the feasibility of the project. But before they arrived, Indonesian officials stalled. It was increasingly clear that the Indonesians expected considerable, probably unrealistic, assistance from the United States in return for their aid to Cambodia.

The American technicians did eventually inspect the Bandung facility and another munitions plant then under construction in Turen and concluded pessimistically that it would take two to three years for the Bandung factory to be converted to produce AK-47 ammunition, while the Turen plant, which was not yet operational, would take even longer to convert and could produce even less than the Bandung facility.

In the end Indonesia did provide some modest, and very secret, military aid to the Lon Nol government, the most significant of which were AK-47 rifles, ammunition, and related equipment sent to the Americans for transshipment to the Cambodians. In exchange the United States provided the Indonesians with M-16 rifles. The Indonesians also secretly trained some Cambodian troops. Still, Indonesian aid was limited and secret, and American hopes to use Indonesia as a significant source of military supplies and the training of Cambodian troops were not to be realized. Other avenues would have to suffice.

More predictable assistance came from Thailand, although in the end Thai support, like Indonesia's, was less than was anticipated. The Thais loaned aircraft to the Cambodian air force but, due to considerable domestic opposition, did not send any regular troops to Cambodia. Some irregular volunteer units did enter the country, however, paid for by the United States. A more promising source of troops were Thai-Khmers (many, perhaps most, of them Khmer Serei). The United States agreed to pay for the training of several thousand. On 23 July Prime Minister Thanom Kittikachorn announced that 3,000 Thai-Khmer would go to Cambodia. But in fact they apparently went to Laos instead.

Still, Thailand provided more assistance to the Lon Nol government than any other Asian country (except for South Vietnam). The Thais trained thousands of raw Cambodian recruits; provided at least 361 technical advisers, nine patrol boats, and clothing and equipment kits for 50,000 soldiers; with American approval, they transferred American-supplied military equipment to the Cambodian armed forces. They also conducted reconnaissance flights over Cambodia and, after the Americans withdrew their troops, flew combat missions in direct support of Cambodia troops. The Americans (who observed many of these strikes from their own observation aircraft) were highly impressed with the accuracy of the Thai attacks. Directly or indirectly, the United States paid for much of the Thai assistance through its Military Assistance Programs (MAP) to Thailand and Cambodia.

In the end, the assistance provided by third countries was of some political significance but, except for that from South Vietnam and to a lesser extent Thailand, militarily unimportant. As an American embassy report put it in May 1972, it "has had only a very marginal impact on FANK [Khmer National Armed Forces] capabilities and operations."[48]

With the withdrawal of American forces on 30 June 1970, Lon Nol was concerned whether direct American assistance would continue. He need not have worried. At the end of August Nixon sent Vice President Spiro Agnew to Phnom Penh to symbolize the continuing American commitment.

The administration wanted to support a Cambodian army of 65,000 by increasing military assistance to Cambodia from $8.9 million in FY 1970 to an initial $40 million in FY 1971. Despite objections from the Office of Management and Budget, Nixon signed the order. Because Congress had not appropriated these funds, the administration had to reallocate funds approved for assistance to other countries. So large cuts were made around the globe with Greece, Turkey, and Taiwan absorbing the largest cuts, though Latin American programs suffered the greatest percentage cutbacks. The reductions brought forth anguished cries from American ambassadors around the world who expressed "shock," "deep regret," and "utmost concern." But the administration was determined to provide the assistance to Cambodia.

In the weeks immediately after the withdrawal, the Americans also continued to pay for the training of Khmer Krom troops in South Vietnam and assisted with their insertion into Cambodia. American Special Forces officers were in charge of the training in at least one camp, Lon Hai. The Americans also sent a "psyops" radio team to Phnom Penh to help Radio Phnom Penh, funded military training centers in Cambodia, sent a team of technicians to service the T-28 aircraft, and provided tens of thousands of M-1 rifles and AK-47 magazines. CIA director William Colby visited Phnom Penh to advise the Cambodian government on pacification strategies. Soon the United States would provide a number of C-47 airplanes.

Although American support in the summer and early fall of 1970 must have reassured Lon Nol, there were those within the Nixon administration who questioned whether the United States should continue its assistance, particularly after the initial $40 million was nearly all spent by mid-September. Neither Rogers nor Laird shared the view that Cambodia's future was of much consequence to the United States, particularly if the administration was unable to convince Congress to approve a supplemental appropriation bill. There were even suspicions, probably well founded, that Laird in particular "wanted to wash his hands of Cambodia" even though he was publicly supporting a supplemental appropriation. Despite some internal doubts, there was no real debate within the administration about whether the survival of Lon Nol's government was important to the United States. Options that suggested otherwise, Kissinger stated, had one major problem: "the President believes the opposite." Therefore the debate was over means and not ends.[49]

The most extreme option, proposed by former MACV Commander William Westmoreland, called for American forces to reenter Cambodia and Laos. This was not given serious consideration, but the administration adopted the next most aggressive (and expensive) strategy, which was to continue to build up the Cambodian armed forces while having South Vietnamese forces defend the Cambodian government and one-half of its territory, if necessary. This was to be funded by a supplemental appropriation along with what the assistant secretary of defense called "some devious procedures."[50]

In November Nixon asked Congress for a supplemental appropriation of $255 million for Cambodia. If the appropriation was not forthcoming, Nixon's operatives were determined to do whatever was needed to get the funds somehow—"Operation Scrounge" they termed it—and they were willing to violate regulations if needed.

Meanwhile the American embassy staff in Phnom Penh had increased, with the assignment of several military personnel. Lieutenant Colonel Jonathan Fred Ladd who, despite embassy objections, reported directly to the White House and MACV, headed the MAP staff. Ladd coordinated the delivery of military supplies and informally advised the Cambodian military. Later, as the American commitment grew, a Military Equipment Delivery Team (MEDT) replaced the MAP. Ambassador Emory Swank and the State Department had strongly resisted the establishment of a MEDT, and the precise authority of the MEDT chief vis-à-vis the ambassador became a source of controversy between the Defense and State departments.

Even more indicative of the growing American involvement in Cambodia was the direct air support provided to Cambodian forces. This represented a departure from the initial American mission, which was to use its air power in Cambodia only to interdict "the movement of supplies and men relevant to the war in Vietnam."[51] Increasingly, however, Americans flew combat missions supporting Cambodian troops.

In September another milestone was passed when some American planes were authorized to conduct operations anywhere in Cambodia, though with restrictions. American forward air controller (FAC) aircraft were still limited to certain parts of Cambodia, with Vietnamese or Thai FACs allowed to operate elsewhere. When Senate staffers visited Cambodia in late November and early December, an American officer told them that the description of American air operations in Cambodia as interdiction missions was simply "camouflage."[52]

In sum, the war had been spread to Cambodia. The United States had now acquired another weak government to defend, a government that controlled perhaps one-quarter of the country. At the end of October enemy shells fell on Phnom Penh. "The local hospitals are filling up," a missionary recorded in his diary. All highways from Phnom Penh had been cut, except for the Route 1 to Saigon. By the fall of 1970 the original rationale for intervention in Cambodia (that American actions were entirely related to the war in Vietnam and that there was no intention of becoming involved directly on behalf of the new Cambodian government) no longer held. As Lloyd Rives advised the incoming ambassador, Emory Swank, the first American objective in Cambodia was to see that the country remained "independent and neutral."[53]

Sticking with Lon Nol

"Anyone who depends on handouts soon becomes a creeper rather than a tree."—Singapore President Lee Kuan Yew, referring to Lon Nol, 7 February 1973

DURING THE NIGHT of 8–9 November 1972, lightning struck the Phnom Penh stupa, causing the top section to collapse. This was widely regarded as an ill omen for the republic. But Lon Nol had an alternative reading of the event. It signified the end of the Cambodian monarchy, the reelection of Richard Nixon, and the survival of the republic, he thought. "We hope he is right," reported Ambassador Emory Swank.[1] But it was the skeptics who were right.

Lon Nol was always optimistic about his prospects. By the end of 1970 U.S. embassy officials were inclined to agree. The government had survived, despite deep pessimism and military setbacks in the weeks immediately following the coup. As a result comedian Bob Hope, then in Bangkok, sent a telegram to the White House saying that President Nixon deserved a medal for bravery. On 31 December 1970 Lon Nol informed Nixon that "popular feeling" was increasingly opposed to the enemy and that "the Khmers are now succeeding in tipping the scales as completely as possible in their favor." With American planes decimating reinforcements coming in over the Ho Chi Minh Trail, the prime minister predicted that his own forces would take back regions of the country currently in the hands of the Vietnamese Communists.[2]

The prime minister's optimism was premature. A few days after his prediction, enemy forces attacked a convoy on the Mekong River that was transporting petroleum supplies to Phnom Penh, sinking two or three barges and other craft. This brought the stocks of petroleum products in the city to a "critical point," according to the American embassy. There were no supplies of kerosene and fuel oil left at all.[3] Fighting was also picking up in various parts of the country. Thanks to heavy American military cover, a new convoy made it up the Mekong to Phnom Penh without incident. But on 22 January 1971 Viet Cong saboteurs infiltrated Pochentong airport and blew up virtually the entire Cambodian combat airforce, including MIGs, helicopters, T-28s, and C-47s. All told, thirty-nine Cambodian aircraft were destroyed, and another nine suffered major damage. Ten South Vietnamese planes were also destroyed, while an American C-47, belonging to the embassy's defense attaché, suffered major damage. The Viet Cong may have lost three soldiers, but fifty Cambodian military personnel died and some 300 civilians, mostly military dependents, were wounded. It was a devastating attack—"the most psychologically sobering experience for population since my arrival last September," Swank reported.[4]

Though these events temporarily sobered Lon Nol, within a few days he had recovered his usual aplomb. But it was hard to find evidence to support his cheeriness. Foreign Minister Kuon Wick told Malaysian officials that Lon Nol was "overly optimistic and militarily inept" and should be kicked upstairs to some kind of figurehead position. The day before, unknown to Kuon Wick, Lon Nol had suffered a stroke; the prime minister was soon taken to Tripler General Hospital in Hawaii for treatment.[5]

Despite these setbacks, the Nixon administration was determined to portray American involvement in Cambodia as a great success. Nixon himself told Agnew, Kissinger, and Pat Buchanan that there was no reason to be defensive on Cambodia, that press attacks were "unfair, irrelevant & inaccurate & conflicting." Administration opponents, he raged on, had a vested interest "in seeing us fail cause they predicted we'd fail." A few days later he told Kissinger that they should not have "a soft-handed defense[;] have to whack the opponents on patriotism—American lives—etc." The next day the president acknowledged that he had "*not* gotten over success to people[;] have to make it very simple . . . . *have* to estab[lish] success of Cambodia[;] public doesn't see it as success[.] They've only heard TV—and it's all unfavorable."[6] Perhaps, as Nixon told Alexander Haig, the problem was that Kissinger's staff had "all turned left. Must examine staff closely. Watch for traitors."[7]

When pessimistic press reports continued to appear, some citing government officials, Nixon was incensed. For example, in response to Terence Smith's story in the *New York Times* headlined "U.S. Aides See Situation in Cambodia Deteriorating," Nixon demanded to know who the aides were. The administration's desire to demonstrate success in Cambodia could not alter the facts on the ground, however. B-52s had to be used to relieve beleaguered Cambodian forces trapped in the Pich Nil Pass on Route 4, the important road linking Phnom Penh with the port of Kompong Som (Sihanoukville), and the Cambodian Army continued to be ineffective.

In effect admitting that the situation was critical without saying so, the administration did all that it could do to prevent Cambodia's collapse. For fiscal year 1971, it managed to pry $185 million in aid for Cambodia out of a reluctant Congress, raided MAP funds intended for other countries in order to get matériel to Cambodia, and waived legal requirements so that it could purchase 600 trucks for use in Cambodia from American subsidiaries in Australia. It put considerable pressure on Australia and South Korea to train Cambodian troops. Over strong State Department objections, the administration assigned more military personnel to the American embassy, while the chief of the MEDT, Brigadier General Theodore Mataxis, deliberately sidestepped the chief of mission and imported materials that he wanted—even when the ambassador specifically vetoed them. (High level State Department officials attempted, unsuccessfully, to have Mataxis replaced.) Skirting the law, Americans provided informal advice and training to Cambodian forces, took in military supplies in the attaché's helicopter, and evacuated wounded government troops back to Phnom Penh. Most important, the United States extended its already extensive air support of Cambodian forces to cover all Cambodian territory. Not surprisingly, the percentage of sorties over Cambodia soared. In 1970, 8 percent of American sorties in Southeast Asia were over Cambodia. In 1971 the figure was 14 percent.

Despite these efforts, officials in both the Department of Defense and the American embassy in Phnom Penh were privately becoming pessimistic about Cambodia's future. For one thing, there was no strong political leadership. While Lon Nol had made a considerable recovery from his stroke, he was still seriously incapacitated. His doctors ordered him to work no more than one hour per day, and in May 1971 he had to accept temporarily a figurehead position in the government. For another, the military situation continued to be problematic. Senior officials in Washington predicted that the military situation would worsen, in part due to the lack of aggressive leadership in the Cambodian Army.

Reports of endemic corruption and some scathing evaluations of the current government only deepened the gloom. Sim Var, Cambodia's ambassador to Japan, commented that the present cabinet looked like it had been "picked from the street," that the National Assembly "lacked political maturity," and that Lon Nol's entourage was "corrupt."[8] Embassy officials did not accept such reports at face value, but their own considered analyses were scarcely less damning.

Meanwhile, the Khmer Rouge Army (officially the army of the *Front Uni National de Kampuchea,* or FUNK) grew at an alarming rate. Thought to be only a nuisance in 1970, it was estimated by Sirik Matak to number 15,000 in August 1971, a figure that the American embassy also used. But the actual figures may have been much higher. By the end of the year the Cambodian government's intelligence service estimated the number at 20,000, which, it thought, would probably grow at some undetermined date to 50,000. American military intelligence analysts thought Khmer Rouge strength was already considerably higher. In August 1971 they estimated it at somewhere between 35,000 and 50,000. One CIA analyst, Sam Adams, thought there might be as many as 150,000.[9] Whatever the precise figure, the Khmer Rouge was no longer just a nuisance, and while the military situation might not be critical in 1971, the future looked ominous. By late November 1971 the American embassy was saying that there was no hope that the government could expel completely the Vietnamese Communists and regain control over all of Cambodia.

The American military's response to this deterioration was to try to build up the Cambodian military at a frantic pace. Little attention was given to pacification. To this end the Department of Defense wanted to increase the number of in-country MEDT personnel to ninety-one—up from the currently authorized figure of twenty-three. Swank and the State Department, on the other hand, thought that the United States should keep as low a profile as possible in Phnom Penh. As Fred Ladd, Swank's Counselor for Military-Political Relations, once put it, increasing the in-country MEDT team would be "like helping a thirsty baby by shoving a fire hose down its throat."[10] Swank and Ladd wanted to provide aid, but they thought the Defense Department's approach was wrongheaded.

In addition to genuine philosophical differences over how the United States should best relate to Cambodia, there were serious turf wars, with the State Department insisting that the ambassador, as chief of mission, had control over all aspects of American relations with Cambodia, including military assistance, while the military officials, feeling that they were running a war, believed they should be the primary actors. General Mataxis was the symbol of this problem. His primary allegiance, as he construed it, was to the military, and so on occasion he ignored or evaded Swank's express wishes. Perhaps his most notorious act of insubordination (in State Department eyes) was his decision to import assault rifles (AK-47s and UZIs) as well as sidearms for MEDT personnel—despite the ambassador's specific prohibition against them.

The bureaucratic and philosophical differences led to strong exchanges, even between secretaries Rogers and Laird, which eventually found their way into newspaper and magazine reports. When Brigadier General John Cleland took over as chief of MEDT, relations seemed to be smoother. Swank agreed to substantial increases in the number of MEDT stationed in Cambodia, for example. But serious differences remained.

If the State and Defense Departments often found themselves at odds, they both believed, along with the White House, that Congress provided inadequate appropriations for Cambodian assistance. They also disliked the congressional prohibition on the use of American advisers and restrictions on the number of Americans in Cambodia at any one time. Consequently, considerable efforts went into trying to convince Congress to increase funding and reduce restrictions. The administration was also not above using devious methods to obtain the funds it sought. Even so, it was not easy.

Toward the end of the year two developments in Cambodia increased antiwar sentiment in Congress and contributed to the pressures to cut aid. The first was Lon Nol's effort to reassert his personal control. Democracy was no longer appropriate for Cambodia, he pronounced, and he began to rule by decree. Though not technically accurate, the popular understanding in the United States was that Lon Nol had abolished the National Assembly and assumed dictatorial powers. More devastating for Lon Nol and his supporters in the Nixon administration was the disastrous Chenla II military campaign, which began in August 1971. Designed to reopen route 6 to Kompong Thom, and personally organized and directed by Lon Nol himself who "brushed aside the concerns of the naysayers," including Americans and some Cambodians, who warned him of serious deficiencies in his blitzkrieg plan, the campaign turned into an utter disaster in November as Communist forces cut the government forces to pieces. Over 3,000 of Cambodia's best troops were killed and thousands more wounded, while 15,000 others fled in disarray, leaving their weapons behind. General Sak Sutsakhan called it "the greatest catastrophe of the war." It would in fact be the last major offensive of Lon Nol's army. Also for the first time large numbers of refugees, many escaping allied bombs and artillery during the Chenla II campaign, streamed in panic along the roads or made do in makeshift camps, getting little if any assistance from the authorities while just trying to stay out of the fighting.[11]

Efforts to achieve a diplomatic solution to the Cambodian crisis were also attempted. In September 1970 the Nixon administration itself considered making a public proposal for an Indochina-wide ceasefire in place to be followed by an international conference that would arrange for the withdrawal of all external forces. Swank was ordered to get Lon Nol's approval of the draft proposal. The Cambodians objected, particularly to the idea of a ceasefire in place, and there were some modifications. On 7 October Nixon made a televised addressed to the nation proposing an international conference on Cambodia. But nothing came of it.

Perhaps because of their doubts about Nixon's proposal, some important Cambodians wanted to sound out Sihanouk about possible terms. Son Sann, in particular, who had served in previous Sihanouk administrations, received encouragement from government officials (apparently including Sirik Matak and Cheng Heng) to contact Sihanouk. In Paris Son Sann met with several of Sihanouk's supporters. But nothing resulted from these contacts. Son Sann hoped to return to Phnom Penh and then go on to Moscow, Berne, and Prague, where he wanted to meet with former Prime

Minister Penn Nouth, the only person worth speaking to, he thought. But when Son Sann returned to Phnom Penn in July, Lon Nol gave him "no encouragement at all." No negotiations could take place until the Vietnamese withdrew entirely from Cambodia, he was informed. Arguing in religious terms, Lon Nol told Son Sann that victory was certain since "the conflict has become a religious war and the reign of Buddha is to last another 2,500 years." Although Son Sann had become a devout Buddhist since the death of his son in 1969, Lon Nol's attitude left him discouraged. He cashed in his unused airline tickets. Nevertheless, Son Sann intended to pursue his contacts when he returned to Paris in August. Asked about the American attitude toward such contacts, Swank responded that the United States had "a sympathetic and positive interest in any serious attempt to contribute to peace."[12] Nothing seems to have resulted from these talks, doubtless in part because the Khmer Rouge also had little interest in negotiating a settlement.

Nixon's impending historic visit to Beijing offered a new possibility for negotiations or at least soundings. A number of rumors surfaced that Sihanouk wanted to meet with Nixon when the president was in China. In an interview in December with the Italian weekly *L'Europeo,* Sihanouk displayed an "obvious eagerness to meet with President Nixon during his Peking visit."[13] Sihanouk's most direct approach to the United States came in January 1972 when he let it be known that "should the President wish to speak to him, he would be pleased to come to Peking."[14] But no Nixon-Sihanouk meeting took place, although there are indications—including a statement by Sihanouk himself—that the Chinese attempted to arrange such a meeting, only to have Nixon veto it.

It is unfortunate that the United States declined to engage the prince. To be sure, any agreement with Sihanouk would almost certainly have resulted in the end of the Lon Nol government. But perhaps an arrangement could have been made that would have kept the Khmer Rouge at arms' length; the results for Cambodia would have been better. Even though there was a sense by then, as Ambassador Swank put it in 1987, that "the Cambodians were doomed," no one in the administration was willing to say so out loud.[15] Despite the public advice of those like Senator Mansfield, who urged that Sihanouk be restored, there was no political will in the administration to forge a solution short of retaining the Lon Nol government. When rumors surfaced in the summer of 1972 that preparations were under way to return Sihanouk to Cambodia, Nixon personally informed Lon Nol that the United States had nothing of the sort in mind.

As the United States continued to negotiate with the Vietnamese Communists, as Nixon prepared for his historic trip to China, and presumably as the full force of the Chenla II disaster began to hit home, Lon Nol himself began to look for a way out. The first hint of this came to the Americans' attention at the end of 1971 when rumors circulated that the Communists had attempted to contact the government about possible peace terms. Evidence for this was in the very low level of military activity and in some comments from Soviet officials. Although the State Department tended to doubt the veracity of such reports, they continued to surface. A flurry of rumors appeared late in January 1972 that North Vietnam, using various Communist embassies in Phnom Penh as intermediaries, was proposing a ceasefire in exchange for the government allowing the North Vietnamese uncontested access to their former sanctuaries and the resumption of shipping supplies through Kompong Som (Sihanoukville). An alternative rumor was that the Cambodians had initiated the soundings.

American embassy officials tended to dismiss a possible Cambodian initiative, since both Lon Nol and Sirik Matak privately denied making one. They put more credence on the former possibility, adducing a number of reasons as to why the Soviets and other Communist countries might have an interest in promoting a settlement. The embassy was frankly uncertain about what was going on and concluded that, while "soundings" of some sort probably had been made, no formal negotiating proposal had been presented.[16]

At almost exactly the same time an intelligence report surfaced that a Lon Nol emissary had approached the Indonesians to see if they would serve as intermediaries with the North Vietnamese. The terms being discussed, the report stated, included a nonaggression pact in return for "North Vietnamese use of logistics corridors in northeastern Cambodia." Swank took this report to be "probably accurate." An even more credible report about the same time stated that Major General Kang Keng, a trusted associate of Lon Nol, had approached Soviet embassy officials to see if they could serve as intermediaries. Swank thought this was "an arresting development." Upon reflection, however, Swank stated it was logical for the Cambodians to develop a negotiating position, given the uncertainties of external assistance in the months ahead. "They see the example of our private talks with Hanoi and Peking," he wrote, and thus had "an understandable motivation to do some exploring themselves."[17]

Although the State Department commended Swank for his cogent analysis, the White House took a very different view of these contacts. With the president's personal approval, it became the position of the United States that it could not "visualize any mutually agreed *modus vivendi* between Hanoi and Cambodia" that would not threaten Vietnamization, weaken the Khmer Republic, and "shake general confidence amongst our friends on the Indochinese peninsula." Reestablishment of the sanctuaries would be "an enormous setback" to American aims. Swank was therefore ordered to see that these contacts ended.[18]

Swank's account of his hour-long conversation with Lon Nol about this required twelve pages of single-spaced text. In the conversation Lon Nol insisted that the overtures had come from the Soviet Union, not from him.

But Swank was not fully convinced. "I think it plausible to conclude that Lon Nol was not being fully candid with us," Swank reported. Using his diplomatic skills, the ambassador kept the conversation pleasant throughout, and the two men parted on friendly terms. But the point had been made, and made clearly. If Lon Nol wanted continued American support, he must stop all contacts of this sort.[19] It may be only a coincidence, but two weeks after the American démarche the lull in military activity came to a sudden end when a rocket attack on Phnom Penh killed over 100 persons.

It was quite clear by this point that the FANK was not winning the war. In April 1972 an interagency review concluded that FANK would be able to hold Phnom Penh for the next eighteen months, but the enemy would "continue to makes gains" in the countryside. FANK lacked good leadership, and Lon Nol interfered "at all levels." Even more troublesome, Cambodia's military strategy was unrealistic, the army's tactics flawed, and its administration "chaotic." Furthermore, the Cambodians knew little about unconventional warfare, their psychological warfare program was "very limited," their intelligence capabilities "only marginally effective," and the highly touted "general mobilization" almost invisible.[20]

Nor did the political future look bright. Given his compromised health, Lon Nol could leave the scene at any moment, and there was no successor in sight. Political instability would inevitably affect the war effort negatively. In a particularly telling admission, the group conceded that "while they had justifiable complaints under Sihanouk, the Khmer were by and large protected from the ravages of war. Now the war has been brought to the countryside and to the capital city." Keeping up enthusiasm for the war among Cambodians, already diminished, would be more and more difficult as the resistance became increasingly "Khmerized." While the administration tried to find points of optimism, the future looked bleak indeed.[21] Some FANK units reportedly were even collaborating with the enemy.

Then in August for the first time the enemy began to use tanks near Kompong Trabek. They cut Route 1 in three places and isolated several FANK units. The use of tanks unnerved the normally upbeat Lon Nol. He began to write directly to President Nixon pleading for more support. Between August 3 and 10, he wrote five lengthy letters—at least one of them handwritten—to Nixon. Swank thought that this was a poor way for Lon Nol to expend his limited energy, but Nixon encouraged this practice, feeling that this helped the Cambodian president deal with his anxieties.

Adding to the sense of gloom, from time to time enemy rockets rained down on Phnom Penh, sometimes aimed accurately at defense targets but often killing civilians and further eroding the already fragile morale. On 6 May twenty-eight persons died and ninety-six more were wounded when 112 rockets and other ordnance landed near the Ministry of National Defense. Sappers also infiltrated the airport and the city, launching attacks against bridges, airplanes, and other convenient targets. Eventually the embassy had to forbid American families with children from coming to Phnom Penh. The situation became so precarious that later in the year Lon Nol himself asked the Australians if he could send his three young sons to Australia to study.

A moment of optimism occurred in May 1972 when FANK troops retook the Siem Reap airport and attempted to surround the enemy in Angkor, but ultimately they did not have the strength to do so. By August FANK was back on the defensive in the Angkor area, and the renowned French archaeologist, B. P. Groslier, who had attempted to continue his work at the ruins, feared that in desperation the army would employ heavy weapons and destroy the priceless monuments. Furthermore, FANK's failure to reopen Route 1 and the enemy's successful blockading of Route 5 to Battambang resulted in severe rice shortages in the capital, leading in September to riots and looting of Chinese shops. Soldiers perpetrated much of the violence until Lon Nol confined them to their barracks. By the middle of September American officials were not certain that Lon Nol could retain the loyalty of the army, as the military leaders increasingly questioned his judgment. "The underlying thread" of this discontent, concluded American Chargé Thomas Enders, was "concern that Lon Nol may be losing the war."[22]

The Americans responded to this situation by reassuring Lon Nol that he retained solid American support, and they took various measures to try and turn the situation around. American planes, including on occasion B-52s, continued to assist Cambodian troops. In the fall a high-level American delegation arrived in Cambodia to develop recommendations on reorganizing FANK to make it more effective—a delegation whose very presence was, according to the State Department's legal office, a clear violation of the law forbidding Americans to advise the Cambodian government. But none of these efforts seemed to make much difference.

Meanwhile the internal political situation was deteriorating. Students, who had once strongly supported Lon Nol, became discouraged when the democratic reforms they expected did not materialize. On 27 April 1972 military police fired on demonstrating students, hitting at least twenty of them, and the American embassy reported that the populace sympathized with the students. More demonstrations and strikes ensued.

Lon Nol, who in March had successfully maneuvered to eliminate Sirik Matak from power, then announced that he would hold presidential elections in which he would run. To his surprise a number of other candidates announced their intention to enter the race, and two, In Tam of the Democratic Party and Keo An, reputed to be a Sihanoukist, refused to withdraw. In the end, the official figures showed that Lon Nol received about 54 percent of the vote; In Tam, who actually won the election in Phnom Penh, received 24 percent; and Keo An, who was popular in the countryside (despite an apparent reputation of being "wildly impractical and unbalanced," according to a later American embassy assessment), received a remarkable 21 percent.[23] Thousands of people simply declined to vote, and in any event the vote was rigged. Had the election been fair, In Tam or possibly even Keo An would have won. One scholar insists that Lon Nol actually received less than 20 percent, and perhaps only 15 percent, of the vote.[24] Clearly Lon Nol's government was in trouble, and there was a great malaise among the population, if not quite yet a sense of defeatism.

In the fall of 1972 more than ever the United States urged national unity. All Cambodian leaders agreed in principle; but in practice unity was difficult to achieve. Lon Nol, for example, blamed Sirik Matak for the military failures, the student riots, and alienation of the Buddhist monks. On 5 October the government closed down Sirik Matak's newspaper because it published an article that the government found offensive. Lon Nol's "ability to govern" was not enhanced, thought the Americans.[25] Little came of their pleas for unity. Meanwhile Lon Nol was losing international support, though his government, with much American help, managed to retain the Cambodian seat at the United Nations.

Things only got worse in Cambodia, despite progress at the Vietnam War peace negotiations in Paris. Indicative of the dangerous situation even in the capital, the American ambassador (or chargé in his absence) rode to work in a heavily armored car. Inside the car was a military policeman armed with an UZI and a pistol. Behind was a second car carrying three Cambodian military policemen armed with M-16s and pistols. Two military policemen on motorcycles rode alongside. The protection was needed. On 24 September Thomas Enders was riding in this fashion to the embassy when a large bomb detonated near his car on a major Phnom Penh thoroughfare. Had Enders been in a regular car, he would have been killed. As it was he escaped unharmed, although one of the motorcycle policemen died at the scene, as did a civilian cyclist. The Viet Cong and Cambodian Communists were blamed, but in retrospect William Harben, chief of the American embassy's political section, suspected that Lon Non, brother of Lon Nol, who had a reputation for viciousness and, as head of Cambodia's covert intelligence operations, was familiar with terrorist techniques, was behind it. It is possible that Harben was right, for the United States generally considered Lon Non's influence detrimental. If Lon Non was responsible, he may particularly have disliked American pressure to obtain an honest count of the number of Cambodian soldiers and in other ways reduce corruption. Or he may simply have objected to American support for his political enemies in Cambodia. In any event, there was much violence in Phnom Penh. All told, by the time of the assault on Enders, twenty-seven terrorist attacks had taken place during the year in the capital.

That number was soon to increase. Early in the morning of 7 October—the second anniversary of the creation of the Khmer Republic—Viet Cong sappers penetrated the northern defenses of Phnom Penh and infiltrated the capital. Achieving total surprise, they destroyed or captured the bulk of a FANK company's much prized M-113 armored personnel carriers (APCs). Equally important, they destroyed the key bridge across the Tonle Sap River. (The bridge was not restored until 1994, largely with Japanese funding.) The government could take some comfort in the fact that the Cambodian Army swiftly rallied, American planes were in action within fifteen minutes, and most of the raiders were killed or captured. But the raid was nevertheless devastating. The incoming chief of staff, Sosthene Fernandez, called it "a disaster." Enders fully agreed.[26] The future looked bleak.

Although there was no dramatic change for the rest of the year, the situation in Cambodia had clearly deteriorated dramatically since the coup that placed Lon Nol in power. In January 1973 the State Department spelled out the situation in stark terms in a document intended as background reading for Vice President Agnew, who was about to visit Phnom Penh. He would find a country different from the one he had first visited in 1970, the department wrote. The government now controlled no more than one-third of the country, perhaps only one-fourth. Furthermore, "the high morale and national dedication present at the time of your first visit has largely disappeared into one of war-weariness, ineffectiveness and considerable corruption." Lon Nol's base of support was "very narrow," most other Khmer leaders having withdrawn from the government. The military leadership has "not been effective." Economically, the country was "not in good shape." There were no exports to speak of, and Cambodia was almost entirely dependent on the United States for trade. The United States was even supplying rice—this to a country which had almost always been self-sufficient in that commodity.

The State Department paper also challenged the long-standing American position that the Khmer Rouge were mere puppets of the Vietnamese. With "apparently little assistance from the NVA/VC" the Khmer Rouge had launched large scale attacks simultaneously in many parts of the country. Although the government army was much larger and better equipped and was able, with considerable air support from the United States, to withstand these attacks, it seemed powerless to defeat the insurgency. This, the vice president was to be informed, was due to "poor leadership, particularly at the highest level; current factionalism within the top military leadership which is intensified by the divisive role of Lon Nol's brother, Lon Non; [and] corruption and a dramatic decline in morale at all levels."[27]

Before the State Department's briefing paper reached the vice president, it went to Henry Kissinger, who changed it in significant ways. In contrast to the State Department's view that the Khmer Rouge were by now largely independent of the North Vietnamese, the vice president was informed that Hanoi controlled most of the "indigenous Communist military and political apparatus in Cambodia." Kissinger's unwillingness to acknowledge that the Khmer Rouge were not dependent on Hanoi—something even in 1975 he would not fully accept—was a major misreading of the Cambodian situation. As William Shawcross put it in 1978, "from Kissinger's refusal to accept that the Khmer Rouge could seriously distrust the Vietnamese communists stems much of the subsequent, continuing disaster."[28]

Kissinger's rewrite did acknowledge that the enemy controlled "most of eastern and northeastern Cambodia and substantial areas in other parts of the country," but government forces also controlled "a substantial part of the country, including the richest rice producing areas, and a majority of the population." Gone were statistics estimating government control at only one-third to one-fourth of the territory. Furthermore, the Cambodian Army, though it had numerous problems, "has been generally successful in keeping open vital lifelines to Phnom Penh and in protecting most of the important population centers."

Gone also were references to the dramatic deterioration that the vice president would see when compared to his earlier visit in 1970. There were no references at all to declining morale or the pervasive war weariness that the State Department had identified. Nor was there any mention of Cambodia's dependence on the United States for rice and trade. In sum, Kissinger's revision of the State Department paper suggested that the country had some important problems and still required American assistance to survive, but it was not in desperate straits. "Most of the country has been spared the ravages of war, since most of the fighting has been along lines of communication, and U.S. air strikes have been conducted in largely unpopulated areas," the vice president learned.[29]

The State Department's view was the more accurate one. The situation was so precarious that the embassy recommended that the plane that brought Agnew to Phnom Penh return to Saigon, or perhaps circle in the air during the vice president's visit. If it were to stay on the ground at Pochentong airport, it might be attacked.

Meanwhile in the fall of 1972 there were expectations that the fighting in Vietnam would soon end, as Henry Kissinger and Le Duc Tho negotiated seriously in Paris. The basic American negotiating position with respect to Vietnam, put forward in the previous May even as Nixon was ordering renewed intensive bombing of North Vietnam (OPERATION LINEBACKER), was a ceasefire in place and the return of prisoners of war, after which the United States would withdraw its troops. After intensive negotiations, most issues were resolved by 12 October. Cambodians were at no point involved in the negotiations directly.

In late October, having initialed an agreement with Le Duc Tho in Paris, Henry Kissinger was dispatched to Indochina to get South Vietnamese concurrence. On 22 October he flew to Phnom Penh where, for three hours, he discussed the agreement with Lon Nol and other Khmer leaders. The main provision affecting Cambodia was an article that called for an end to military actions and the withdrawal of all foreign troops. It contained no specific deadline. It is not clear how much detail Kissinger shared with the Cambodians, though he certainly informed Lon Nol that the agreement contained a provision for the withdrawal of foreign troops. Two weeks later Lon Nol told a *New York Times* reporter that Kissinger had not informed him in any detail about the Paris agreement.

It was probably no coincidence that three days after the *Times* story, Alexander Haig, Nixon's deputy national security adviser, and John D. Negroponte of the NSC showed up in Phnom Penh to discuss the tentative peace accords with Lon Nol and Prime Minister Hang Tun Hak. The agreement did not yet specify when hostilities in Cambodia would cease, but the Americans told the Khmer leaders that they would press the North Vietnamese on this issue at the next meeting. Nixon planned to guarantee the enforcement of the agreement, in part by keeping "a massive air and naval presence in the area," which, after an agreement was reached with Vietnam, would be "even more at your disposition." The American MAP program would also continue.[30]

The Cambodian government wanted the agreement to provide for the withdrawal of all North Vietnamese troops, the evacuation of all sanctuaries and arms caches, a prohibition on the North Vietnamese taking Khmers with them for training in North Vietnam (which had happened after the Geneva Conference of 1954), and a requirement that North Vietnam use its influence with the Khmer Rouge to end hostilities in Cambodia. The Americans responded that they doubted they could get the North Vietnamese to agree to the last of these items. But they did encourage the Cambodians to improve their own bargaining position by taking the offensive militarily to open as many lines of communication as possible prior to a ceasefire. Beyond that, the United States counseled caution. Not only would immediate military efforts to establish control over enemy-occupied areas be counterproductive in a political sense, but they risked humiliating defeat. Better to wait until the North Vietnamese had withdrawn according to the peace agreement, the Americans thought, before expanding government control.

But for the moment all of this was academic. South Vietnamese President Nguyen Van Thieu had refused to sign the peace agreement, despite great pressure from Kissinger, and Nixon had ordered his national security adviser back to the conference table. Difficult negotiations continued into December, but a settlement was not reached, and Nixon resorted to another round of intensive bombing in North Vietnam—the infamous Christmas bombings, or LINEBACKER II.

Actually, the prospect of a peace settlement in Vietnam was unnerving for the Cambodian government (as indeed it was for the Khmer Rouge). The government feared that the American departure from Vietnam would inevitably lead to decreasing American support, if not abandonment. The Khmer Rouge feared North Vietnamese and Chinese pressure to accept a ceasefire and negotiated agreement.

In any case the Lon Nol government never put all of its negotiating eggs into the Paris talks basket. In addition to urging the Americans to get acceptable terms for Cambodia in Paris, the Cambodians again attempted to contact the North Vietnamese and the Khmer Rouge to see whether a negotiated settlement of the war was possible. Son Sann, with his government's approval, resumed his efforts to find a peaceful settlement. He was given implicit authority to contact officials in Sihanouk's government in exile in Paris.

Meanwhile Sihanouk himself, despite his fiery public rhetoric, was dropping numerous hints again that he would like to meet with American officials. It is not impossible that there was some American consideration given to a negotiated settlement at this time involving the prince. There surely was some informed speculation about this. But the bulk of the evidence suggests that the Nixon administration had committed itself to the Lon Nol regime and was not about to turn back toward Sihanouk. Sihanouk, the American officials thought, was finished. He ought to retire to a nice villa in France, they said.

That the Americans never seriously contemplated discussions with Sihanouk at this time is evident in their complete disregard of the prince's efforts later in the fall of 1972 to open communications. Perhaps the most serious effort to get negotiations going came from the French, who offered to help the Americans establish a private channel of communications with Sihanouk. In December similar offers from Sihanouk to talk with the American surfaced in Guyana and Mauritania. Not only did the United States decline to pursue these soundings: it did so vigorously and contemptuously.

During the latter stages of the Vietnam peace negotiations, the Chinese indicated to Kissinger that they would be willing to arrange a meeting with Sihanouk. Kissinger acknowledged it was possible to arrive at a solution that would take Sihanouk's concerns into consideration. However, he did not envisage negotiations directly between Sihanouk and the United States but rather among the Khmer parties themselves. Only after a ceasefire in Cambodia might the Americans talk with Sihanouk. The lack of American diplomatic imagination was unfortunate. To be sure, it would have been politically difficult for the Americans to turn to Sihanouk. But the United States had no treaty obligations to the current Cambodian government and was not in theory tied to any particular personality; it might have been possible to separate Sihanouk from his murderous allies the Khmer Rouge who, the prince well knew, had no long-term use for him or the monarchy.

As William Shawcross put it eloquently in 1978, "but for the contempt with which Henry Kissinger always dismissed him, Sihanouk—who understood the nature of the Khmer Rouge—might have been able to avert the dark savagery which has been visited upon his people since April 1975."[31]

Finally on 27 January 1973 the final peace accords to end the war in Vietnam were signed. With them came some optimism that the fighting in Cambodia might also stop. However, the Paris accords were vaguer about Cambodia than about Vietnam and Laos. Article 20 called upon the parties to respect Cambodia's independence, sovereignty, territorial integrity, and neutrality, as had been delineated in the Geneva agreements of 1954. It required all foreign countries to end their military activities in Cambodia and withdraw their troops; foreign countries were also not to use Cambodia to encroach on the sovereignty or security of other countries, and Cambodia was to settle its own internal affairs without foreign intervention. There was, however, no timetable nor a specific agreement for a ceasefire.

In this circumstance, the Americans wanted Lon Nol to declare a unilateral ceasefire and insist on a Vietnamese withdrawal from Cambodia, while at the same time refraining from taking provocative actions against their positions. He would continue his efforts to seek a negotiated settlement with the insurgents. The United States would temporarily halt the delivery of military supplies and air support but would quickly resume delivery if the fighting began again. American air support would be used initially only against Khmer Rouge positions, thus not impeding any Vietnamese withdrawal. In compliance with the accords, the United States quickly shut down training facilities in Vietnam, returning some Khmers to Cambodia and transferring others to Thailand.

The peace settlement in Vietnam, along with Lon Nol's unilateral ceasefire declaration, temporarily put the insurgency on the defensive, politically. On 26 January Sihanouk, Khmer Rouge leader Khieu Samphan, and Sihanouk's Prime Minister Penn Nouth signed a statement (broadcast on 30 January) welcoming the ceasefire in Vietnam and asserting that they too cherished peace. The next day Sihanouk reiterated his willingness to meet with Kissinger.

This relative moderation may have been due in part to pressure from the North Vietnamese. Although in Paris they had told Kissinger frankly that they had little control over the Khmer insurgents and were unable to deliver a ceasefire in Cambodia (there had even been fighting at times between the Khmer Rouge and the North Vietnamese), they, and the Chinese as well, attempted to moderate Khmer Rouge intransigence and encourage a negotiated settlement. In fact there was clearly a difference of opinion in the insurgent ranks. Sihanouk called for negotiations with the United States and a decrease in military activity, while the hardliners had little desire for a ceasefire and wanted to press their military advantage. That the

North Vietnamese and Chinese basically agreed with Sihanouk and made some attempts to get the Khmer Rouge to negotiate eventually widened the growing gulf between the Khmer Rouge and the North Vietnamese.

But the United States never made any attempt to exploit this rift by attempting to arrange the talks for which Sihanouk had asked. On the contrary, as Swank told journalist Stanley Karnow, "the reimposition of Sihanouk's rule is not an acceptable political solution for the majority of the Khmer nation." Foolishly lumping the Chinese, the North Vietnamese, and the insurgents together, Swank told Karnow that until they all moved away from "their current intransigent stance, the possibility of even beginning meaningful negotiations on Cambodia is remote." As it was, Sihanouk withdrew (for the moment) his offer to meet with Kissinger because, as he informed *Baltimore Sun* reporter Eddie Wu, "the US government has refused any meeting with him and had refused to have any dialogue with his government. Under these circumstances, he said, the war in Cambodia would continue."[32]

The Chinese, however, who were at this point not wedded to the Khmer Rouge, believed that direct negotiations between Sihanouk and the United States should take place and might result in a genuinely independent and neutral Cambodian state led once again by the prince. "Why can't you accept to have negotiations with Norodom Sihanouk as head of state?" Zhou asked Kissinger, who was in Beijing. "How can we, when we recognize one government, engage in a direct negotiation with Sihanouk?" Kissinger said. "This is out of the question." Zhou, however, kept pushing. Both France and the Soviet Union had managed to maintain ties with both sides, he pointed out. Furthermore, Lon Nol—an opportunist who over the years had personally benefited from both the Communists and the Americans—was not worthy of support, he said. Finally, he pointed out, a major flaw in Kissinger's position was that Sihanouk would never negotiate with those who overthrew him. But the Chinese leader did not convince Kissinger.[33]

Nothing might have come of an American effort to begin talks, but, as Kissinger put it later in another context, by urging the talks and offering to act as the intermediary, Zhou was putting his personal prestige on the line. He probably would not have done so if he had thought that direct talks between Kissinger and Sihanouk could not succeed, and it is unfortunate that such talks were not attempted before the Khmer Rouge hardliners became even stronger.

The fighting resumed in a major way on the night of 7–8 February 1973 when Khmer Rouge forces attacked all sides of the FANK perimeter around the besieged city of Kompong Thom. For the first time since the Paris Accords, the Cambodians requested, and received, tactical American air support. Ten days later the American embassy reported that Kompong Thom had become very largely a city of refugees, soldiers, and military dependents. Supplies were very low, with only a two-day supply of gasoline to power the communications center and the hospital. The military garrison had perhaps one week's worth of ammunition left. The lone doctor was so busy he could not attend to refugees. The airport had been closed since 8 December 1972. Morale was understandably low, and some refugee families had been allowed to leave to go back to their homes in enemy-controlled territory. (The airport was reopened in March 1973, but the city was still surrounded and besieged.)

Enemy attacks spread to other regions of the country. Even with little or no assistance from the North Vietnamese (the Lon Nol government could not discover any evidence of Vietnamese involvement in any of these new actions), the Khmer Rouge once again attacked a variety of targets, interdicting highways and the Mekong River corridor. The FANK response was not impressive. At the end of February 1973 the American embassy reported that even commanders refused orders to fight. After tactical airstrikes, they seldom followed up on the ground. Furthermore, little seemed to have been done about payroll padding and other forms of corruption within the military. All in all, the embassy rated FANK's battlefield performance "poor." Military ineptitude, combined with Lon Nol's refusal to broaden his government, led Swank to conclude, "we must recognize the possibility that time is not necessarily on the side of the GKR [Government of the Khmer Republic]."[34]

The embassy had little to suggest by way of improving the situation. All they could propose was withholding the economic aid promised to North Vietnam in the Paris Accords as long as Hanoi did not respect the agreement, including the provisions relating to Cambodia. And they urged additional pressure against the Vietnamese by increasing the bombing of the logistical network in Cambodia. Together with additional tactical air and B-52 strikes against the insurgency, this pressure might improve the bargaining position vis-à-vis Hanoi and the Khmer Rouge, resulting eventually in a tacit or explicit reduction of hostilities. It was not a cheery conclusion or one that promised results. That same day (6 March) the enemy sank another munitions barge—the second one in a month—resulting in the loss of $2 million in MAP-supplied ammunition.

In Washington State Department officials read Swank's reports with increasing concern and began to consider the dramatic possibility of removing Lon Nol. What, they asked the ambassador, would he think if Lon Nol traveled abroad on the recommendations of doctors ("which we could arrange") for medical attention and rest?[35]

Swank was not yet ready to recommend such a drastic measure—in effect a soft coup. A better alternative, Swank thought, was to insist that Lon Nol appoint Sirik Matak vice president. This would bring into the government a competent administrator and counter Lon Non's influence. It would not be a panacea, Swank quickly acknowledged. Sirik Matak did not have widespead popular appeal, and Lon Non, who would resist Matak's appointment, "could prove to be a ruthless and malevolent opponent of our interests and position here." Still, Swank offered to speak to Lon Nol along these lines. He hoped he would be able to invoke President Nixon's name to add extra weight to the American insistence that Sirik Matak be appointed.[36]

But if the ambassador was not yet ready to recommend that Lon Nol be forced to leave, he came to believe that Lon Non had to be removed from the political scene. The ambassador was willing to threaten to withdraw American aid to accomplish this, but the State Department would not agree. What State Department officials hoped would happen was that Lon Nol would insist on seeking additional medical treatment in the United States. In return for arranging this, the United States would insist that Lon Nol leave the government in the hands of a "group of executors, to include Sirik Matak" and that Lon Non leave the country at the same time. The United States was even willing to have Lon Non appointed ambassador to Washington.[37] Swank pointed out that the American unwillingness to threaten a withdrawal of aid left only his powers of persuasion to convince Lon Nol, whom he described as a "willful and obstinate man" who would not do anything he considered to be against his own interests.[38]

The day after Swank's proposed approach to Lon Nol, two dramatic events occurred that threatened to upset American calculations. Late in the morning of 17 March three of Lon Non's agents entered a meeting of striking university teachers at the Faculty of Pedagogy, where they assailed a teacher who was denouncing the government. The crowd locked the agents in a room, but then fifty plainclothesmen (also from Lon Non's forces) forced their way in and threw hand grenades into the crowd, killing two persons and wounding eight.

Then at 1:20 p.m. that same day a Cambodian Air Force pilot, So Photra, stole one of the American supplied T-28 airplanes from Pochentong Airport and dropped two bombs on the Chamcar Mon Palace compound, Lon Nol's official residence. One of the bombs landed in a military compound of wooden barracks. A third bomb hit the nearby Chrui Changwar peninsula, causing casualties, while a fourth landed in a flooded area on the northwestern outskirts of the city, causing no damage. At least forty-three people, most of them dependents of military personnel, died in the attack. Lon Nol and members of the government's inner circle escaped harm. The plane then flew away from Phnom Penh toward insurgent-controlled areas.

Initially both the embassy and the government assumed that So Photra was acting on behalf of the insurgents. Because So Photra was either the husband or (more likely) the boyfriend of Princess Botum Bopha, one of Sihanouk's daughters, Lon Nol concluded that this was a royalist-Communist plot to take over his government, and he responded by suspending civil rights, prohibiting meetings on the street of more than five people, requiring anyone (including foreigners) who planned to leave the country to have their papers revalidated, incarcerating or placing under house arrest at least sixteen members of the royal family and grounding a number of pilots of royal birth, arresting former presidential candidate Keo An (who had once suggested that Sihanouk ought to be allowed to return as a private citizen), firing Air Force Commander So Satto and placing him under house arrest, arresting leaders of the teachers' strike, closing newspapers and hauling editors before military courts, and, potentially the most serious of all, placing Sirik Matak under house arrest and cutting off his telephone. Lon Nol told the Indonesian ambassador that "he had tolerated dissent long enough and would tolerate it no longer."[39]

Swank and other embassy officials tried to moderate Lon Nol's actions. But the ambassador had to admit that there was now no more point in urging the president to appoint Sirik Matak as vice president. The events of 17 March had overtaken the planned American démarche. When opportunities arose, however, Swank continued to suggest that Lon Non might want to leave the country.

For the next week a series of devastating reports poured into the State Department beginning with an embassy assessment of Lon Non that, when telegraphed to Washington on 31 March, consisted of seven sections totaling twenty-two pages. Lon Non, the report stated, was a man of "unusual energy and initiative" who unfortunately applied those qualities toward furthering his own personal ambitions "restrained neither by good political judgement nor moral scruples." He was "an inadequate administrator" and "a poor and probably dishonest manager of men and materiel." In a particularly biting criticism of Lon Non's military abilities, the report stated that he was "by Cambodian standards, a poor commander" who "sought maximum exposure to publicity and minimum exposure to the enemy." He could not be trusted with American-supplied equipment and had, in fact, been cut off from those supplies. He was a political agitator who was behind the student strikes of 1972 that led to Sirik Matak's resignation as prime minister-designate, and he had been involved in the recent disturbances at the Faculty of Pedagogy. The Australians reported that he used an assassination unit called the "Republican Security Battalion," which drove around in a fleet of yellow Hondas. The purpose of all of this was to keep his brother in power and further his own interests. "Those who dislike and fear Lon Non," the report concluded, "among who must be counted many if not most of the best military and civilian leaders, are aware of this. Increased reliance upon Lon Non has thus decreased to a dangerous level Lon Nol's ability to rely on others."[40]

Meanwhile, things seemed to be falling apart in Cambodia. Troops refused to fight and soldiers looted market stalls in Phnom Penh. The Mekong River corridor remained closed to convoys, since the government controlled no more than 30 percent of the river between Phnom Penh and the Vietnamese border, and elsewhere enemy forces made advances. The one bright spot was the advance by Brigadier General Chantarangsey, who had developed about the only successful pacification program in the entire country and whose forces had recently occupied the Kirirom Plateau, an area under enemy control since 1970. But typical of the country's internal politics, Lon Nol ordered Chantarangsey to withdraw from Kirirom because he did not want a potential rival to be successful when other FANK units were doing so poorly.

Adding to Cambodian and State Department woes was the realization for many that the war was increasingly a civil conflict. Most North Vietnamese and Viet Cong combat troops had withdrawn from Cambodia (thus putting American operations there on a shaky legal and political foundation). All main force units had pulled out, and only about 7,000 combat troops remained (although there were as many as 20,000 administrative and logistical personnel still there). It was increasingly difficult to get the Cambodian government forces to fight their fellow Khmers.

The flurry of negative reports demanded action at the highest levels, and Nixon dispatched Alexander Haig to Phnom Penh for a first-hand assessment of the situation. Stopping first in Vientiane, where Prime Minister Souvanna Phouma told him emphatically that Lon Nol had to broaden the base of his government and bring back In Tam and Sirik Matak, Haig arrived in Phnom Penh on 10 April 1973. Though details of the Haig visit are unaccountably sketchy, Haig apparently told Lon Nol that the United States would cut off all economic and military assistance unless he brought opposition leaders into the government and ended Lon Non's activities.

The threat—which the State Department had previously told Swank it would not use—worked. A few days after Haig's departure it was announced that Lon Non would depart on a three-month trip to France and the United States. In addition the current Hang Thun Hak government resigned. Cheng Heng, Sirik Matak, In Tam, and Lon Nol agreed to form a High Political Council that would rule by decree for six months. The National Assembly would be suspended during that time. This was very largely a victory for the opposition, whose demands Lon Nol—under strong American pressure—had accepted. It might even be characterized as an American-driven soft coup, since Lon Nol's power had been dramatically reduced. On the other hand, as two senior Senate staffers observed, now that Lon Nol had done what the United States demanded, he had every right to expect continued American military support, support which, all observers agreed, was the only reason his government had so far been able to survive.

Despite the apparent political progress in Phnom Penh, as the military situation worsened some officials recommended taking a step that had been heretofore resolutely rejected: negotiating with Sihanouk. As the Under Secretary of State for Political Affairs William J. Porter wrote, "sometimes we must think the unthinkable." But the administration remained unwilling to alter course. State Department officials pointed to Sihanouk's inbred anti-Americanism, his antagonism toward all of his neighbors, the hostility of the Khmer Rouge (which Kissinger still mistakenly believed were under North Vietnamese control), and the fact that the prince could never again regain the respect of the Cambodian military. But the main reason not to negotiate Sihanouk's return was that it would appear to the international community that Lon Nol had lost his struggle against the Communists, and the United States would have suffered a loss of prestige by appearing to capitulate.

Kissinger himself professed to believe that Sihanouk was already a Khmer Rouge prisoner. "Sihanouk understood that the Khmer Rouge and Hanoi were determined to block" attempts to return him as head of state, Kissinger wrote in his memoirs. And even though the prince of course hoped that this would not be the case, "he was too weak to abandon the only base he had—whatever his convictions. . . . So much for the argument that it was American opposition that prevented the return of Sihanouk to power in Cambodia," Kissinger concluded.[41]

The flaw in Kissinger's assertion is that he had repeatedly refused Sihanouk's offers to negotiate directly and so could not be certain how much freedom of action the prince enjoyed. Kissinger did continue to tell the Chinese privately that the United States was not committed to any particular Cambodian leader and encouraged negotiations between Sihanouk's representatives and "other forces"; and on 24 April, again using "one of its most highly sensitive channels," the United States reiterated to China its willingness to work toward a solution for Cambodia that would include "all political forces, including those of Prince Sihanouk." But the Americans were not yet willing to meet with Sihanouk or his representatives.[42]

Shortly thereafter Sihanouk, who had recently returned from a visit to the "liberated areas" of Cambodia and feeling that he had strengthened his influence with the insurgents, stated unequivocally that he would "negotiate directly with President Nixon or his representative." He said he had "received carte blanche from the GRUNK/FUNK forces to negotiate with the United States."[43] The United States again did not respond. If it had, it might have found out just how much leeway Sihanouk had, whether he really was a prisoner of the Khmer Rouge at this point, and whether it was possible to lure him away from the most radical insurgents. In sum, Kissinger's assertion that it was not American opposition that prevented Sihanouk's return to power in April 1973 is unproven. Later (nearly two years later), when Kissinger changed his mind and agreed to meet with Sihanouk, it was too late.

Meanwhile the military situation became increasingly difficult. Communist forces again cut Route 1 and recaptured territory along the Mekong River that they had lost only a few weeks before. Mekong River convoys again stopped, and the United States had to airlift fuel to the capital. By late April 1973 enemy troops surrounded Phnom Penh, which was well within their artillery range. Bombs and shells became a part of daily life in the capital. As Wilfred Deac writes, "The enemy seemed to be everywhere."[44] American embassy officials told the Korean defense attaché that it would be prudent to send dependents out of the country.

With the Khmer Rouge pushing in on Phnom Penh from all directions, the Americans unleashed the air force. The bombing was so close to Phnom Penh that the force of the explosions damaged buildings in the city itself. It caused "major damage" to a gate at the Alliance mission's compound, for example. By late July the State Department felt compelled to urge all civilians to leave. The Americans feared the consequences when the bombing ended on 15 August as Congress had required. "This is the most pessimistic report I have ever gotten in many contacts with the State Department regarding this situation," wrote an Alliance official. "There were no tempering, optimistic statements." Early in August a political officer at the American embassy in Phnom Penh told missionaries to "get out immediately."[45]

In the end the calls to leave Phnom Penh turned out not to be immediately necessary, for the most intense bombing in military history finally stopped the FUNK advance and prevented an insurgent victory in the summer of 1973. Still, if the bombing prevented an immediate takeover of Phnom Penh, the GKR appeared at the time to be on the brink of defeat anyway. To the surprise of many, the Khmer Republic survived for nearly two more years. But it was nevertheless a losing cause. Even if the bombing had continued, it is unlikely that the GKR would have survived in the long run. Furthermore, the intense bombing may also have undercut relatively moderate forces within the revolutionary movement and strengthened the hand of the radical Pol Potists, thus ensuring extreme outcomes (such as the evacuation of the cities) when the revolutionaries triumphed in 1975.

The increased bombing also caused difficulties for the administration at home. Despite safeguards, there were horrendous civilian casualties. In one incident, for example, some 250 civilians were killed or wounded in a B-52 attack near the Vietnamese border town of Chau Doc. Estimates of the number of civilians killed by the American bombing from 1969 to 1973 run as high as 150,000.[46]

The bombing produced two other areas of concern. Its original justification—that the bombing protected the withdrawal of American forces from Vietnam—no longer held since the last American troops had departed on 28 March 1973. Now the administration claimed that the bombing must continue to force the North Vietnamese to respect the Paris Accords. Because the fighting in Cambodia threatened the settlement in Vietnam, the air operations in Cambodia should be viewed not as a commitment to Cambodia per se but rather as "a meaningful interim action to bring about compliance" with Article 20 of the accords.[47]

Central to the administration's legal argument was the contention that the Khmer Rouge were creatures of the North Vietnamese—created, led, and sustained by them. For example, Deputy Assistant Secretary of Defense Dennis J. Doolin testified that the Khmer insurgents were "directed and controlled and organized by the North Vietnamese" and that, "if it were not for the North Vietnamese leadership, North Vietnamese advisers and cadres, North Vietnamese heavy weapons support and logistic support[,] there would be no Communist insurgency in Cambodia outside of the capability of the Government to handle it." Congressman Gerald Ford (R-MI) made the same point in a letter to his fellow Republican legislators. "Cambodia is not experiencing a genuine civil war but a classic Communist insurgency controlled and supported by Hanoi," he wrote.[48]

But such a view was long outdated. At the Paris peace talks Le Duc Tho contended that he could not control the Khmer Rouge, a statement that Kissinger in his memoirs acknowledged was accurate. In fact according to a later JCS report, most Vietnamese Communist forces withdrew from Cambodia in May 1972, well before the Paris peace agreement. As the JCS put it later, by early 1973 the Khmer Rouge "by and large, were responsible for their own war effort."[49] By June 1973 the Khmer Rouge were in the process of driving out the remaining North Vietnamese troops, as well as ethnic Vietnamese civilians. But this did not change Kissinger's mind. "Even after I returned to Washington in May 1974," recalled Kenneth Quinn, who had been reporting about these developments from the field, "I could not convince top policy officials that there had been a fundamental change in the situation."[50]

Whatever the relationship of the North Vietnamese and the Khmer Rouge, some Vietnamese troops did remain in Cambodia. Was this a violation of Article 20 of the Paris Accords? The agreement required both a North Vietnamese withdrawal and an end to American military actions in Cambodia. It set no timetable, however, and so the North Vietnamese were technically no more in violation of the Paris Accords than was the United States. In May Secretary Rogers, in testimony before the Senate Foreign Relations Committee, agreed that this was the case which, as White House aide William E. Timmons put it in a memorandum to President Nixon, undercut the "Administration's rationale for continued air operations."[51]

A related matter of concern to legislators was the increasingly deep involvement of the American embassy in Phnom Penh in directing the air strikes. To many in Congress this was a violation of American law that prohibited the presence of American advisers in Cambodia. Opponents of the administration believed that the embassy's intimate involvement also violated various other laws that made it clear that the United States had no commitment to defend the Cambodian government. Pressure was growing for a legislative end to American involvement in what was increasingly a

Cambodian civil war, and it was only a matter of time before Congress cut off all funds for military actions in Cambodia.

Adding to the administration's frustration, the new political arrangement to which Lon Nol had agreed under American pressure was not functioning well. Despite the agreement, Lon Nol was increasingly ruling by himself. The high hopes of the Americans that the new Cambodian council would bring a sense of unity had been dashed. The department had little to offer as to how the situation might be improved. Swank was instructed only to keep emphasizing the dire necessity of unity. The Americans were clearly hoping that Lon Nol might decide to seek treatment abroad for his paralysis.

With a difficult military and political situation and the likelihood that Congress would soon legislate an end to the American air war, the possibility of a negotiated settlement warranted renewed exploration. The United States now gave more serious consideration to a settlement that might involve Sihanouk's return in some capacity (although officials were still unwilling to speak with the prince or his representatives directly). On several occasions in May 1973 Sihanouk again made it clear that he was willing to negotiate with the United States. On 6 May in a lengthy and revealing interview with Stanley Karnow in Peking, Sihanouk stated that he had offered to reconcile with the United States if the United States would deal with his government and end its intervention in Cambodian affairs. But the previous February, he said, Nixon had not let Kissinger see him when he came to Peking. Sihanouk said he had proposed meetings as early as 1972 and had repeated the proposal in 1973 but to no effect. He would still be willing to meet with Nixon or Kissinger or with his friends Averell Harriman and Mike Mansfield, he stated.

Shortly thereafter Sihanouk left for a trip to Africa and Europe, where he hoped to gain the political support of a number of countries. At virtually every stop in Africa he repeated his willingness to negotiate with American officials. In Senegal he offered to negotiate directly with the United States. In Guinea he told President Sékou Touré that he had no current complaints against the United States, and Touré, who was also friendly with the United States, offered to help bring about negotiations. In Rabat, Morocco, Sihanouk proposed "direct and bilateral negotiation to end the unjust war." The result, he said, playing on Nixon's own rhetorical approach to peace in Vietnam, would be "a peace with honor."[52] In Mauritania, where the American ambassador condescendingly reported that Sihanouk "giggled his way" through the airport ceremony, the prince asked President Ould Daddah to pass a note to President Nixon stating that if Nixon would negotiate with him, he would reestablish diplomatic relations with Washington and make "generous arrangements" for the present Cambodian leadership in Phnom Penh.[53]

The United States responded negatively to all of Sihanouk's offers. The administration took an almost contemptuous attitude toward the offers of African leaders to assist in reaching a settlement, probably because the Nixon-Kissinger administration had little interest in Africa or respect for its leaders. Later Kissinger told a group of high-level advisers, "the idea that we had to communicate with Sihanouk through Mauritania was absurd."[54]

Instead of negotiating directly with Sihanouk, the United States tried once again to negotiate a settlement indirectly—in this case with Hanoi. On 23 May 1973 in Paris Kissinger proposed to the North Vietnamese an end to the U.S. bombing of Cambodia, a withdrawal within sixty days of all American and North Vietnamese personnel, and a ceasefire to last sixty days during which negotiations would take place among the Cambodians. The North Vietnamese agreed only that both sides would do their best to bring about a peaceful settlement. To Kissinger, this meant that nothing would happen. Nothing did. In August Kissinger told Singapore's Prime Minister Lee Kuan Yew the reason that nothing had happened was that the Watergate scandal had so weakened the administration that it was unable to bomb North Vietnam for a week, as planned. Had the bombing taken place, Kissinger said, North Vietnam would unquestionably have agreed to a temporary settlement in Cambodia. Such a statement was speculative in the extreme. It assumed North Vietnamese control over the insurgency and that North Vietnam would have succumbed to such pressure. More likely, nothing would have happened in any case since the proposal did not include negotiations between Sihanouk and the United States. Vietnam would not have acted after a week of bombing, there would have been strongly negative domestic and international reactions, and Sihanouk would never have agreed to negotiate with the GKR.

Four days after Kissinger's approach to Hanoi, however, the United States significantly modified its position. To Huang Hua, the Chinese ambassador to the United Nations, Kissinger proposed a sixty- to ninety-day ceasefire, during which the United States would withdraw its personnel and arrange for Lon Nol to leave Phnom Penh for medical treatment in the United States. Discussions would then take place between Sihanouk and the GKR. And for the first time the United States would engage in "some discussions" with Sihanouk's representatives. At the end of the process the United States "would not oppose the return of Prince Sihanouk." Chinese officials pointedly reminded Kissinger that Premier Zhou Enlai had previously told the Americans that Sihanouk and the Khmer Rouge were willing to negotiate directly with the United States.[55]

This was the first time the United States had proposed any discussions, however limited, with Sihanouk or his representatives. On 4 June, according to Kissinger's memoirs, China "was now prepared to: 'communicate the U.S. tentative thinking to the Cambodian side'" once Sihanouk returned from his African and European tour.[56]

Kissinger chose to interpret the Chinese action in very positive terms. Zhou, he wrote in his memoirs, "had clearly committed himself to a compromise that preserved key elements of the Lon Nol structure," and he would not have agreed to act as an intermediary unless he thought a settlement probable. Furthermore, Kissinger stated, Zhou privately wanted the American bombing to continue since this was his major bargaining chip with the Khmer Rouge. Zhou could tell them that he could bring about an end to the bombing in exchange for negotiations. "In mid-June," Kissinger recalled, "we believed for better or worse that we were on the homestretch. We could envisage a cease-fire, Sihanouk's return, and then Sihanouk's dealing with existing political forces so as to give himself room to maneuver between them and the Communists. We nearly made it, with all that it would have meant for Cambodia's future."[57] On 19 June Kissinger went a step further. If a ceasefire was in effect later in the summer, he would personally meet with Sihanouk "for political discussions."[58]

But the optimism soon faded. Sihanouk and the Khmer Rouge seemed to back away from negotiations, as did the Chinese. Kissinger was bitter. "This is the first time in the development of our new relationship that the Chinese word has not counted," Brent Scowcroft angrily told the Chinese.[59]

According to his memoirs, however, Kissinger, while upset with the Chinese, believed that the real cause of the impasse was not Chinese untrustworthiness but congressional ineptitude. In cutting off funds for American military actions in Cambodia, Congress had ended the prospect of fruitful negotiations, he believed. Kissinger had frantically tried to prevent a bombing halt. But Congress, seething with anger about the recent revelations of the secret bombing of Cambodia, finally legislated an end to American military actions. On 29 June Nixon was forced to sign legislation that would end the bombing on 15 August.

Kissinger maintains that the imminent termination of the bombing not only ended his own bargaining power but privately enraged Zhou Enlai, who learned about the legislation from a visiting congressional delegation. Since China had publicly criticized the bombing, Zhou's growing agitation when he learned that the bombing would soon end mystified the delegation. But Kissinger claimed to understand: "Zhou saw emerging before him his geopolitical nightmare: an Indochina dominated by Hanoi and allied with the Soviet Union, brought into being by an obtuse superpower that did not deign to give its own diplomacy a chance to succeed." The premier had lost leverage with the Khmer Rouge. Up to this point, Zhou could tell the Khmer Rouge that he could gain an end to the bombing in exchange for negotiations, Kissinger contends. But now the Khmer Rouge could simply wait out the remaining weeks of American bombing. "There was no way for even the best-intentioned Chinese leader to ask the Khmer Rouge to forgo the total victory we had handed them," Kissinger writes.[60]

Sihanouk during his March/April 1973 "secret" visit to "liberated" Cambodia in the company of Khieu Samphan and Son Sen, two senior Khmer Rouge leaders. From the Private Collection of Ambassador Julio A. Jeldres.

Kissinger's interpretation of the Chinese actions is open to question. Unfortunately, Chinese accounts of their policy toward Cambodia and their interaction with the Americans over Cambodia have not been published, and thus any interpretation cannot be definitive. But the contemporary American documents cast some doubt on Kissinger's memoir account. For example, the Chinese commitment to pass along American thinking to Sihanouk may not have been as firm as Kissinger contends. More significantly, it is not certain that the revelation that the bombing would soon end was the cause of Zhou's visible agitation at the congressional action. Instead Zhou's being placed in a position where he would have to agree with a congressional delegation against the president may have been the source of his agitation.

Most fundamentally, Kissinger's assertion that Zhou wanted the bombing to continue because it gave him leverage with the Khmer Rouge, and that the decision to end it was the fundamental reason for China's refusal to pass along the American position to Sihanouk and its plan in general to cool its relations with the United States, is debatable. Kissinger may well have exaggerated China's interest in helping the United States achieve a settlement on terms acceptable to the Americans. At one point Kissinger even argued that Sihanouk also secretly approved of the bombing because, as with the Chinese, it gave him some leverage with the Khmer Rouge.

China and Sihanouk had always condemned the bombing, and to assert that they privately liked it because it gave them leverage with the Khmer Rouge is speculative and probably wishful thinking, Kissinger's way of demonstrating the wisdom of his own approach that an allegedly short-sighted, ignorant Congress had thwarted. Nor were Kissinger's aides as convinced as he was that the Chinese decision not to pass along the American negotiating position to Sihanouk resulted from the bombing cut-off. Lawrence Eagleburger summed it up this way: "we were simply not going to be able to answer Mr. Kissinger's question as to why the Chinese had behaved in this way."[61]

Kissinger's case that the end of the bombing halted promising discussions is also called into question by the fact that the administration at the time apparently did not inform appropriate congressional committees (or anyone in Congress) about any "progress" in negotiations. In March 1975 the State Department released a brief account of various negotiating efforts; it included the allegation that the bombing halt had thwarted promising discussions. But John Sparkman (D-AL), who chaired the Senate Committee on Foreign Relations (and who appears to have been angered at this effort to blame Congress), and Senator Clifford Case (R-NJ) told President Ford that in 1973 they were unaware of any negotiations. And in a press conference Assistant Secretary of State Philip Habib had to acknowledge that "key members of Congress" were not informed. "How could these folks who did what they did do anything else," asked a reporter, since they were unaware of the purported negotiations? It was a pertinent question, but Habib did not respond.[62]

Regardless of whether Kissinger is correct that congressional action to end the bombing stopped all hope of a negotiated settlement in the summer of 1973, he is on particularly shaky ground when he defends the administration's negotiating record in previous months. The United States, he writes, had "agreed with the desirability of a neutral Cambodia ruled by Sihanouk. Our diplomacy had for six months painstakingly put the pieces in place for such an outcome."[63] In fact, it is not at all clear that the United States had for six months been working for Sihanouk's return. If true, this meant that Kissinger had been working for Sihanouk's return from the very moment the United States had signed the Paris Accords in January. But for most of this six-month period the United States had given unswerving (albeit sometimes frustrated) support to the Lon Nol government. As the situation worsened in the spring of 1973, some American officials did begin to think about the "unthinkable"—a possible Sihanouk return to Phnom Penh. But there is no evidence that Kissinger and Nixon were among them—unless, of course, it came about through negotiations between Sihanouk and the GKR, which was unlikely.

Furthermore, Kissinger's claim that his compromise proposal "had been made not once but several times since the beginning of the year" is not true. The United States had no objection to negotiations among the Khmers, but it was not until 27 May 1973 that the administration said the United States itself would engage in "some discussions" with Sihanouk's representatives—and then only with low-level American diplomats in Beijing and as a part of a parallel negotiation in which Sihanouk would negotiate with GKR representatives (something the prince had consistently refused to do). But despite the conditions, this was nevertheless the first time the United States had expressed a willingness to have any discussions with Sihanouk's representatives, and this explains why the Chinese for the first time explored the possibility of assisting the United States. Only in July did Kissinger himself agree to meet with Sihanouk later in the summer, and then only if a ceasefire was already in place.

Indeed, early in August Kissinger indicated to Singapore's President Lee Kuan Yew that he was not that eager to be involved in bringing Sihanouk back to Phnom Penh. "Our present strategy is that if someone brings him back, we'll be delighted to deal with him," Kissinger told the Singaporean. "But we don't want to be the ones to do it."[64]

In sum, Kissinger's diplomacy always offered too little and was too late and too secretive. Perhaps the national security adviser was correct in stating that if he had tried to arrange a meeting between Americans and Sihanouk in February, the Khmer Rouge would have blocked it. But we will never know because it was not tried. Sihanouk continued to seek a meeting for months thereafter. By the time Kissinger finally did express a willingness to meet him, the Congress (which was not informed of the negotiating efforts) had taken matters into its own hands, the GKR appeared to be on its last legs, and the more radical Khmer Rouge had more power in the revolution than they had previously enjoyed.

On 21 October 1973, while he was floating in his swimming pool in California, Nixon informed Kissinger that he was naming him secretary of state. Both recognized that this was a confession of Nixon's weakness as the Watergate affair continued to undermine his presidency. He had never wanted a strong secretary of state, but there was no other way for Kissinger to retain any authority with the rest of the government. Shortly thereafter Lon Nol congratulated him and commented that he hoped Kissinger's forthcoming trip to Beijing would "help end the bloodshed in Cambodia, bring the parties to the negotiating table, and bring a more secure peace."[65] In fact, after the August debacle the Nixon

administration's interest in negotiations had cooled. The United States had no interest in speaking directly with Sihanouk.

Instead of rethinking its negotiating stance, the Nixon administration determined to support the GKR to the limit. "This Administration will do everything at the edge of legality to support Phnom Penh," Kissinger told Lew Kuan Yew in August. He had broken off discussions with the Chinese, he said, because he did not "want them to think we are too eager."[66]

Nixon's decision to relieve Swank early in September 1973 was another sign of the administration's determination to pursue as aggressive a course in Cambodia as possible. Not only had Swank wanted a relatively inconspicuous American presence in Cambodia, but he had grown increasingly disenchanted with the war. As he told a farewell press conference on 4 September, the war was "losing more and more of its point and has less and less meaning for any of the parties concerned."[67] In 1975, in a particularly dishonorable action, Secretary of State Kissinger could find no assignment for Swank in the department.

A month after Swank left Cambodia, Kissinger told GKR Foreign Minister Long Boret that the administration had reversed the "low profile" policy. "Our policy now is to help to the maximum extent possible . . . ," he said. "There will never be negotiations in Cambodia unless you are strong." Long Boret need pay no attention to rumors that he would meet with Sihanouk when he went to Beijing in November, Kissinger added. "I am going to Peking but I have no intention of talking to him in Peking or in the foreseeable future."[68]

Because of his renewed emphasis on support for the GKR instead of negotiations, Kissinger quickly put aside suggestions from others that he rethink his position, notably from Senator Mansfield who had received a cable from Sihanouk. Mansfield had previously informed the prince that he would be going to Beijing soon and would welcome the opportunity to visit him. Sihanouk responded that he would be very pleased to see Mansfield and included a specific proposal for peace. Kissinger could have taken advantage of Mansfield's impending trip to see how much room for maneuver Sihanouk had by this point. Instead, he warned Mansfield not to become involved. Furthermore, a month later when Kissinger went to Beijing himself he belittled Mansfield to the Chinese leaders. The senator "has a sentimental attachment to Prince Sihanouk which is not related to reality and is not reciprocated in any way," he informed Zhou. When the Chinese leader returned to the subject of Mansfield's forthcoming visit (something that obviously interested the Chinese), Kissinger said, "it could help us if he does not receive too much ammunition from the Chinese side on Cambodia."[69]

It is hard to say what the administration really expected to accomplish by its own singleminded support for the GKR. To be sure, in September FANK had surprised everyone with a successful defense of the important city of Kompong Cham—although the Khmer Rouge forces took 15,000 people with them as they retreated. Phnom Penh also had a breathing spell for a time, as fighting virtually ended, though most major highways remained interdicted.

But the political situation had not improved. GKR Air Force Lieutenant Pech Lim Kuon was one of many Cambodians who disliked Lon Nol's leadership. On 19 November 1973 he climbed into his T-28 and dropped four bombs on the royal palace. Lon Nol and his entourage were unhurt, and Kuon flew his plane to Kratie, where he defected to the Khmer Rouge. (He later served as a helicopter instructor for the victorious Khmer Rouge, before he stole a helicopter in 1976 and defected to Thailand.)

Even though the GKR managed to survive for the rest of the year (and indeed for an additional sixteen months), Kissinger later wrote that he knew Cambodia was doomed after the summer of 1973. Why, then, did he not acknowledge defeat and save Cambodia the additional agony that it had to endure in 1974 and 1975, before the Khmer Rouge finally took over? Why did he not try to work out some arrangements with Sihanouk that might, at least, have given some power to non–Khmer Rouge elements before the Khmer Rouge had complete control of the insurgency? Perhaps the most candid answer was given to Zhou Enlai. Why, the prime minister asked Kissinger in November 1973, did he persist in supporting Lon Nol who headed a government with which the United States had no treaty obligations? "I will speak frankly," Kissinger replied. "Our major problem with Cambodia is that the opponents of President Nixon want to use it as an example of the bankruptcy of his whole policy. So if there is a very rapid collapse, it will be reflected in our other policies. That," he said, "is our only concern."[70] Several thousand more Cambodians would have to die because Nixon's political enemies might benefit if the war ended too soon and Nixon's other policies might suffer as a result. The Cambodians did not forget. When Nixon died in 1994, a newspaper published in Cambodia put it this way: "Though many Cambodians may now be inclined to forgive and forget, few tears will be shed here for Richard M. Nixon."[71]

Dénouement

GERALD FORD, HENRY KISSINGER,
AND THE FALL OF CAMBODIA

"The obstacle to Sihanouk coming back is the Communists, not us."
—Henry Kissinger to a congressional delegation recently returned from Indochina,
5 March 1975

"When I was in Congress, I was known as a Hawk, and I can't change now that I am in the White House."—Gerald Ford, 27 June 1976

"Our strategy is to get the Chinese into Laos and Cambodia as a barrier to the Vietnamese. . . . They [The Khmer Rouge] are murderous thugs, but we won't let that stand in our way. We are prepared to improve relations with them."—Henry Kissinger, 26 November 1975

ON 7 JANUARY 1974 American Chargé Thomas Enders informed Ambassador to Vietnam Graham Martin that he was receiving "daily representations" from his family to get out of Phnom Penh.[1] His family's concerns were understandable. In the previous ten days at least twenty-nine rockets had hit Phnom Penh, killing over twenty people. The day before Enders' message to Martin, an assassination squad had tried to kill FANK's commander-in-chief, and a large Khmer Rouge force began to assault the capital's perimeter. Over 100 persons died in the shelling that accompanied the assault. The situation became so serious over the next several days that fistfights broke out in the French embassy to obtain the limited number of airplane tickets out of Cambodia. The Khmer Rouge also attacked Kampot and Oudang, the latter a symbolically important former royal capital. Half of Kampot's civilian population fled into the countryside to escape the shelling. After horrific fighting, Oudang fell to the besiegers late in March.

Despite this situation, Enders kept telling his family that things were not as bad as they seemed. In some important respects this was shown to be a correct assessment as the year progressed. Although the Khmer Rouge controlled most of the countryside, the government was holding its own militarily and even made some limited gains. It eventually pushed the enemy back from Phnom Penh, repulsed the attack on Kampot, and managed to hang onto Prey Veng and Kompong Cham. In July government forces liberated 14,300 people from Khmer Rouge rule near Neak Luong and recaptured the devastated Oudang in July. Security around the Great Lake, the Tonle Sap, improved to the point that badly needed agricultural commodities could be shipped to Phnom Penh.

Nevertheless, the overall military situation was no better than a stalemate, as the U.S. military acknowledged. FANK, though it had more firepower than the Khmer Rouge and completely controlled the air, was unable to launch large-scale offensive operations. It had little chance to retake significant amounts of territory that were under the insurgents' control. The Americans were well aware of the various FANK weaknesses, including pervasive corruption. But they nevertheless believed that it was strong enough to prevent a defeat.

Henry Kissinger hoped that the military situation was sufficiently favorable that they could get negotiations going. But the Watergate investigations, which in August would force Nixon to resign and be replaced by Vice President Gerald Ford, increasingly occupied the president's time and made it difficult to forge any new paths. Almost nothing was done to explore negotiations during the first several months of 1974. By April the chances of a successful negotiation seemed even less, as Khieu Samphan, with Chinese support, pushed Sihanouk aside to become the opposition's leading spokesperson. It may be, as French diplomat Etienne Manac'h believed, that Chinese policy changed because the Americans showed no interest in negotiations with Sihanouk. Khieu Samphan visited China, where he was given "the red carpet treatment," while Sihanouk's role during the visit was "very modest." Sihanouk, characteristically, acknowledged that he "knew where the power was" and that the Khmer Rouge could "bump him off any time." Shortly thereafter China facilitated an eleven-nation tour for the Khmer Rouge leader in which Sihanouk "found himself relegated to role similar to that of an extra."[2] Negotiations were not necessarily out of the question, though, for it may be that in return for their support for the Khmer Rouge, the Chinese expected an openness to a negotiated settlement.

In June Ambassador John Gunther Dean told the administration that time was working against the United States, and efforts to find a peaceful solution were urgent. Graham Martin, the normally hard-line ambassador to Saigon who fancied himself "one of the best intelligence officers this government ever had," agreed. In June he recommended via a back channel to Kissinger

John Gunther Dean meets with Cambodia's Prime Minister Lon Nol. Courtesy of the Jimmy Carter Presidential Library.

personally that he seek a solution involving Sihanouk. "We are running out of time," Martin told the secretary of state. A solution involving Sihanouk, Sirik Matak, and General Sosthene Fernandez ought to be attempted. It had to be worked out with the USSR and China, Martin insisted, and while it certainly would be difficult, it would be easier to accomplish than the successes that Kissinger had just achieved in the Middle East.[3]

Unfortunately, the administration did not share the ambassadors' sense of urgency. For the rest of the summer, whenever the possibility of negotiations was discussed, the American position remained unchanged. While not absolutely wedded to Lon Nol, and willing to accept a role for Sihanouk as the result of negotiations and indeed to accept any solution negotiated directly by the Khmer parties, the United States would not itself agree to propose that Lon Nol leave, nor would it agree in advance to a coalition government. Indeed, the Martin proposal does not seem to have had any serious consideration until September when W. Richard Smyser, a senior staff member of the NSC, informed Kissinger that the staff disagreed with it. "There seems little reason to talk to Sihanouk or any Cambodians on the other side before the UN credentials fight," he wrote.[4] Since the fight over who would represent Cambodia at the United Nations would not end until late November or early December, Martin's proposal (if Kissinger accepted the NSC advice)—based on the ambassador's assessment that time was of the essence—would not even be considered until many months after it was first put forward. Additional pressure for negotiations came from the JCS. However, the military leaders had no more influence than the ambassadors. "It is rather a worthless paper," wrote one official, referring to the chiefs' analysis.[5]

Sometime in the summer (just when is not clear from the currently available materials), Dean floated another idea. Could not an international conference on Cambodia be called, he asked? The State Department was supportive but the NSC—in a pattern that was becoming increasingly apparent—expressed reservations. If the conference included Viet Cong representatives, that would have the effect of destabilizing South Vietnam, a price not worth paying, thought Smyser. In addition, Smyser objected to the apparent willingness of the State Department to dump Lon Nol. "At the first hint of a meeting, everybody at State wants to scuttle our friends," he complained.[6] But in fact the administration followed up on Dean's ideas, at least to a limited extent, for it discussed a possible conference with two countries that had relations with GRUNK. How serious these approaches were, however, cannot be determined from the available documentation.

Whether or not a conference was the solution, Dean desperately wanted what he called a "controlled solution" as quickly as possible. An uncontrolled solution, in which American assistance would end, the embassy would shut down, and personnel would be withdrawn while the GKR and FANK simply disintegrated, would, he stated in memoranda to Kissinger in September, have a devastating impact on the U.S. image that would have ramifications well beyond Indochina. He suggested the respected Lieutenant General Saukham Khoy as a possible transitional leader whenever it became appropriate for Lon Nol to step aside. But the administration did not think the Cambodian situation sufficiently serious to change course. "I think we should not undertake diplomatic initiatives right now," stated Kissinger.[7] Furthermore, Kissinger basically disliked Dean's efforts to insert himself into the negotiation process.

Meanwhile, the annual, bitter fight was underway as to who would represent Cambodia in the United Nations General Assembly. This was important symbolically, as well as in terms of international assistance that might be provided to the GKR. The GRUNK had increased its international respectability to the point where more countries now recognized it than the GKR, and few gave the Phnom Penh government any chance of prevailing at the United Nations. But in this context Ambassador Dean thought he saw a possible compromise that would further his idea of an international conference. Dean suggested that the United States agree to keep the Cambodian seat vacant in return for Chinese assistance in arranging a Cambodia conference. With the seat vacant, GRUNK would be on a more equal footing with the GKR and would therefore be more likely to negotiate, thought Dean. The United States would benefit by getting real negotiations started, "an achievement," argued the ambassador, "beside which the question of the UN seat pales into relative insignificance." Dean also made the radical proposal that he be authorized to meet directly with GRUNK officials, including Khieu Samphan. This was something that GRUNK had publicly advocated on various occasions. A meeting could be arranged in Laos, he contended.[8]

Whether any of these proposals for new approaches to peace in Cambodia would win out, as against the NSC's status quo attitude, depended very much on Henry Kissinger, who, late in November was in China for talks. In Beijing Kissinger went farther than before in willingness to dump Lon Nol and accept a coalition government headed by Sihanouk. The coalition would emerge from a peace conference "whose practical result would be the return of Sihanouk, the transformation of the existing structure in Phnom Penh, and the participation of the resistance forces." In sum, Kissinger had moved slightly beyond his previous positions but had made no fundamental changes, and indeed his statement to Deng Xiaoping that the Khmer insurgents were still under Hanoi's control was outdated, as Deng pointed out in no uncertain terms.[9]

Deng gave no hint that he would follow up on Kissinger's suggestion of a peace conference that would result in bringing Sihanouk back to Phnom Penh as part of a coalition government. Instead he told Kissinger that his information about Hanoi's involvement in Cambodia was completely erroneous. "There is not a single Vietnamese soldier fighting in Cambodia," he told Kissinger. There was no meeting of the minds.[10]

Aside from being more forthright in his willingness to facilitate Lon Nol's removal following a peace conference, Kissinger had not put forward any new American ideas about how to settle the Cambodian war. He had not proposed direct talks with Sihanouk and had not offered State Department–suggested concessions to get a conference going nor proposed keeping the UN seat vacant in exchange for Chinese help in arranging a settlement. Nor had he authorized Dean to try to get discussions going with GRUNK officials. These proposed solutions might not have worked, but they were not attempted. Instead, the administration continued to push hard to obtain additional funds to support the GKR, hoping that eventually the GKR would be strong enough to demonstrate to the other side that it would have to negotiate. Given the war weariness in both Cambodia and the United States, the ever present problem of corruption in the Cambodian military, and the concomitant growing congressional unwillingness to continue, much less increase, funding for Cambodia, the administration's approach was unlikely to succeed.

In September the Senate Foreign Relations Committee prepared a bill that provided $347 million in aid, with a cap of $200 million in military assistance. This was some $200 million less than the administration had requested. The administration soon decided that it would have to ask for $223 million in additional aid for Cambodia. To persuade Congress to go along with this request, the president discussed the issue with a bipartisan group of senators and representatives. In the course of the discussions, Kissinger hinted that efforts to seek a negotiated settlement were underway. "We can't discuss it in this broad a group," he said. There were in fact indications that the United States had by now begun to modify its long-standing refusal to speak with Sihanouk or Khmer Rouge officials. According to an administration source, in December 1974 an unsuccessful attempt was made through an unidentified neutral country to open a channel to Khmer Communists. Also in December and again in January 1975 the United States "concurred" in a French initiative to open a dialogue with Sihanouk. According to a later administration summary of negotiation efforts, at first the prince agreed to receive an emissary but later backed away.[11]

The French initiative dated from Giscard d'Estaing's accession to the presidency in May 1974.[12] Wanting to act as a statesman, Giscard wondered if his government might be able to play a constructive role in settling the Cambodian problem. His ambassador in Beijing, Etienne Manac'h, thought that the best option was to get Sihanouk back to Phnom Penh prior to a Khmer Rouge military victory. That would require that the United States arrange for Lon Nol's departure and for massive demonstrations in favor of the prince's return. The Chinese, Manac'h thought, might go along since they were leery of a complete Communist victory that might ultimately result in aligning Cambodia with China's nemesis, the Soviet Union. Giscard signed on to the scheme. The Chinese seemed willing to go along, as long as a Khmer Rouge victory was not imminent, although their position was hedged and ambiguous. On 25 November 1974 Sihanouk told Manac'h that he agreed with the plan but insisted that it had to be kept secret. If the United States removed Lon Nol, he was prepared to return to Phnom Penh and establish a government of national unity. The Khmer Rouge would dominate but would not have complete power.

Giscard presented his proposed solution at a previously scheduled meeting with Ford in Martinique. But the final communiqué—which should not have said anything at all about Cambodia if the parties wanted to keep the matter secret as Sihanouk had demanded—urged that the two Cambodian parties negotiate with each other. Drafted by Kissinger's staff, it appeared to be a complete rejection of Giscard's proposal. Although this snafu was most likely the result of a hurriedly drafted communiqué that was not reviewed by any French Asian experts, Kissinger retrospectively blamed the French. "I think maybe the French screwed us in December," he told the president shortly before the Khmer Rouge moved into Phnom Penh. Wherever the blame lies, the effect on Sihanouk was devastating. He had no choice but to condemn French meddling in Cambodian affairs. When Manac'h next saw the prince, he was depressed because his hopes of fashioning a moderate solution, something like Yugoslavia in eastern Europe, would not happen. Now there would only be force; something akin to Stalinist Albania would be the result, he feared.[13]

Although Kissinger had shown some interest in the French plan, the administration had no interest in Dean's suggestion, also made in December, that the ambassador meet with Khieu Samphan. Dean's efforts to inject himself into the negotiating process only irritated the administration. He nevertheless sent increasingly angry telegrams to Washington, virtually demanding movement toward negotiations. On 4 February 1975 he informed the State Department that GKR officials realized that only the United States, in whom they had placed their trust, could bring about peace. The administration talked about getting additional funding, which was all well and good. But what the Cambodians wanted to know was "what we were doing to make the further financing of the war unnecessary. . . . They are certainly not holding us back, and if they are not, who or what is?" he continued. "I must say I do not have the answer to these questions." Later the same day, after reviewing the deteriorating military situation and pointedly recalling that the previous September he had called for "a controlled solution" as quickly as possible, he reiterated his recommendation that the United States contact the insurgents "so that we can have some voice in working out the terms of the denouement." It would be unworthy for the United States to simply withdraw and leave the Khmers to their fate, he stated.[14]

Two days later, Dean's frustration overflowed. It appeared that the administration was not going to try to find a solution to the war, at least until the dry season campaign ended the following August. This was foolish, he told the State Department. The Cambodian government might well not survive until then, and even if it did it would probably be in a weaker situation than currently. Sihanouk had made it perfectly clear that he would only talk to Americans, on the single condition that Lon Nol leave, something that Dean thought could be easily arranged. It might be true, as the State Department pointed out, that Sihanouk would not be able to get support from his Khmer Rouge colleagues to negotiate—in which case the United States ought to try to separate Sihanouk from the Khmer Rouge. "If we could wean Sihanouk away from the Khmer Rouge," he wrote, "it would be a brand new ball game in Cambodia." Thus he urged "in the strongest possible terms" that the United States "undertake immediate direct contact" with the prince. If the effort failed, no one would be the worse. "But if we decline to make the effort now we are wasting precious time, and I am afraid that we have precious little time left in Cambodia." In more normal times, Dean went on, it would be appropriate for him to resign since he disagreed with Kissinger's policy so fundamentally. Given the dire circumstances, he had decided not to take that step. But he did want to register his "profound disagreement with what appears to me to be Dept's reasoning, i.e. that we will be in a better position for negotiations some months from now or that developments will have occurred in the US or in Cambodia which will shed a kinder light on our five year effort in Cambodia."[15]

Although Dean's telegram provoked an angry reaction from Kissinger himself, who told the ambassador to "resist the urge to read the department lectures," in fact Dean's strongly worded representations appear to have moved the administration for the first time to try to make direct contact with Sihanouk.[16] The day after Kissinger's strong telegram to Dean, the secretary informed the ambassador that the Americans were going to try to contact Sihanouk. The ambassador quickly informed the Cambodian president who, according to Dean, looked relieved that the Americans were finally going to try to speak to the prince.

Thereafter, Dean's dispatches were more measured. But when he had heard nothing more for ten days, even as the military situation continued to deteriorate, he could contain himself no longer and proceeded to give Kissinger his advice on how to conduct talks with Sihanouk. Above all he wanted the United States to throw its entire support behind Sihanouk, "not reluctantly but willingly."[17]

Unfortunately, Sihanouk did not, or could not, respond to the American effort. It is likely that his unhappy experience with the French intervention, which had put the Khmer Rouge on their guard about Sihanouk, immobilized him. Had the United States tried to talk with Sihanouk in the months, and even years, earlier, when he had clearly indicated his willingness to meet with the Americans, or even if it had carefully and discreetly followed through on the French proposal the past December, the story might have been different. But the United States never attempted to contact Sihanouk directly until February 1975, when the Khmer Rouge were on the brink of a military victory. There was never a sufficient sense of urgency at the highest levels. Dean had it right, even though Kissinger told the president that the ambassador had "gone wild and is writing for the record."[18]

By February the military situation was desperate. The Khmer Rouge, with Chinese help, had blocked and mined the Mekong River. Lloyds of London stopped issuing insurance to river convoys at any price, and virtually none were now attempting the deadly journey. Oudang fell back into enemy hands, and the front around Phnom Penh was again in danger of collapsing, with fighting taking place only a few kilometers from the city. When rockets fell on a market on 18 February, a missionary clinic "was turned into a bloody mess." On 23 February, after being briefed by military officials, the president of the Christian and Missionary Alliance ordered the organization's missionaries to depart within five days. An American military official told the missionaries that the situation was "on a downhill trend and beyond the point of retrieving."[19]

Sir Robert Thompson, who had often advised the American government about developments in Vietnam, visited Cambodia in March and arrived at equally pessimistic conclusions. Lon Nol "seemed out of touch with reality," he informed the Americans. If the Mekong were not opened soon (and he doubted FANK's ability to do that), the end was in sight. "It is an agonizing situation with possible tragic ending," Thompson reported. "In view of KC behaviour in the countryside it could end in massacre. . . . Any means of avoiding a bloodbath should be urgently sought."[20]

By this time it was clear to Dean that the end was near. In a moving telegram Dean reported that an enemy breakthrough around the Phnom Penh perimeter was now a "distinct possibility." FANK did not have the means to clear the Mekong, and military and civilian morale was at "an all-time low." Even if the Congress approved additional assistance, it was doubtful that it would do much good. If an "uncontrolled solution" was to be avoided, Dean wrote, "we must establish contact with Sihanouk despite all the obstacles in the way so that he can return to Cambodia while there is still an army, navy, airforce and government in being in Phnom Penh."[21]

But the administration had given up on negotiations, even those that might provide for the kind of "controlled solution" that Dean wanted, at least until Congress voted additional assistance and the GKR made it through the dry season. Talk of negotiations in the immediate future was little more than a public relations maneuver. The one initiative that momentarily aroused some excitement in Washington came toward the end of March when Sihanouk appealed to President Ford to get his films and other personal cultural effects out of Phnom Penh. The United States agreed to do what it could and hoped that this might lead to talks with Sihanouk about a peaceful solution. But when George H. W. Bush, head of the liaison office in Beijing, asked for a personal meeting with the prince, Sihanouk refused to discuss political matters. The incident reflected Sihanouk's inability by this point to do anything to stop the Khmer Rouge, whose destructive nature he fully understood. The United States nevertheless saved at least some of Sihanouk's films.[22]

Meanwhile, the administration continued to hope that Congress would approve additional emergency aid for Cambodia. Congress had not provided any new funding, and the shipment of military supplies—which were being funneled into Phnom Penh in an emergency airlift—would have to end sometime in April. (Food supplies could go on for a few more weeks.) If only the GKR could make it through the dry season, it continued to argue, negotiations would take place and a peaceful, if not very satisfactory, solution would be worked out, hopefully involving Sihanouk and some members of the current government.

This was not an easy position to sell. Did not a lot of the American assistance end up on the black market in Phnom Penh, asked the critics? Would not more money only prolong the bloodletting? As Senator Mansfield put it late in February, he was "sick and tired of pictures of Indochinese men, women and children being slaughtered by American guns with American ammunition in countries in which we have no vital interests and which are not tied to our security or our welfare." Even with the new funds, and even if the GKR survived to the rainy season when fighting would recede, the Cambodian government would be (as Dean had long maintained) considerably weaker than it already was.[23]

The administration was nevertheless committed to finding additional assistance, and Ford went to great lengths to persuade the Congress. His most successful approach was to convince an unenthusiastic congressional leadership to send a bipartisan fact-finding mission to Vietnam and Cambodia. Evenly divided between supporters of aid and those who opposed it, the members of Congress who went were all moved by the tragedy they encountered in Phnom Penh, and most returned willing to provide some additional aid. But despite immense efforts, Congress recessed without taking action. Congress would not resume deliberations until 7 April.

Even as the debate on aid continued, the thought of replacing Lon Nol seemed increasingly attractive. Lon Nol's departure might contribute to getting Congress to enact emergency aid, since many members saw him as incompetent and an impediment to a settlement. Lon Nol's departure might also improve Khmer morale. A number of influential Cambodians were carefully trying to arrange his exit. But the State Department was resolutely opposed to this kind of pressure on Lon Nol. Dean was only to listen and report and not take any position on the possible removal of the chief of state. When Cambodians discussed this with Dean, they were mystified at the neutral attitude of the Americans who, over the years, had not been at all shy about telling the Khmers exactly what they wanted them to do. "For the last two years we have done everything for the Khmer except blow their noses for them," Dean wrote. Under the circumstances, he reported, to do nothing would probably be interpreted as supporting Lon Nol's position.[24]

In this case the State Department's caution proved to be the right policy, for instead of the United States, the Japanese and ASEAN states made it clear to Lon Nol that he must go. Dean was then allowed very cautiously to nudge the Cambodian leader. For a time Lon Nol balked (despite his own repeated assurances over the years that he would step aside if circumstances required it), but after requesting (and presumably getting) $1 million from what must have already been a nearly barren Cambodian treasury to provide for his needs abroad, the Khmer leader left Phnom Penh for Indonesia. He subsequently flew to the United States, where he planned to settle in Maryland. By the time he left, advanced Khmer Rouge elements were only two and one-half miles from Phnom Penh.

Dean hoped against hope that Lon Nol's leaving would allow for a negotiated transfer of power, preferably to Sihanouk, who would retain some acceptable members of the GKR. Meanwhile, however, the embassy began quietly planning for an emergency evacuation. On 10 February spouses began to leave Cambodia, and on 14 February the embassy posted a letter urging nonofficial Americans to leave. The time for activating "Operation Eagle Pull," the contingency emergency airlift out of Phnom Penh, was reduced from 48 to 24 hours. There was much discussion about how many persons were to be evacuated. If Khmer officials, embassy employees, and their families were taken out, along with American diplomats, third-country nationals, personnel at other embassies for whom the United States had responsibilities, and the Americans from voluntary organizations, the figure came to well over 3,000. Eventually the estimated number of people to be evacuated was trimmed back to something under 1,200, although Dean acknowledged that even this figure was little better than a guess. The preferred plan was to evacuate people with fixed-wing aircraft. But the airport was already suffering from sporadic shelling and was constantly in danger of being closed. The helicopter alternative posed its own logistical problems.

On 31 March Dean wrote that the situation was falling apart. American military officials in Phnom Penh predicted that FANK would probably collapse sometime between 6 and 17 April, and anti-American sentiment was on the rise. The airport could be closed at any time, as FANK had not been able to disrupt enemy positions nearby. The ambassador was soon given permission to begin a gradual, quiet evacuation of some personnel. In this way 130 Americans, 577 Khmers, and 297 third-country nationals were flown out prior to the final evacuation. On 5 April Dean was granted authority to call for Eagle Pull with only three hours' notice if necessary. On 7 April Sihanouk sent telegrams to Cyrus Eaton and Senator Mansfield warning the Americans to shut down their embassy at once. The Khmer Rouge had deliberately not taken the airport, Sihanouk said, to allow for an American departure.

While the administration had approved withdrawing many personnel from Cambodia, it hoped to postpone a final departure as long as possible. The initial reason for this was to allow for Congress to act on the administration's aid request. If the embassy was abandoned, there was no possibility of a favorable vote. "We have two nutty Ambassadors," Kissinger stated, referring to Dean in Phnom Penh and Martin in Saigon. "Dean wants to bug out," he told President Ford.[25] Kissinger's comments were egregiously unfair to Dean but indicated the administration's current desire to keep an American presence in Phnom Penh a little longer. But the next day CIA director Colby told the NSC that Cambodia could not last more than a week, and the next day the administration ordered an evacuation.

In the meantime there were some last-minute contacts with Sihanouk's representatives in Beijing. George Bush wrote a letter to Sihanouk, and at least one meeting, and probably more, took place between Sihanouk's representative, a Mr. Phung (possibly a pseudonym), and American diplomat John Holdridge. On 10 April Phung told Holdridge that it was important to reach a solution before the fall of Saigon (which was also imminent), that Sihanouk could not do anything while he was in China but that he did not want "the Red Khmer to take over the country completely," and that the prince wanted FANK kept intact. The American response was to ask Sihanouk to request transportation to Phnom Penh from the Chinese. If this could be arranged, the United States would facilitate a ceasefire so that the prince could land safely in the capital.

Unfortunately, nothing came of these late contacts with Sihanouk, and the military situation in Cambodia did not improve. At 5:00 p.m. on 10 April Dean reported that the northern defenses of the capital were disintegrating and that it was likely that the airport would not be usable the next day. The previous day Dean had told Acting President Saukham Khoy and Foreign Minister Long Boret that if the last-minute effort to arrive at a political solution with Sihanouk failed, there would be an evacuation. The Americans would take with them a limited number of Khmers if they wished to go. They would have no more than two hours' notice, and one of their trusted aides should come by the ambassador's residence at 6:30 a.m. to carry a note back to them. Both Cambodian leaders fully understood what was being conveyed to them.

The next day at daybreak the first of thirty-six large helicopters carrying 360 marines left the USS *Okinawa* in the Gulf of Thailand for the flight to Landing Zone Hotel (a soccer field adjacent to the unfinished luxury Cambodiana Hotel) to pick up the assembled Americans and Cambodians. While they were on their way, Dean met with Saukham Khoy and Long Boret. Saukham Khoy was not certain if he would go with the Americans and thought that "mostly women and children of Khmer VIPs would take advantage of our offer."[26]

Fewer people wanted to leave than was expected. In the end this final evacuation included about 82 American citizens, 159 Cambodians, and 35 persons of other nationalities. Among them was Saukham Khoy. Former Prime Minister Sirik Matak chose not to leave. "I never believed for a moment that you would have this sentiment of abandoning a people which has chosen liberty," he wrote in an eloquent, if not entirely accurate, letter to the departing ambassador. "You have refused us your protection and we can do nothing about it. You leave and my wish is that you and your country will find happiness under the sky. -/-/- But mark it well that, if I shall die here on the spot and in my country that I love, it is too bad, because we all are born and must die one day. I have only committed this mistake of believing you, the Americans."[27] (Sirik Matak was in fact one of the first victims of Khmer Rouge vengeance, as were Long Boret and Lon Non, who also chose not to leave.)

The evacuation went smoothly. The Cambodians who crowded around the soccer field were curious, not hostile. There was no American gunfire.

But toward the end of the operation Khmer Rouge guns opened on the field. At least one Cambodian boy watching the spectacle was killed. No Americans or others being evacuated were injured, though at least two of the departing helicopters suffered damage from ground fire. The American presence in Cambodia was now gone, and the killing fields were about to begin.

Except for one final drama. On 12 May at about 2:15 p.m. (local time—3:15 a.m. in Washington) a Khmer Rouge gunboat approached an American merchant ship, the SS *Mayaguez,* which was steaming from Hong Kong en route to Sattahip, Thailand. The ship was approximately seven miles from the Cambodian island of Poulo Wai when Khmer Rouge sailors took command of the ship, and gunboats began escorting the captured vessel toward the Cambodian island of Koh Tang.

Although it took the administration several hours to understand the seriousness of the situation, the president decided to engage the Cambodians with military force if the crew was not immediately released. The administration hoped to avoid another *Pueblo* incident. (In January 1968 North Korea seized this American military ship and held the crew for several months as hostages.) At 2:25 a.m. (Washington time) on 13 May an American reconnaissance plane found the *Mayaguez* anchored at Koh Tang Island. Orders were then issued to prevent the ship from being taken to the Cambodian port of Kompong Som. At 6:04 a.m. the ship's crew was transferred to a Cambodian gunboat and taken to the island. That evening the *Mayaguez* crew boarded a Cambodian gunboat to be taken to Kompong Som. Fortunately, even as American planes were attacking and destroying some Cambodian patrol boats, the boat with the *Mayaguez* crew on board made it to shore unharmed—thanks only to Secretary of Defense James Schlesinger who refused to implement literally a presidential order to stop any boats leaving the island.[28]

Despite some congressional criticism, Ford then decided to attack Koh Tang and bomb Kompong Som. Unfortunately twenty-three American soldiers died when their helicopter, on its way to the battlefield, crashed in Thailand. The assault nevertheless began at 5:42 a.m. (local time) on 15 May. The marines quickly secured the *Mayaguez,* and the *Holt* towed the ship away. But the landing on Koh Tang did not go easily. Given the considerable distance between the American air base at U Tapao, Thailand, and Koh Tang (about 190 nautical miles) and the limited number of helicopters available, only one-third of the landing force could be brought in during the initial landing. Two helicopters were quickly shot down, and the marines who landed encountered fierce resistance.

Four hours after the landing on Koh Tang, the Cambodians released the *Mayaquez* crew from Kompong Son. They were taken to an American warship, the USS *Henry B. Wilson,* on a Thai fishing vessel flying a white flag. But the bombing of Kompong Son and the Ream naval base continued (despite

Schlesinger's objections—he may have been responsible for countermanding orders to employ the B-52s), as did the fierce battle of Koh Tang where the Khmer Rouge soldiers fought bravely and well. Eventually the Americans dropped a huge, 15,000-pound bomb on the center of the island, which may have affected Khmer Rouge morale but did not break their ranks.

The Americans were ready to evacuate by now, but the Cambodians made this very difficult and dangerous. Had they pressed their attack, they might have driven the Americans into the sea, but they were apparently reluctant to leave their concealed positions and open themselves to air attacks. They did, nevertheless, shoot down additional helicopters that were trying to evacuate the hard-pressed marines. In the end, fifteen American soldiers died in the battle. In all probability three additional marines were left behind, only to be killed by the Khmer Rouge over the next several days.[29] Including those killed in the helicopter crash in Thailand, more Americans died in the rescue attempt than there were *Mayaguez* crew members freed. American bombing of the Cambodian mainland destroyed several Cambodian buildings, and nine Cambodian boats were destroyed as well.

Despite the losses, Ford considered his response to the *Mayaguez* affair a great success. And, despite the doubts of some prominent political leaders, public opinion seems to have been very much on his side. As a military action, however, the Koh Tang operation was nearly disastrous—complicated, ironically, by the use of modern communications technology that actually increased friction in the chain of command and interfered with battlefield actions. Furthermore, the bombing of Kompong Som put the *Mayaguez* crew in great danger, and little attention was given to a possible diplomatic solution, partly out of fear of another *Pueblo* incident but also because Kissinger wanted a strong military response to restore American "credibility."

> The red, red blood splatters the cities and plains of the Cambodian fatherland,
> The sublime blood of the workers and peasants,
> The blood of revolutionary combatants of both sexes.
> That blood spills out into great indignation and a resolute urge to fight.
> 17 April, that day under the revolutionary flag
> The blood certainly liberates us from slavery.
> —Cambodian national anthem under the Khmer Rouge

With Phnom Penh in its death throes, Gerald Ford might have exploited the opportunity to blame Congress and others for the outcome, as Kissinger surely would have. Instead he followed the counsel of Senator

Mansfield, majority leader of the Senate. "We paid a high price for our participation in the Indo-China tragedy in men and money," the senator said. Acknowledging the complicity of six administrations, Mansfield told his colleagues that "this is not the time for either the Executive or the Legislative Branch to begin pointing the finger. If there is any blame to be attached, and there is a great deal," he stated, "we must all share in it. None of us is guiltless." To this Ford responded simply, "I accept my wise friend's counsel."[30] Not giving in to the temptation to assign blame was one of Ford's most important legacies to the country.

With the fall of Phnom Penh on 17 April, the administration correctly feared a bloodbath. Over the previous months the administration had received various intelligence reports of conditions in areas controlled by the Khmer Rouge that varied from unpleasant to savage. In February 1974 foreign service officer Kenneth Quinn (who later served as ambassador to Cambodia from 1995 to 1999) completed an especially thorough analysis of Khmer Rouge rule in areas of southern Cambodia that they controlled. This was a particularly valuable study because in this area the Khmer Rouge (or Khmer Krahom—"Krahom" means "red" in the Khmer language) had broken with other insurgents (the Khmer Rumdoah), who were loyal to Sihanouk. How the Khmer Krahom operated in the area they controlled, therefore, provided a reliable basis for projecting what would happen in the larger society if an unadulterated Khmer Rouge regime materialized.[31]

Based on interviews with refugees, other reports from American and South Vietnamese sources, and a lengthy interview with a former Khmer Rouge leader in Kampot Province who had fled to Vietnam after three and one-half years as village chief, Quinn was able to identify a number of characteristics of Khmer Rouge rule. Among other things they tried to eliminate completely any vestiges of Cambodian royal society. To do this they destroyed most government schools and offices, eliminated any references to "royal" in their governmental arrangements, and even changed the names of provinces and districts, substituting numbers for names. They then began a program of land reform, set up cooperative stores, and outlawed colorful dress. Once they had defeated FANK in the spring of 1973 they accelerated efforts to communize the society and began a vitriolic anti-Sihanouk campaign.

The Khmer Rouge took various steps to control the population. They required passes to travel outside of the villages; to go outside of the local district required higher-level approval. Patrolling was constant, and repeat offenders were executed. A secret police apparatus was also established. Local residents were "reeducated" through intimidation and terror and were required to attend propaganda sessions at night. Young men and women were removed from their homes for intensive political training, from which they returned condemning religion, traditional ways, and parental authority. To obliterate class lines, educated or wealthy individuals were forced into agricultural labor. For those who refused to conform, terror was employed. Harsh punishment was "widespread" and the death sentence was "relatively common" for those who attempted to flee, questioned Khmer Rouge policies, or were accused of espionage. Those arrested usually just disappeared. Because the jail was in malaria-infested mountains, those sent there for any length of time were likely to die.

In addition to suppressing dissent, Khmer Rouge terror was intended to break "down traditional social and communal bonds" and to leave individuals "alone to face the state." They changed traditional approaches to religion, marriage, and certain customs. Marriage was actually forbidden for the time being so that all energies could be devoted to the war. When it was allowed again, the minimum age was to be raised to twenty-five and elaborate marriage ceremonies were to be prohibited. Traditional dancing was totally forbidden, as was "the singing of religious and folk songs." All ethnic festivals were outlawed, and religious activity, Theravada Buddhism in particular, came under attack, with faith in the revolution being the substitute—although the pagodas had not yet closed. Monks were forced to perform manual labor, stripped of their robes and, if recalcitrant, sent to reeducation centers. Some monks who refused to support Khmer Rouge policies were tortured to death. The practice of Islam—the religion of the Cham minority—was totally forbidden, and Chams were not allowed to practice various customs mandated by their religion.

Economically, the Khmer Rouge attempted to level the condition of the people. They confiscated mechanized transportation (motor scooters and motorized sampans, for example), along with material goods, houses, furniture, family heirlooms, and so forth. Anyone caught trading illegally was subject to stiff penalties. Finally, in a chilling presentiment of what was to come, Quinn reported that the Khmer Rouge were engaged in "a program of population relocation and the creation of uninhabited buffers zones around areas they controlled."

The most obvious popular reaction to Khmer Rouge policies was flight. Despite the knowledge that those who tried to escape would be killed if captured, about 28,000 fled to South Vietnam in 1973 and another 20,000 to 25,000 fled to GKR-controlled territory within Cambodia. According to Quinn, the most important motivation for fleeing was the forced relocation, though restrictions on trade, forced sales of crops, religious persecution, and the verbal attacks on Sihanouk were also factors. There were some acts of rebellion, particularly by armed insurgents loyal to the prince. Many were killed in the fighting, and some pro-Sihanouk people were executed. But overall active opposition to Khmer Rouge rule was insignificant.

Quinn's careful analysis depicted a totalitarian society that could be chillingly brutal, though the picture he presented was not one of totally unmitigated savagery. He noted, for example, that some of the Khmer Rouge practices were not uncommon in other Southeast Asian societies.

Subsequent reports, many of them in mainstream American newspapers, focused on savage repression. To the administration, reports of this sort settled the question about whether there would be a bloodbath once the Khmer Rouge won. In the final weeks of the GKR's existence, reports of Khmer Rouge outrages were used to try and secure additional assistance from Congress.

When the Khmer Rouge entered Phnom Penh in victory on 17 April, they executed many people, including GKR officials. A French priest, François Ponchaud, who traveled around Phnom Penh on 19 April "saw many dead bodies along the road" and "many bodies floating in the Mekong River in front of the palace."[32] The new rulers also emptied the city, driving the people into the countryside. Even those in hospitals had to leave, regardless of their condition. The Americans quickly had reports, albeit initially unconfirmed ones, about these developments.

Although such reports were accurate, there was considerable skepticism about them at first. This was not entirely surprising since Khmer Rouge brutality had surprised even many Cambodians initially. "When the Communists seized control of Phnom Penh on April 17 my first reaction was relief that the fighting was finally over," recalled one GKR soldier. "With my comrades-in-arms, I planned to give the victors a hearty welcome." He was surprised and disappointed, he said, at the ruthless behavior that ensued.[33]

Those Americans who had opposed American actions in Vietnam and Cambodia were among the most skeptical of administration claims of atrocities. They knew that refugee reports, the source of most such stories initially, were often inaccurate or exaggerated. But more to the point, they had grown cynical of anything the government claimed to be true in relation to events in Southeast Asia. Given the many instances when Johnson and Nixon administration officials had lied to the public (the memory of the administration's denying that it was bombing Cambodia was still fresh, for example), there was an inclination to disbelieve administration claims.

Even after the fall of Phnom Penh, skepticism continued. Some of the administration's allegations were based on confidential intelligence sources that were not revealed. Given the Vietnam War–induced distrust of governmental statements, the critics doubted assertions about Khmer Rouge atrocities, especially on the scale being reported. Was this not just a post-hoc effort to discredit the antiwar movement?

This skepticism was also reflected in some contemporary scholarly works. Gareth Porter and G. C. Hildebrand's monograph, "The Politics of Food: Starvation and Agricultural Revolution in Cambodia" (later published as *Cambodia: Starvation and Revolution*) is perhaps the best example. Completed in September 1975 for the Indochina Resource Center in Washington (a church-sponsored research organization with an antiwar posture), the work included a foreword by respected Cornell University historian George McT. Kahin, coauthor of an early account of American involvement in Vietnam.

Prince Sihanouk meets with Mao Zedong for the last time in September 1975. From the Private Collection of Ambassador Julio A. Jeldres.

Porter and Hildebrand's account was based on genuine research and contains important information on the state of the country the Khmer Rouge inherited. It is also worth pointing out that the Khmer insurgency was not entirely unified and that not all of the new rulers were satanic. Nevertheless the authors accepted much too uncritically Khmer Rouge statements and documents. The Khmer Rouge regime was one of the most brutal in memory, and comparisons with Nazi Germany's or Stalin's terror were apt, even if the American administration did sometimes publicize atrocities to serve its own policy and political interests. Yet "The Politics of Food" reflected, in an extreme sort of way, the lack of trust in the American government, something that several administrations had brought on themselves through misstatements and outright lies. As *New York Times* columnist Anthony Lewis put it in 1977, "When Henry Kissinger cries for Cambodia, there is room for scepticism."[34]

In addition to being brutal, the Khmer Rouge regime of Democratic Kampuchea (DK) was one of the most isolated in the world, with DK having serious ties only to China and North Korea. Despite the new regime's terror and its xenophobic outlook, the United States debated whether to try to establish contact with DK. In September the Americans, urged by China, considered approaching the DK delegation at the United Nations to see if bilateral relations could be improved. Quinn thought the approach premature and not in American interests. But his objections were not persuasive, and on 2 October Philip Habib approached the DK representative to the United Nations, Sarin Chhak, while a high-level State Department official met Sihanouk at the airport when he arrived in New York to attend the United Nations meeting. It is not clear what Habib's meeting accomplished, but it must not have been entirely without results, for two weeks later NSC official Thomas J. Barnes suggested to Kissinger that he take up with the Chinese the issue of 125 Cambodian refugees residing at Camp Pendleton who wanted to return to Cambodia. This "could serve as a useful follow up to Assistant Secretary Habib's approach to Sarin Chhak," Barnes wrote. It would also "be a good test of whether the Chinese are sincere in wanting us to develop this relationship, and of whether the Khmer·are prepared to take small steps in helping us"; this might result in "a new relationship," he concluded.[35] Kissinger let the Thais and Chinese know that he favored a Chinese presence in Cambodia to counter the Vietnamese. The Khmer Rouge were "murderous thugs," he told Thai Foreign Minister Chatichai Choonhavan in November 1975. "But we won't let that stand in our way."[36] It seems likely that the subsequent decision in 1976 to allow limited humanitarian assistance to DK (the administration approved a license to allow a humanitarian organization to provide $50,000 in malaria medicines to DK, assistance that the Khmer Rouge never acknowledged) reflected the whispered, scarcely articulated view that DK served American interests by containing a newly unified Vietnam, toward which the United States was hostile. Thus when in July 1976 the Australians reported that the Cambodians had approached them about establishing diplomatic relations, Kissinger was intrigued. "Anything that would help to contain Vietnam would be good," he stated.[37] Kissinger foreshadowed what would become American policy for the next fifteen years: supporting anti-Vietnamese elements in Cambodia, including the "loathsome" Khmer Rouge.

The American public slowly became aware of the nature of the Khmer Rouge regime, notably from an exposé in *Time* magazine and a book by *Reader's Digest* editors Anthony Paul and John Barron, *Murder in a Gentle Land*, which served as the basis of congressional hearings in 1977. But despite the extreme nature of Khmer Rouge rule and the outrage that resulted, there was little stomach to take strong action. The American public wanted nothing more to do with Southeast Asia. The Ford administration declined to go further than issuing occasional condemnation of the regime, urging the admission of refugees, supporting international organizations that chose to undertake investigations, and wishing the best to those private humanitarian organizations who worked to alleviate conditions in Cambodia.

Jimmy Carter, Human Rights, and Cambodia

"I hoped and believed that the expansion of human rights might be the wave of the future throughout the world, and I wanted the United States to be on the crest of this movement."—Jimmy Carter

A FOREIGN POLICY that placed the defense of human rights at its center characterized the administration of Jimmy Carter—at least rhetorically.[1] Most popular and scholarly commentators have been critical of Carter as a foreign policy leader, but his devotion to human rights, the degree to which he made it a central aspect of American foreign policy, and the successes he had bringing about real changes abroad figure prominently in recent efforts to rehabilitate the former president's reputation.

Unquestionably Carter gave more prominence to human rights than any recent previous administration. According to historian Douglas Brinkley, in fact, human rights was the "paramount" consideration in determining American policy.[2] Even Carter's critics acknowledge that there are instances where his emphasis on human rights resulted in significant changes and even saved thousands of lives. Yet in the case of the murderous Khmer Rouge regime in Cambodia human rights considerations hardly entered into the administration's calculus, despite the fact that Carter himself characterized the Pol Pot regime as the "worst violator of human rights in the world today." Not surprising, Carter scarcely mentions Cambodia in his memoirs, nor do revisionist scholars discuss his policy toward that country.

The administration's failure to elevate human rights concerns in its policy toward Cambodia can be attributed to several factors. After the recent traumas caused by the debacle in Vietnam, most Americans wanted to forget about Southeast Asia. There was also a sense that the United States could exert no influence on the secretive and xenophobic Khmer Rouge regime. Major issues of more

Human skulls and bones at what was called Sang Prison during the Khmer Rouge rule. It is located near Trapeang Sva Village, Trea Commune, Kandal Stung District, Kandal Province. The stage upon which the bones were positioned was part of the central administrative building of a teachers training college built by USAID in the early 1960s. The bones were exhumed in 1979 from a killing field that is about one kilometer west of the former college, on the shore of the lake. Photo by Kenton Clymer. Thanks to Craig Etcheson and Sorya Sim for information about the location.

immediate importance to the United States also deflected attention from Southeast Asia: forging a new Panama Canal treaty, trying to bring an end to the Israeli-Palestinian problem, responding to the Soviet invasion of Afghanistan, and dealing with the Iranian hostage crisis, for example. But in the final analysis old-fashioned geopolitical considerations, in particular the desire to oppose the perceived expansion of Soviet influence in Southeast Asia at the expense of America's new friend, China, won out over human rights in Carter's Cambodia policy. In a final irony, after the Vietnamese drove the Khmer Rouge from power at the end of 1978, the United States secretly supported efforts to resuscitate and sustain their remnant military forces. For this, National Security Adviser Zbigniew Brzezinski, with Carter's at least tacit approval, bears primary responsibility.

When Carter took office in January 1977, he immediately addressed issues remaining from the Vietnam War. The new president pardoned those who had resisted the draft and began the process (ultimately abortive) of restoring diplomatic relations with Vietnam. But Cambodia received little attention. The decision in 1977 to approve three licenses to ship DDT to Cambodia to ease the country's problem with malaria may have been simply a matter of humanitarian concern, although providing the aid might also have reflected the belief by some officials—first adumbrated by Kissinger in the previous administration—that DK served American interests by helping to contain Vietnam. In any event, no policy initiatives were taken in 1977 to try to mitigate the terror.

The administration's inattention to the tragedy in Cambodia soon caused a growing number of people to point out that the administration's silence belied its rhetoric about the centrality of human rights to its foreign policy. Such sentiments resulted in the first congressional hearings on Cambodian developments since the victory of the Pol Pot forces in 1975. In May 1977 the Subcommittee on International Organization of the House International Affairs Committee heard from four witnesses: *Reader's Digest* editor John Barron; scholar Gareth Porter; and former foreign service officers Peter A. Poole and David Chandler, both of whom had previously served in Cambodia. Porter defended the Khmer Rouge decision to evacuate the cities; Poole and Chandler offered cautious assessments of the situation and thought past American military actions were substantially responsible for bringing the Khmer Rouge to power. But beyond agreeing that some humanitarian assistance (such as additional shipments of DDT, along with food and medicine) might be helpful, none of the witnesses initially offered any suggestions on how the United States could significantly change the Cambodian situation, and all except Barron opposed strong public condemnation. "You have no specific recommendations for the U.S. policy which you would put forward as a means of ameliorating or encouraging moderation in the regime there," committee chairman Donald M. Fraser (D-MN) stated in apparent frustration.[3]

The witnesses' testimony appalled Representative Stephen Solarz (D-NY). Although Solarz, who was quickly becoming the leading congressional authority on Cambodia, agreed that the American bombing of Cambodia had been "contemptible," what was now happening in Cambodia was "one of the most monstrous crimes in the history of the human race." To stand by and say nothing betrayed "a kind of implicit racism." If the victims were white, he went on, the United States would not be talking "about sending DDT to the offending nation in an effort to ameliorate the situation." The situation was so horrendous and unprecedented, Solarz thought, that it required "an exceptional and maybe extraordinary response on our part," and he suggested looking at an international boycott or even an international police action.[4]

The administration responded that it had "no leverage to affect the human rights situation in Cambodia."[5] But such expressions of impotence did not assuage the critics. On 28 February 1978, for example, Solarz wrote directly to the president condemning the flagrant violations of human rights, and Carter then directed Brzezinski to prepare a strong condemnation of Democratic Kampuchea. When the statement finally emerged on 21 April 1978, it condemned the Cambodian government as "the worst violator of human rights in the world today." The Khmer Rouge were accused of causing "hundreds of thousands" of deaths. A reference in an earlier draft to one to two million people perishing because of genocidal policies was not included, although the controversial term "genocide" did survive in a subsequent section that called attention to a recent Canadian House of Commons resolution condemning the "acts of genocide" in Cambodia. Even in this slightly watered-down version, the condemnation of Cambodia earned Carter much applause, and the president soon asked for recommendations on ways to encourage change in Cambodia.[6]

However, attention soon focused mostly on the plight of the Cambodian refugees who had managed to escape to Thailand. (There was virtually no interest, it might be noted, in the tens of thousands of Cambodian refugees for whom Vietnam was caring.) Within a few months legislation passed allowing approximately 15,000 Cambodian refugees to resettle in the United States. Such legislation did not, however, address the plight of the millions of Cambodians still living under the Khmer Rouge government. Although some, like Senator George McGovern (D-SD), eventually called for armed intervention to end the suffering, most of those who wanted stronger action believed that the most effective way was to have the United States persuade the People's Republic of China, the Khmer Rouge's only real ally, to end Cambodia's reign of terror. In 1978 this seemed more realistic than in the past because the Carter administration hoped to establish full diplomatic relations with China. In July a bipartisan group of eighteen congressional representatives urged Carter to make Cambodia a part of the discussions aimed at normalizing relations with China. Pointing out that the United States had already indicated its willingness to cooperate with the Chinese on regional problems, the legislators urged that China be asked to reciprocate.

The representatives' suggestion did not commend itself to Brzezinski. The National Security Adviser was fiercely anti-Soviet and a strong proponent of improving relations with the Soviet Union's bitter antagonist, China. Just as he would soon end talks on restoring relations with Vietnam because he feared normalization with Vietnam might complicate negotiations with China, so too he did not want to make China's intervention with Pol Pot a condition of normalization.

To give first priority to the geopolitical advantages inherent in normalizing relations with China, however, belied the Carter administration's insistence that concern for human rights was the primary determinant in its foreign policy. To many, the policy of seeking to normalize relations with China without calling on its government to pressure the Khmer Rouge seemed hypocritical. China was the only country in the world that might be able to influence a regime that Carter himself had accused of being the world's worst violator of human rights. By not linking the two issues, American policy appeared to be based purely on realpolitik calculations and, in particular, a desire to play the China card in the strategic battle with the Soviet Union. Even Carter found Brzezinski's fascination with China irritating at times. "Zbig," the president jotted on one of Brzezinski's papers advocating a delay in normalizing relations with Vietnam, "you have a tendency to exalt the PRC issue."[7] But Brzezinski held firm. He regarded the establishment of full diplomatic relations with China as his crowning achievement, but there was no respite for Cambodia.

Relief for Cambodia finally came in December 1978 when Vietnamese troops (along with some Cambodians who had taken refuge in Vietnam) invaded Cambodia and drove the Khmer Rouge regime out of Phnom Penh. Soon Pol Pot controlled only a small part of the country near the Thai border, as well as some refugee camps inside Thailand. The Vietnamese installed Heng Samrin as the prime minister of the new government, the People's Republic of Kampuchea (PRK). Several months after the invasion, Vietnamese Prime Minister Pham Van Dong told a visiting group of Americans representing Church World Service (the overseas relief and development arm of the National Council of Churches) that Vietnam had acted to "salvage a nation. . . . We have brought that nation from death to life," he said.[8] Vietnam's motives were actually considerably more complex. Among them were disagreements over the border between Vietnam and Cambodia (which had led to episodes of armed conflict between the two countries over the past three years), fear of encirclement by China, and anger at Cambodian raids into Vietnam that had killed thousands of villagers. But regardless, Vietnam ended the murderous rule of the Khmer Rouge. Despite the distrust that most Cambodians historically had for the Vietnamese, on this occasion their hereditary enemy was their liberator. As Sihanouk himself put it many years later, "If they [the Vietnamese] had not ousted Pol Pot, everyone would have died—not only me, but everyone— they would have killed us all."[9]

The Carter administration did not see it that way, however. Only a couple of months before the invasion the Americans had been close to normalizing relations with Vietnam, only to have Brzezinski stop the process. After it was clear that the United States was backing away from normalizing relations, Vietnam signed a treaty of friendship with the Soviet Union (something it had carefully refrained from doing up to that point) and prepared to drive the Khmer Rouge out. When Vietnam invaded Cambodia, the United States condemned the act. Even the Khmer Rouge regime's "unparalleled crimes," the Americans told the Vietnamese, did not justify a "military violation of Kampuchean sovereignty and replacement of the government by force."[10]

To the Carter administration and especially to Brzezinski, the Vietnamese action had the deleterious effect of expanding Soviet influence in Southeast Asia. Pol Pot's regime was despicable but it was allied with China, which the United States now supported. The diplomatic calculus quickly became more complicated, for during his visit to Washington at the end of January 1979, China's Vice Chairman Deng Xiaoping asked Carter how the United States would respond if Chinese forces attacked Vietnam. Carter personally urged Deng not to do it. But, as Brzezinski put it, Carter "did not lock the United States into a position which could generate later pressures to condemn China in the UN."[11] When China invaded Vietnam on 16 February 1979, the president reportedly told the NSC that "the Soviet-backed . . . Vietnamese invasion of Cambodia gave the Chinese little choice but to invade Vietnam." This remained at the heart of the American view of Indochina. As one official put it, "the Vietnamese invasion of Kampuchea is the root cause of the tensions in the region."[12] Not surprisingly, in the immediate aftermath of the Chinese invasion, Brzezinski met almost daily with the Chinese ambassador and provided him with intelligence reports on Soviet troop deployments. Thus, as historian Qiang Zhia writes, "the US was secretly assisting China as it delivered its 'punishment' to Vietnam."[13]

As these developments unfolded, nothing indicates that the administration gave any thought whatsoever to trying to prevent Pol Pot from resuming his murderous rule. What would happen to the Cambodians if the Vietnamese withdrew? The question was not raised. Legitimate questions of international law served as a basis for U.S. criticism of Vietnam's action. But the real concern of the United States was geopolitical. Soviet influence in Southeast Asia appeared to have been expanded at the expense of China's. From such a perspective the fact that Pol Pot's forces had not been completely destroyed cheered the administration.

Once again it was up to Congress to try and force action on behalf of the Cambodians. On 22 February 1979, Solarz and eight other members of Congress called the administration on its failure to address the issue of the possible return of the Khmer Rouge to power. If the Vietnamese withdrew from Cambodia without an international force of some kind in position, they stated, "the genocidal Pol Pot regime" would reestablish itself in Phnom Penh, and the suffering of the Cambodian people would continue, as would regional instability.[14]

The administration responded that it did not disagree with many of the representatives' sentiments. But there is little evidence that the Carter administration devoted much energy to trying to prevent the Khmer Rouge from returning. This was evident on 1 March 1979 when Assistant Secretary of State for East Asian and Pacific Affairs Richard Holbrooke called for the withdrawal of Vietnamese forces from Cambodia but said nothing about how the Khmer Rouge would be prevented from resuming control if they withdrew. It was left to Solarz to make the point that the administration had no plan to prevent Pol Pot's returning to power if the Vietnamese left. The administration's major goal was to get the Vietnamese to leave Cambodia because their presence there, and the regime they had installed and supported, represented in the administration's view a gain for Soviet influence in the region at the expense of the Chinese. From this perspective, keeping Pol Pot's forces in the field where they could fight the Vietnamese was in the administration's interest, despite the embarrassment of supporting, if only indirectly, a man who had perpetrated mass murder and produced immense suffering in Southeast Asia. The interest of ordinary Cambodian people was of little concern.

Meanwhile the plight of the hundreds of thousands of Indochinese refugees continued to attract attention. Tens of thousands of Cambodians were fleeing to Thailand to escape the Khmer Rouge and the continued fighting in their country. But the unrelated but simultaneous exodus of large numbers of "boat people" from Vietnam complicated the international situation of the Cambodian refugees. Sometimes rescued half dead on the high seas by merchant vessels or American warships, frequently suffering from horrific attacks by pirates and marauders before reaching Malaysia, Indonesia, Thailand, or elsewhere (where they were forced to live in often wretched refugee camps, if they were not actually pushed back out to sea), the plight of the boat people was an embarrassment to Vietnam. A great outcry to assist the boat people arose.

It was more comfortable for the American government to focus attention on the boat people (it was easy to blame the government of Vietnam directly for causing the problem) than on the Cambodian refugees (the "land people"). But the latter could not be ignored altogether. Stories about their harrowing lives under the Khmer Rouge and traumatic accounts of escape through minefields into Thailand began to appear in American publications. When in June 1979 Thailand forced about 45,000 Khmers back into Cambodia with tragic results, there was a strong outcry. Carter unconvincingly blamed the PRK and the Vietnamese for the tragedy, but the United States worked with the Thai government and voluntary organizations to deliver food and other relief supplies to the border, where they were simply left to be picked up by needy refugees on the Cambodian side. In addition, the United States encouraged Thailand to allow those refugees who had been forcibly repatriated to return to Thailand by assuring them that the United States would relocate up to 10,000 of them in the United States.

Attention to the Khmers soon increased dramatically when reports of imminent famine inside Cambodia itself began to appear. It was estimated that tens of thousands, perhaps as many as 200,000, were starving every month. The Carter administration had largely ignored warnings of impending famine, including those from its own ambassador in Thailand as early as April. But in late July Secretary of State Cyrus Vance acknowledged that there was now "a serious threat of famine."[15] Even with the emergency now acknowledged, however, the Carter administration was hardly in the forefront of the relief effort. It criticized the Heng Samrin regime (and its Vietnamese supporters) for insisting that all aid be channeled through the PRK, which it claimed was hindering distribution. But what most concerned the United States was that food shipments through Phnom Penh might be diverted to Vietnamese soldiers or be used in other ways to bolster the PRK.

The failure to get aid into Cambodia generated heated criticism. If the British development agency Oxfam and the American Friends Service Committee could manage to get some food into Cambodia, the critics charged, why could not the United States government? Within the government, the Presidential Commission on World Hunger, headed by Sol M. Linowitz, encouraged the administration to address the food crisis. In response, the administration initially committed $7 million. Under pressure from Linowitz and various voices outside the government (most notably that of Theodore M. Hesburgh, president of the University of Notre Dame and chairman of the Overseas Development Council), the administration soon increased the figure to $30 million.

In addition to the new financial commitment, Carter sent letters to other countries urging them to increase their own contributions. He also formed an interagency working group to coordinate relief efforts, naming former senator Dick Clark (D-IA) to head the group. Carter also issued a proclamation calling on all Americans to contribute generously to Cambodian relief and designating each Saturday and Sunday until Thanksgiving as times when Americans might contribute through their houses of worship. All in all, it was a major administration effort. Even Sihanouk's wife, Princess Monique, the former head of the Cambodian Red Cross, was impressed. From Beijing she praised "la générosité du peuple américain et . . . l'action magnifique de son président."[16]

Important as the administration's new commitment was, it still lagged behind public opinion on the issue. After Senator John C. Danforth (R-MO) gave a "chilling report" to his colleagues about his recent visit to Phnom Penh where his delegation saw Cambodians "literally dying before our eyes," Congress approved an additional $30 million "with unanimous whoops of approval." Congress had doubled the amount requested by the administration.[17]

Even with the new commitments and the enthusiastic public support for assistance, just how forthcoming the United States would be in allowing funds to be spent inside Cambodia (as opposed to along the border) remained uncertain. Politics still mattered. On 29 October syndicated columnist Jack Anderson alleged that State Department officials had "deliberately sabotaged" the relief effort insofar as it applied to aid being provided to those inside Cambodia itself. Lower-level officials, especially those at the "East Asian desk," were allegedly most culpable, he charged, though the larger problem was the "deep-seated anti-Vietnam bias in the State Department."[18] Anderson may have exaggerated State Department obstructiveness, but his insight that anti-Vietnamese sentiment informed American policy toward the region was on the mark.

In sum, although the administration had taken important steps to increase assistance to Cambodia, its willingness to address the tragedy in a forceful fashion remained in doubt. As a member of Vice President Walter F. Mondale's staff put it in a letter to Carter's chief of staff Hamilton Jordan, "there is little sense of the Administration having acted decisively. On moral, humanitarian and political grounds, it should be otherwise."[19]

By late November 1979 those within the administration who wanted a strong public policy of blaming Hanoi, the PRK, and the USSR felt emboldened (probably because the Iranian hostage crisis had distracted attention from the Cambodian tragedy). Brzezinski led the charge and had the NSC draft a militant statement accusing Vietnam, with Soviet backing, of denying the relief agencies access to hundreds of thousands of Cambodians. Vance and the State Department objected. It was, after all, hard to sustain the charge that the Vietnamese, who had rescued the country from the real perpetrator of mass murder, Pol Pot, were themselves guilty of genocide. Even within the NSC there were prominent voices who acknowledged that the relief supplies were now arriving in Cambodia, and that problems of distribution were at least in part logistical in nature.

But Brzezinski was intolerant of ambiguity. He preferred propaganda. Thus on 3 December he again ordered the State Department to explain what it was doing to publicize Vietnamese efforts to deny food to needy Cambodians. To the CIA he was even blunter. The agency was directed "on an urgent basis" to publicize as widely as possible the Vietnamese "starvation policy." Not surprisingly, the official White House "Statement on Kampuchea," issued on 6 December 1979, reflected Brzezinski's tough approach. The Vietnamese invasion of Cambodia had brought to that country "a new wave of oppression, hunger and disease," the statement read. The Vietnamese and the Heng Samrin authorities had "deliberately blocked and obstructed" the flow of aid to Cambodia, exacted taxes on relief goods ("in effect imposing a surcharge on human survival"), diverted relief supplies to the military, and even mined fields so that the crops could not be harvested.[20]

Brzezinski's views prevailed within the administration, but they did not go unchallenged. Influential columnist Mary McGrory immediately responded that "if the Carter administration put as much effort into feeding the Cambodian people as it does into trying to discredit the Cambodian government, the famine would be over in a month." All agreed, McGrory stated, that distribution of food was inadequate and that people were starving as a result. But while the administration charged that the PRK was "deliberately starving the Cambodians for political purposes," she wrote, international relief administrators blamed "the inexperience of the green and jumpy young managers of Cambodia and the total absence of any technology, beginning with telephones, trucks and railway lines."[21]

McGrory's column correctly portrayed the views of many relief workers on the ground. Reports from the field also cast doubts on the accuracy of American claims that Soviet assistance was virtually nonexistent. Charles Twining recalled speaking with a Russian who had been in Phnom Penh as early as February 1979 to bring in "some urgent supplies."[22] The USSR did not channel its supplies through the international relief agencies, but it did provide equipment and food independently, which was reported in the American press (although often buried in other stories with other focuses). Henry Kamm, for example, in a story about Cambodian authorities blocking aid supplies, reported that, contrary to the American view, Vietnamese soldiers were helping distribute rice and that the USSR had provided some corn. In addition, both the International Committee of the Red Cross (ICRC) and the United Nations Children's Fund (UNICEF) pointed out that over 200 Soviet trucks arrived in December and that they, along with the trucks recently imported by the international relief organizations, would speed up delivery of food and other relief supplies.

Others complained that, not only did the United States distort the situation inside Cambodia but that American policy itself contributed to the inadequate distribution of supplies. For example, the United States funneled aid into Cambodia only through UNICEF and the ICRC because those organizations had permission (albeit unwritten) not only from Heng Samrin but also from Pol Pot to distribute supplies in the areas they controlled. But the United States refused to work with Oxfam because that organization had reached an agreement only with Heng Samrin. Furthermore, the critics pointed out, by focusing on aid on the border, the United States was in effect encouraging Cambodians to flee toward the border where they could get food. Oxfam America's director complained that the United States could dramatically improve the logistics situation inside the country by supplying additional equipment for unloading ships at Kompong Som, for example, but had refused to do so.

The critics also complained, quite correctly, that the United States employed a double standard when it came to monitoring the distribution of supplies. Inside Cambodia, the United States insisted that no aid whatsoever get to the Vietnamese troops and that monitoring mechanisms be in place. But along the border aid was simply left for people to come and retrieve, with much of it taken back into Cambodia where it could be used by military forces, including those of Pol Pot. Even when relief operations became more systematized and aid was delivered to the refugee camps, much of it ended up in the hands of various warlords and military forces, including the Khmer Rouge. One UNICEF survey documented that 87 percent of the food aid in one sector of the border was misappropriated. In other words, the United States used inadequate monitoring of aid delivered inside Cambodia as an excuse to limit assistance there but was unconcerned about the lack of monitoring along the border, even if some of the food got to Pol Pot's forces.

The administration nevertheless continued to disparage the internal relief effort, instead focusing attention on the plight of the refugees along the Thai border, whose presence it continued to blame largely on the PRK and Vietnam. Brzezinski hoped to undertake highly publicized, dramatic efforts to provide food in this area. Although there was unquestionably a need for food along the border, Brzezinski's intentions were at least as much political as they were humanitarian. For the most part he would be feeding people who were not under PRK control. Efforts to get assistance deeper into Cambodia, including PRK-controlled areas, such as with truck convoys from Thailand, were designed in part to embarrass the PRK. All in all, the administration had thrown down the gauntlet to Heng Samrin and his Vietnamese and Soviet supporters. Though couched in terms of getting vitally needed food to starving Cambodians, administration pressures on the PRK had political motivations.

The critics eventually had some impact on the administration, however. Some administration officials now acknowledged that some relief supplies sent to Phnom Penh were getting distributed, and to the extent that there were distribution problems it was at least in substantial part due to logistical roadblocks. In an implied criticism of Brzezinski, Victor H. Palmieri, Carter's new coordinator for refugee affairs, suggested several ways to improve distribution, including avoiding diplomatic positions that might negatively affect the process. Even Ambassador to Thailand Morton L. Abramowitz reported that the distribution system in Cambodia operated at near capacity. Though the priorities of the PRK did have an impact on distribution, the "terrible transportation system, [and] inexperience" were major reasons for the distribution problems.[23]

But if the administration had been forced to acknowledge that logistical problems, inexperienced officials, and an infrastructure destroyed by the Khmer Rouge were at least partially, and perhaps primarily, responsible for the delays in distributing food; and if they had to agree that the situation had improved in recent weeks with more food getting through, this did not change the political calculus. Although the United States might have to funnel some assistance through Phnom Penh because of the immensity of the humanitarian disaster and domestic pressure, it remained American policy to force the withdrawal of the Vietnamese and, with them, the government they had installed in Phnom Penh. In sum, the administration would accept some challenges to its view of the relief situation, but it would not accept suggestions that it change its basic policy toward the region. American policy remained to end Soviet military involvement in Vietnam, end Vietnamese military operations in Cambodia, and replace the Heng Samrin regime with one that represented the will of the people. It failed to address how this could be accomplished without running the danger that the Khmer Rouge would reassert their terroristic rule over Cambodia.

A further indication of American priorities was evident in the nascent effort to build political and perhaps a significant military resistance to the forces of the PRK and Vietnam. Because many documents remain classified, the details of this effort are not all known. But Sihanouk was one important key. After his ouster in 1970 the prince had thrown his support to the Khmer Rouge resistance. But he knew that in the final analysis the insurgents would have no use for him; when they were finished with him they would "spit me out like a cherry stone," as he once put it.[24] During Khmer Rouge rule Sihanouk had been in effect their prisoner, and several members of his family, including seven children, died at their hands. He had no trouble breaking with them after their defeat in 1979. He welcomed the Vietnamese invasion that drove them from power, but he had no love for the PRK. Therefore the Carter administration looked favorably upon the prince's aspiration to replace Heng Samrin and once again lead his country. Consequently the Americans maintained contact with Sihanouk almost from the moment the Vietnamese pushed the Khmer Rouge out of Phnom Penh.

It is likely that Carter wanted to encourage Sihanouk, who had only a very small armed force loyal to him, to cooperate with the remnant Pol Pot forces as a way of resisting the PRK and Vietnamese, for on 14 January 1980 Vance wrote a personal memo to Carter in which the secretary of state did *not* think (as apparently Carter did) that the United States should urge Sihanouk "to cooperate with the Democratic Kampuchea (DK) regime as long as Pol Pot and his Khmer Rouge henchmen continue to control that regime." The Khmer Rouge had not changed their nature, Vance pointed out, and therefore if Sihanouk were to ally with them "he would undermine his ability to rally support among Kampucheans and his prospects of being eventually accepted by the Vietnamese as an alternative to Pol Pot and Heng Samrin."[25]

Although the administration courted Sihanouk, the prince's views were not entirely in accord with those of the United States. Despite his dislike of the Vietnamese, he knew better than to equate their influence in Cambodia with Khmer Rouge rule. "The fate of the Cambodian people is, it appears," he wrote to Carter in April 1980, "much better than that known under the yoke of the Khmer Rouge." Furthermore, Sihanouk was very concerned about the insecure position of refugees along the Thai border. They were at the mercy of various Cambodian warlords, to whom the people were "humiliated slaves." But what must have been particularly embarrassing to American officials was Sihanouk's charge that aid supplies along the border were not being equitably distributed but were instead diverted away from the starving people. "The humanitarian aid (that of UNICEF, the Red Cross, etc.) which was destined for them has been in large part diverted by those 'war lords,' by the [Thai] 'government,' and by the Cambodian 'resistance,' protected by China and Thailand," he wrote.[26]

By May 1980 Vance, who served as a cautionary force in the administration, was gone, having resigned in protest over the attempt to rescue American hostages in Iran. Brzezinski was pleased. With Vance gone he became an even more dominant figure in the administration, which meant that Cambodia would be viewed even more completely through a geopolitical Cold War lens. Carter's anger at the Soviet Union's invasion of Afghanistan earlier in the year hardened the administration's approach to any issue that involved the Soviet Union. "Softer" approaches, such as an emphasis on human rights or a willingness to accept ambiguity in Vietnam or Cambodia, were of little consequence. This was seen in two interrelated issues that came to a head in the summer and fall of 1980: the perennial question of who would represent Cambodia in the United Nations, and the issue of whether to give support to—or encourage others to support—the remnants of the Khmer Rouge in their resistance to the PRK.

In 1979 the United States had reluctantly voted to allow DK to retain the United Nations seat—this despite Sihanouk's plea that the seat be kept vacant. Within the administration Assistant Secretary of State for Human Rights Patricia Derian had argued passionately against the vote, as had others, including Donald McHenry, who represented the United States at the United Nations. Those who favored seating DK argued that a government imposed by a foreign invasion was illegitimate, and that it was consistent with international law and practice to seat the predecessor government. But the more important reasons were frankly political: it was important to resist the extension of Vietnamese (and therefore Soviet) power, and the United States did not want to alienate China and America's friends in the Association of Southeast Asian Nations (ASEAN), who also opposed Vietnam's actions in Cambodia. "We made the only decision consistent with our overall national interests," wrote Vance. It was, however, an embarrassing posture clearly at odds with Carter's professed devotion to human rights. As NSC official Lincoln

Bloomfield put it, "the technical grounds for our role have proved extraordinarily difficult to explain to the concerned lay public."[27]

Now in 1980 the issue was about to emerge again. And despite Brzezinski's dominance of the foreign policy agenda, this time there was even more sympathy within the administration for a change in policy. In June Bloomfield argued forcefully for keeping the U.N. seat vacant on the grounds that neither the PRK nor DK had a legitimate claim to represent Cambodia. "There is just too great a gulf between our expedient policy [of supporting DK representation] on the one hand, and the moral posture frequently enunciated by the president, featuring frequent denunciations of the Pol Pot-Khmer Rouge as the most genocidal since Adolph Hitler," he wrote to Brzezinski. If Pol Pot actually controlled Cambodia, he went on, then "we would have to hold our nose and accept its technical legitimacy." But the Khmer Rouge controlled almost no territory and, according to U.S. intelligence reports, had "virtually no political support within Kampuchea."[28]

But Roger W. Sullivan, another of Brzezinski's assistants at the NSC, disagreed. Sullivan wanted the United States to stand staunchly behind ASEAN and China. Any hint of American wavering, he said, would be read by all parties as indicating that the United States had decided to accommodate itself to Vietnamese rule in Cambodia.

With the U.N. vote scheduled for September 1980, important humanitarian and religious organizations lobbied furiously for a change in American policy. All of them threw back at Carter his famous words that the Pol Pot regime was the "worst violator of human rights in the world." Even more significant, politically, was the position of the International Rescue Committee. The IRC's executive committee voted unanimously to support an open seat at the United Nations, despite the fact that its executive director, Leo Cherne, was a strong administration supporter.

Public outrage at a possible U.S. vote to seat the Khmer Rouge also resulted in strong protests by some members of Congress, while within the administration Sam Brown, a Carter appointee who directed ACTION (the domestic peace corps), sent in last-minute appeals to the president and Secretary of State Edmund Muskie imploring them to reconsider the decision. "It is wrong substantively and can only further alienate many people who are already concerned about the consistency in U.S. policy . . . ," he wrote. "This decision is the most fundamental test of our commitment to human rights. In a broader sense, it is a test of the morality and integrity of all our actions abroad."[29] The NSC did not forward Brown's letter on to the president, nor did Brzezinski sign a proposed reply to Brown that had been prepared for him. A few days later the United States joined ASEAN and China in voting again to let the Khmer Rouge represent Cambodia.

The United States also continued to support the Khmer Rouge with humanitarian assistance. Everyone knew that the Khmer Rouge survived only because of food they received from the international community, aid that the Thais in particular insisted they must have, but aid that the United States also supported. The feeding program along the border unquestionably resuscitated the Khmer Rouge (and also helped build up the less important, non-Communist resistance groups), thus paving the way for much stronger armed resistance against the PRK during the 1980s. The best humanitarian argument in favor of this was that one could not simply ignore the thousands of civilians, including children, in the Khmer Rouge camps. But the United States and others might have attempted to pressure the Thais to disarm the Khmer Rouge. "I have asked myself a thousand times whether that is what we should have done," said Ambassador Abramowitz in 1980. Abramowitz listed a number of reasons why disarming the Khmer Rouge had not been pursued, including that the Thais and the Chinese were friends of the United States and that they had far greater interests in Southeast Asia than did the United States. But the primary reason was the Vietnamese presence in Cambodia.[30]

Instead of disarming the Khmer Rouge, the Carter administration secretly supported Thai and Chinese efforts to provide military assistance to them. The Chinese had determined to rebuild the Khmer Rouge almost from the moment they were driven out of Phnom Penh. Just exactly when the United States decided to lend its support is not yet clear. But by the early summer of 1980 the policy had been in place for some time, for in June Roger Sullivan became alarmed that some State Department officials were urging that the United States vote against the Khmer Rouge at the United Nations and distance itself from ASEAN and Chinese policy on this issue. "There is confusion over our policy toward Pol Pot and his resistance forces," Sullivan wrote to Brzezinski. Sullivan's letter revealed that Brzezinski had long encouraged the Thais and Chinese to provide enough support to the Khmer Rouge to make life difficult for the Vietnamese. But, Sullivan went on, the State Department now appeared to favor a new policy of opposition "to the DK forces." As a result the Chinese and the Thais were "particularly confused and alarmed." If the United States now intended to discourage "the Thais from cooperating with China in support of Pol Pot forces, then we are moving from a difference of tactics to a conflict of major interest," Sullivan wrote. He urged Brzezinski to make it clear to the Chinese "that we do not seek to discourage the Thais from supporting the DK resistance forces. On the contrary, as you told [Thai Foreign Minister] Sitthi [Savetsila], we do not want the Vietnamese to consolidate their control if we can prevent it and, if we cannot prevent it, we want it to be a protracted and expensive business for them." The next day Brzezinski, Muskie, and Secretary of Defense Harold Brown agreed that the United States was "not against military aid by the Chinese to the Cambodian rebels."[31]

The revelation that the United States actually wanted the Chinese and Thais to assist the Khmer Rouge with military assistance as a means of putting pressure on Vietnam lends support to those who charged at the time that the United States helped structure the international relief effort in such a way that it intentionally helped the Khmer Rouge. The critics were on solid ground when they charged that the monitoring of aid distribution was actually better in Phnom Penh than it was on the border, where it helped sustain the Khmer Rouge. They were also correct in believing that, for strategic reasons, the United States really did want to see the Khmer Rouge resuscitated. British journalist John Pilger, a leading critic of American policy, was remarkably prescient in stating that he thought the United States would insist that the Khmer Rouge be cleaned up and come back "in the guise of a 'non-aligned' coalition."[32] Two years later the United States helped engineer the Coalition Government of Democratic Kampuchea (CGDK), a "coalition" controlled by the Khmer Rouge.

Administration supporters resented this kind of criticism. But the Carter administration *had* decided to encourage China and Thailand to support the Khmer Rouge remnants (even to supply them with weapons) and to use Pol Pot's forces as a counter to the Vietnamese who had liberated Cambodia from their clutches. Although the administration could not ignore the humanitarian outcry and thus did provide some assistance through the PRK (under strict guidelines), its fundamental orientation was geopolitical, as the critics charged. The United States was engaged in a worldwide struggle with the Soviet Union, which had raised international tensions to the boiling point by invading Afghanistan. Carter had responded with his boycott of the Moscow Olympic Games. The Soviet Union supported Vietnam, and thus the administration—and in particular Brzezinski—viewed the Vietnamese invasion of Cambodia as an extension of Soviet influence detrimental to the interests of the United States and its allies. While the administration piously condemned the Vietnamese invasion on the principle of noninterference, it was the geopolitical factors that really mattered.

Brzezinski's proudest accomplishment was the normalization of relations with China and the subsequent American tilt toward Beijing. China, which was engaged in a bitter ideological struggle with the Soviet Union, had supported the Khmer Rouge (in spite of Pol Pot's murderous policy toward the ethnic Chinese living in Cambodia) and, like the United States, viewed Vietnam's invasion of Cambodia as an unacceptable extension of Soviet power. Unable to remove the Vietnamese by persuasion or force, the Chinese, working with the Thais, set about to resuscitate the Khmer Rouge in the hope that they would eventually be able to force the Vietnamese out. The United States explicitly encouraged them and, at the very least, assisted the Khmer Rouge with relief aid.

From time to time and place to place, the defense of human rights was a significant feature of Jimmy Carter's foreign policy. But it was not a primary consideration for National Security Adviser Zbigniew Brzezinski, and to the extent that Carter allowed Brzezinski to formulate foreign policy, the defense of human rights faded as a central administration concern. Nowhere was this more clearly seen than in Cambodia.

Toward a New Beginning

"I feel that we [Cambodia and the United States] now have a good relationship compared with the last two decades in which we seemed to be enemies."—Cambodian Prime Minister Hun Sen, 1999

IN AUGUST 1981 the Southeast Asia Resource Center (formerly the Indochina Resource Center) devoted the tenth anniversary edition of its journal, *Southeast Asia Chronicle,* to the debate over developments in Kampuchea. The organization, which had its origins in the antiwar movement, acknowledged that differences among its members were "deep and sharp." Basically, the editor stated, it came down to whether one emphasized the immediate welfare of the Cambodian people (in which case one supported the Vietnamese occupation of the country), or the consequences that a long-term Vietnamese occupation would have on national sovereignty (in which case one would oppose the Vietnamese).[1] However one responded, people associated with the Resource Center thought in terms of what would be best for the people.

By contrast, officials in the new Ronald Reagan administration displayed almost no concern for Cambodia (or other third world countries), and the people who lived there, per se. Rather they sought to create an international environment that would best benefit of the United States, its allies, and the survival of its political values and economic system. This was not, of course, in itself unusual. "Realist" scholars and practitioners from George Kennan onward have always emphasized the pursuit of national interest, enlightened or otherwise. What set the Reagan administration's foreign policy apart was, as conservative columnist Charles Krauthammer put it in 1985, that it turned "on its head . . . accepted thinking on geopolitics." Unlike earlier realist administrations, Reagan's administration scorned containment as a defeatist strategy, just as had some Republicans (but not Eisenhower himself) in the 1950s. Earlier administrations sought to prevent Communist expansion, observes James M. Scott, while the Reaganites "emphasized cure." They would liberate areas under Soviet, or Soviet-proxy, domination.[2] Consequently Reagan's foreign policy evinced a hard-edged, crusading mentality (an approach condemned by traditional realists). This was the essence of what became known as the "Reagan Doctrine." American actions thus might result in instability, violence, and suffering in the short run. But in the long run the United States would benefit from a diminished Soviet threat. As Reagan administration official Peter W. Rodman entitled his insightful book about the Cold War in the third world, to the administration, defeating Soviet Communism was "more precious than peace."

The Reagan Doctrine's single-minded approach almost required a lack of interest in, or even awareness of, regional realities; it disparaged nuance and displayed almost complete indifference to human rights (except insofar as this issue could be used to criticize the USSR), or any of the "softer" elements that often are a part of foreign policy formation, even in "realist" administrations. Thus in Cambodia the Reagan administration would continue the Carter-Brzezinski policy of supporting the Cambodian resistance groups, though perhaps in a more systematic way.

American aid centered on the non-Communist resistance elements. Several of these had united late in 1979 to form the Khmer People's National Liberation Front (KPNLF), headed by Son Sann, who had served in several Sihanouk governments in the past. Sihanouk himself led a smaller group, the National United Front for an Independent, Neutral, Peaceful, and Cooperative Cambodia (FUNCINPEC), which was founded in March 1981; its armed forces were the Armée Nationale Sihanoukiste (ANS).[3] Together these groups were usually designated as the Non-Communist Resistance (NCR). The KPNLF had perhaps 12,000 soldiers, while 3,000 were loyal to Sihanouk.

Some American support to the NCR was political and symbolic. The United States assisted Sihanouk and Son Sann when they traveled abroad. American embassies provided contacts and sought diplomatic support for the NCR. All resistance forces also benefited from American assistance to the border camps in Thailand. Whether the United States provided additional material support, including perhaps military aid, to the resistance prior to 1982 is a matter of dispute. The matter was undoubtedly discussed. Carter reportedly turned down a request from Sihanouk to fund an army of 100,000, but in March 1981 Reagan's CIA director William Casey argued that the United States should provide weapons to the NCR. The conventional wisdom, based on public testimony of administration officials, is that Casey's advice was rejected and that no aid was extended until late 1982 when Son Sann and Sihanouk, responding to pressure from the United States, ASEAN, and China, joined the Khmer Rouge to form the Coalition Government of Democratic Kampuchea (CGDK). With the NCR now a part of an internationally recognized government (albeit one that controlled almost no territory), the United States could provide assistance more comfortably. Casey presumably continued to argue for military aid, while the State Department remained opposed, fearing that this would hinder the prospects for negotiations. The result of this internal debate was a compromise: the United States would provide covert, nonlethal aid to the NCR, channeling it through Thailand. By one account the United States provided $4 million shortly after the coalition was formed.

Although American aid was ostensibly nonlethal, there were reports that the United States paid for at least one shipment of military supplies sent by Singapore in 1982 and that the CIA provided logistics and ammunition experts to evaluate the military needs of the NCR. In August 1984 Nayan Chanda of the *Far Eastern Economic Review,* the first journalist to uncover the covert aid program, reported that even nonlethal assistance could be used to obtain weapons. The NCR could simply trade it for military supplies from Thailand and Singapore, for example. Or if American funds were used for nonlethal aid, this freed up ASEAN funds to purchase weapons. State Department officials termed American aid of this sort "fungible." In addition, American aid to Thailand for use along the border had little American oversight. The Thais could use the funds as they pleased, including for sending weapons to the resistance forces. Finally, American military aid to Thailand increased substantially—by 1985 it had tripled to nearly $100 million—leading to speculation that the United States was replenishing Thai stocks provided to the Cambodian resistance. In sum, American aid, directly or indirectly, contributed to the military strength of the NCR. As one ASEAN official told Paul Quinn-Judge of the *Christian Science Monitor* (who was one of the first journalists to report on a possible American role in supplying the NCR), the General Accounting Office was "not likely to come out here and audit the KPNLF." If the funds went for guns and ammunition, he stated, the United States would "probably not object, although it would probably prefer not to know."[4]

Nevertheless, ostensibly American aid was nonlethal, and some in Congress, notably Stephen Solarz, the best-informed representative on the Cambodian situation, began to think that overt, lethal assistance might be the better course. Why, he wondered, could the United States provide military assistance to the Nicaraguan contras and the mujahedeen resistance in Afghanistan but not to the NCR? Military assistance, he thought, might help get the Vietnamese out of Cambodia, although the congressman was quick to add that he did not want the withdrawal of the Vietnamese to be followed by the return of Pol Pot. Furthermore, he argued, military assistance to the NCR would help strengthen the non-Communists vis-à-vis the Khmer Rouge and thus help prevent a Khmer Rouge return whenever the Vietnamese left.

The Reagan administration responded to such ideas with a policy review, but in the end it did not change course. Despite its reputation as a "Rambo" administration, intervening far and wide to stop perceived Soviet adventurism in the third world, the wounds of the Vietnam War were still too fresh to permit a more forceful policy in Indochina. The administration would continue to support the NCR politically and with limited covert, nonlethal assistance (thought to have been about $12 to $15 million per year).

In addition to the covert assistance to the NCR, American actions also benefited the Khmer Rouge. They certainly continued to benefit from overt American assistance along the Thai border. Solarz, who seemed genuinely surprised to learn that any American aid went to the Khmer Rouge, responded angrily that this was unacceptable. "It is not in our interest to encourage support for the Khmer Rouge in any way, shape, manner or form," he responded.[5] The aid continued nevertheless. But beyond the covert, nonlethal aid to the NCR and the border relief programs, which benefited all resistance groups, including the Khmer Rouge, the administration was unwilling to go.

Except, perhaps, in deeply secret ways. Although the administration acknowledged that the Khmer Rouge benefited from border relief funds, it adamantly denied providing them with military assistance. "It bears repeating—one can't say it often enough," Assistant Secretary of State for East Asian and Pacific Affairs Paul D. Wolfowitz stated, "that we give no support of any kind to the Khmer Rouge."[6] The majority of scholars and other writers find little evidence to support accusations of American complicity in providing military supplies to the Khmer Rouge. But there are a number of "anomalies," as Cambodia expert Craig Etcheson puts it, suggesting the possibility, perhaps even the probability, that there was unreported American assistance to the Khmer Rouge.

Perhaps the most persuasive indication that the United States may have supported the Khmer Rouge prior to 1985 was U.S. Public Law 99-83, which made it illegal to spend any funds to bolster the Khmer Rouge's military capacity. This was part of the legislation that ultimately allowed lethal assistance to the NCR; Solarz introduced it. Why, one might ask, was such a law needed if aid had not been getting to the Khmer Rouge? Even more significantly, one section of the act "deobligated" funds already "obligated but not yet expended" to promote the Khmer Rouge's military capabilities. Though not entirely conclusive, the passage of this law suggests, as Etcheson puts it, "that the United States has in fact provided military assistance to the Khmer Rouge, and that the conventional wisdom about US policy toward the Khmer Rouge is wrong."[7]

In any event, any military aid provided to any elements of the resistance was very secret. And by 1985 Solarz in particular had concluded that the United States should supply lethal aid to the NCR and should do so openly. Aid was needed, he argued, to help persuade the Vietnamese to withdraw from Cambodia, to build up the NCR as a creditable counter to the more powerful Khmer Rouge, and to show American support for ASEAN. He convinced the House Subcommittee on Asian and Pacific Affairs to support legislation authorizing $5 million in overt aid. The aid would be channeled through the Thais who could, if they chose, use the funds for lethal assistance. Solarz's subcommittee acted without hearings, but in February and March 1985 the Solarz proposal was the subject of spirited debate before the full Committee on Foreign Relations. Wolfowitz testified that other countries should supply whatever military assistance was required. Solarz, however, refused to accept administration assurances that the NCR was already getting all the aid it could use effectively from other sources.

Speculatively, one of Solarz's concerns was that he might have known about deeply secret CIA efforts to support the Khmer Rouge in the early 1980s—aid that would have been consistent with the visceral anti-Vietnamese feelings of Brzezinski and Casey—and that he wanted this brought into the open and stopped. Covert assistance to the Khmer Rouge might also explain why the Reagan administration was reluctant to support an overt aid program to the ineffective NCR.

In any event, siding with the administration (though certainly not because he supported covert aid to the Khmer Rouge) was Representative Jim Leach (R-IA), who introduced an amendment limiting NCR assistance to humanitarian aid. Though sympathetic to the NCR, Leach, like Wolfowitz, argued that no clear need for military aid had been demonstrated. ASEAN and China could and, being on the front line, should supply whatever military requirements existed. More significantly, Leach argued that a greater U.S. role would make a Vietnamese withdrawal and a negotiated settlement more difficult. The $5 million would have no military effect, would signal an unwise resumption of military involvement in the region, and would supply arms to forces over which Washington would have little control. Furthermore, routing the aid through Thailand was bad for the United States, he argued, because of the lack of accountability.

But Solarz had the votes. The committee rejected Leach's call for caution 24–9 and approved instead the Solarz plan by a convincing vote of 24–5. Thus, as James M. Scott has written, the initiative passed from the executive branch to the legislative. The vote pleased ASEAN and Son Sann, who said, "The tap is open, and even if in the end only a drip comes out, I will be happy. Perhaps later we will receive water."[8]

While the lethal aid proposal was making its way through the legislative process, there was for the first time a meaningful public debate on the question. Solarz and Leach began the public discussion by presenting their contrasting views in side-by-side columns in the *Washington Post*. Among the few to support Solarz publicly were Marvin Ott, then a fellow at the Carnegie Endowment for International Peace, and author and Vietnam veteran Al Santoli. But Leach's critical perspective was more commonly echoed in the public debate. Among the critics was Dith Pran, whose struggle to survive during the Pol Pot years was chronicled in the film *The Killing Fields*. Pran stated that "giving U.S. weapons [to the Khmer resistance] is like pouring gasoline on a fire. . . . Cambodia needs humanitarian relief— not military aid."[9] Historian David P. Chandler agreed. American policy was "encouraging Cambodians to kill each other," while failing to recognize that the Vietnamese dominance in Cambodia could be advantageous, he stated. Many of the critics feared that much of the $5 million in aid would, as Holbrooke put it, "end up going to Pol Pot and his people."[10]

In the Senate, meanwhile, there were no hearings on Cambodia policy. But senators Robert Dole (R-KS), Robert Kasten (R-WI), Jeremiah Denton (R-AL), and Nancy Kassenbaum (R-KS) introduced an amendment on the floor identical to the Solarz provision. The limited discussion that the amendment engendered revealed considerable ignorance about Cambodian developments. But on 15 May 1985 the Senate approved lethal aid by a voice vote. Apparently the critical reaction to the proposal from important newspapers and by humanitarian organizations had had little impact.

In July the drama moved to the House. Unlike in the Senate, the debate was unusually well informed and passionate. But in the end, Solarz prevailed by a vote of 288–122. Reagan signed the bill on 8 August 1985. For the first time, overt aid to the Cambodian resistance had been authorized, with the administration having the option of providing lethal or nonlethal assistance. The actual authorization to spend the funds, made on 19 December, directed the president to spend no less than $1.5 million and no more than $5 million for the NCR.

As Nayan Chanda put it in the *Far Eastern Economic Review,* Congress had gone "Rambo," a phenomenon best understood in the context of events in 1985. It was a year of international frustration for the United States, with a number of terrorist attacks, revelation of an extensive Soviet spy network in the United States, and, in the pre–Mikhail Gorbachev years, renewed fears of Soviet expansion. Congress had lashed out in response.

The vote put the administration in a difficult position. Although the administration was on record as opposing lethal aid, given its ideological commitment to resisting Communism anywhere in the world, its opposition would be tenuous. "My own guess," Leach stated, was that the amendment would "give license to the forces in American society that want to ideologize our foreign policy. Pat Buchanan, and not George Bush" would now be in charge of American policy in Southeast Asia. Indeed, the administration's apparent timidity on the lethal aid question led to attacks from ideological militants within the Republican Party, just as Leach feared. Despite such criticism, however, the administration, moved in part by a desire not to jeopardize the slowly improving relationship it had developed with Vietnam on the question of the Missing in Action American soldiers (MIAs), decided to expend the funds for nonlethal assistance only.

For the next three years Congress appropriated annually approximately the same amount of money for the NCR and continued to give the administration the option of including military aid. Covert aid, presumably non-lethal, continued as well at about $12 million annually. Probably because the administration stuck with its decision to provide only nonlethal assistance, the issue attracted little congressional or public attention—although at times the distinction between lethal and nonlethal aid was, as Solarz himself once put it, "a distinction without a difference."[11]

In the meantime, conditions were developing that would eventually lead to a negotiated settlement. Since 1985 there had been a number of contacts among the Vietnamese, ASEAN, the CDGK, and the United States. None of these had produced significant progress. The Vietnamese refused to deal with the Khmer Rouge, for example, and insisted that negotiations take place with the PRK. But Vietnam was beginning to moderate its positions. Its occupation of Cambodia was costly, both in human and economic terms. The United States and ASEAN were blocking aid to Vietnam from international agencies. The Soviet Union, under Mikhail Gorbachev's reformist leadership, was no longer a certain source of assistance, having announced in 1985 that it could no longer afford to support Vietnam at current levels. And finally, the PRK itself was increasingly in charge of Cambodia and demonstrating that it might be able to withstand an assault from the Khmer Rouge on its own, if it had to. Vietnam had already withdrawn some troops from Cambodia and announced early in 1988 that it would withdraw all of its troops by the end of 1990.

Serious negotiations began about the same time. In December 1987 Sihanouk met for the first time with PRK Prime Minister Hun Sen at the prince's Paris residence; the two leaders met again in January 1988. This began the "formula seeking" phase of the conflict, as the parties searched for a way to bring peace to Cambodia. In July 1988 representatives of the PRK and the three factions who constituted the CGDK met in Indonesia for what became known as the first Jakarta Informal Meeting (JIM). No agreements were reached, but the issues were defined, and there was forward movement. Furthermore, Cambodia was the subject of serious discussions between China and the Soviet Union, as well as among the ASEAN states.

The possibility of a Vietnamese withdrawal, movement toward a settlement in Cambodia, and renewed criticism that the United States was supporting the Khmer Rouge—either intentionally or inadvertently, including its support of the Khmer Rouge as the appropriate claimant of Cambodia's U.N. seat—led the House Subcommittee on Asian and Pacific Affairs to hold hearings in June and July 1988.[12] The focus of the hearings was how to prevent the Khmer Rouge from returning to power. "I tremble with fear," Solarz said, "not only for the people of Cambodia, but for the entire world, for what it would mean to mankind, if the Khmer Rouge were ever to come back to power again."

Prince Sihanouk meets Hun Sen, prime minister of the People's Republic of Kampuchea, for the first time in 1987. From the Private Collection of Ambassador Julio A. Jeldres.

The committee expressed concern that the ASEAN countries and China were more interested in getting the Vietnamese out than in preventing the Khmer Rouge from returning, and since the United States generally deferred to these powers it was, the critics charged, also culpable. Representative Chester G. Atkins (D-MA) in particular charged that the administration considered the return of the Khmer Rouge a "subsidiary" concern. Instead of standing forthrightly against the Khmer Rouge, Atkins charged, the administration pursued a policy of "wink and blink and nod."

While Atkins and other critics thought the United States should distance itself from the NCR because it was allied with the Khmer Rouge, Solarz argued that, on the contrary, the NCR might be "the last best hope of preventing the Khmer Rouge from returning to power" and wondered if the United States should increase its support. It was "essential," he argued, that the NCR "be in a position to make a credible effort to prevent the Khmer Rouge from seizing power, which does come out of the barrel of a gun."[13]

During the hearings, Reagan administration officials indicated that they were considering asking for substantial funding increases for the NCR to encourage a settlement and also to help prevent a Khmer Rouge return to power. But efforts to increase the *overt* funding fell afoul of embarrassing disclosures about the *covert* program. The *Far Eastern Economic Review* revealed that the Senate Select Committee on Intelligence had uncovered corruption connected with the distribution of the covert assistance. Within a week, both the *Washington Post* and the *New York Times* reported that Thai officials, and perhaps businessmen, had stolen at least $3.5 million. The scandal ended administration efforts to provide dramatically higher levels of funding for the NCR, although there was some increase.

As the George H. W. Bush administration took office, the pace of international diplomacy on Cambodia intensified. An important new element was Chatichai Choonhavan, a flamboyant general who in August 1988 became the first elected prime minister of Thailand in a dozen years. Chatichai, intent on turning Indochina from a battlefield to a marketplace, as he liked to put it, quickly softened his country's hardline approach to the PRK (which in 1989 changed its name to the State of Cambodia [SOC]) and Vietnam. On 25 January 1989 he invited Hun Sen to Bangkok for direct talks, thus giving a considerable boost to the PRK/SOC's claims of legitimacy. Chatichai's change of policy irritated the United States, which "disparaged Chatichai personally and criticized his policies."[14]

In February 1989 the parties gathered again in Indonesia. Again, no agreement was reached, although the points of difference were further defined. Shortly thereafter the PRK/SOC announced that Vietnam would withdraw its troops by the end of September 1989—a year earlier than previously expected—even if a political settlement were not achieved.

The next major development was a month-long conference in June 1989 in Paris of the Cambodian parties organized by France and Indonesia. Indicative of the conference's significance, for the first time representatives of the five permanent members of the U.N. Security Council (the Perm 5), the ASEAN states, India and Canada (former ICC members), Zimbabwe (representing the Non-Aligned Movement), and U.N. Secretary General Javier Pérez de Cuéller took part. Much to the distress of the organizers, the Paris conference failed to achieve a settlement.

The failure of the Paris conference occurred in the context of the Bush administration's decision to seek authorization for lethal aid for the resistance forces. Although a major argument in favor of lethal aid had been that it would pressure Vietnam to withdraw, now that Vietnam had announced its intention to do just that, the administration was nevertheless more determined than ever to secure such assistance. The major justification for lethal aid now became to prevent the Khmer Rouge from regaining control. "History will not forgive us if we fail to do everything in our power to keep the Khmer Rouge from once more turning Cambodia into an Asian Auschwitz," Solarz stated. At the same time military assistance to the NCR would signal American unwillingness to accept Hun Sen's government "as an accomplished fact." Since the SOC was the most promising bulwark against the Khmer Rouge, the twin objectives appeared at odds. It was hard to see how dismantling the SOC would help keep the Khmer Rouge out.

Nonlethal aid had considerable support, but lethal aid was, as it always had been, much more controversial, and opposition soon developed. As in 1985, there was a spirited public debate, with most articulated opinion opposed to sending military aid to the NCR. Perhaps the weightiest testimony against aid came from Westerners with recent, firsthand experience in Cambodia, including representatives of religious and humanitarian organizations, journalists like Elizabeth Becker, and John Pedler, a former British diplomat with extensive experience in Southeast Asia. Eight humanitarian organizations that had a presence in the refugee camps, for example, appealed to Vice President Dan Quayle not to send military aid. Pedler, asked by several voluntary organizations to survey conditions in Cambodia, probably spent more time inside Cambodia than any other Westerner (except for a few relief workers) during this period. Besides touring the country extensively in 1989, he met with Hun Sen and other SOC officials, as well as with leaders of the NCR, including Prince Norodom Ranariddh (Sihanouk's son) and Son Sann. His lengthy, informed, and sensitive report (completed in April 1989), along with subsequent updates, strongly advised against providing military assistance.

The arguments against lethal aid to the NCR, if now familiar, were often compelling. It would invite shelling of the refugee camps and increase civilian casualties and strengthen the NCR's Khmer Rouge partners. More fundamentally, those who wanted a political solution without a role for the former perpetrators of mass murder hoped for an agreement between Hun Sen and Sihanouk that would freeze the Khmer Rouge out. Noting the several meetings between the two leaders, they wanted the United States to foster a cooperative dialogue, something the United States had always resisted.

Part of the debate focused on the character of the SOC and its prime minister, Hun Sen. Those who favored military aid asserted that the regime was nothing more than a Vietnamese puppet government, with little if any support among the people. More extreme advocates of military assistance even equated the SOC and the Khmer Rouge (something one still sees), charging that Hun Sen and other SOC leaders, who were Khmer Rouge before they defected, had a record of human rights abuses comparable to that of the Khmer Rouge.

Opponents of lethal aid argued that the PRK had emerged as a government in its own right, was effectively in control of almost all of Cambodia, and brought the full range of normal services to the people. Its record on human rights was not nearly as good as it should be, but after ten years in power it bore no resemblance to the genocidal Khmer Rouge regime. It was difficult to know precisely how much support it enjoyed, but the restoration of a functioning civil society, a growing economy increasingly oriented toward private enterprise, the restoration of basic family life and of Buddhism as the state religion, and perhaps above all its fierce opposition to the return of the Khmer Rouge, suggested it governed by more than coercion. As syndicated columnist Georgie Anne Geyer put it in February 1989, "for the first time since 1975 when the Khmer Rouge took over, Cambodia is alive, a decent country."[15] To attempt to dismantle this government, opponents of lethal aid argued, was folly when the almost certain successor would be the Khmer Rouge.

The Bush administration nevertheless wanted to provide lethal aid. It preferred to avoid public debate by providing the aid covertly. Though covert nonlethal aid had been approved (apparently routinely) for many years, the request for direct covert lethal aid was new, and the Senate Select Committee on Intelligence refused to give its approval, arguing that an important policy change of this nature deserved public debate. In response, on 30 May 1989 the administration sought congressional support for covert lethal aid, insisting that such assistance would strengthen Sihanouk's hand in negotiating with the PRK and the Khmer Rouge. It was a startling development, the public debate of a covert program.

Perhaps because most public discussion of lethal aid had been in opposition to it, congressional opponents believed that they had won the fight. "Lethal aid, covert and overt, is dead," said one knowledgeable senatorial aide.[16] But then Senator Charles Robb (D-VA), not previously identified as someone with a deep interest in Cambodia, introduced an amendment providing for lethal aid. After a spirited, sometimes angry, sometimes irrational debate, the Senate approved lethal aid by a surprisingly comfortable margin of 59–39. The legislation did not contain any specific dollar amount.

Democratic leaders were furious at Robb, but they had underestimated the administration's determination to prevail on this issue. Although the legislation approved by the Senate never became law, as the Paris conference opened, both houses of Congress were now on record in support of lethal assistance. Passage of the Robb amendment allowed the administration to approach the Senate Intelligence Committee and again seek approval for lethal aid.

Whether the possibility of lethal aid would enhance the prospects of successful negotiations soon met its first test. Shortly after the Senate and the House went on record in support of such aid, the Paris conference opened. There was a great deal of hope that this conference would finally end the strife in Cambodia. The foreign ministers of several states, including Secretary of State James A. Baker, addressed the conference. Baker condemned the Khmer Rouge in unusually strong language. But in the end the conference failed to produce a settlement.

Did the administration's efforts to obtain congressional approval for lethal aid contribute to the failure? Had it made the NCR less willing to compromise, as the critics charged?

Doubtless the reasons for the conference's failure were complex. The United States tried unconvincingly to blame Hanoi and Hun Sen, but it appears that the primary cause of the failure was Sihanouk's unwillingness to separate himself from the Khmer Rouge, much to the embarrassment of lethal aid supporters. Although at Jakarta only a month before the prince had in effect agreed to break from the Khmer Rouge if they proved to be intransigent, he now reneged. Perhaps, as historian Ben Kiernan wrote in a biting assessment, Sihanouk "lost his nerve" and demonstrated that he was "a genuine puppet of the Chinese and the Khmer Rouge."[17]

Official Peter Rodman disparagingly termed these developments "Snooky Shock" and recalled that "it was a public relations disaster." Proponents of lethal aid had insisted that such aid was necessary to allow the NCR to stand up to its Khmer Rouge partners and would enhance the prospects of successful negotiations. But the critics appeared to be right: there was even less flexibility on Sihanouk's part than before. Sihanouk, the *New York Times* editorialized, caused the conference to break down by insisting on a role for the Khmer Rouge, something that Hun Sen rightly rejected. Senator Robert Byrd (D-WV), a strong opponent of lethal aid who chaired the Appropriations Committee, then blocked any military aid, and the disheartened administration "made no further effort to salvage lethal aid for the non-Communist resistance."[18] Shortly after the conference, Vietnam withdrew its last forces from Cambodia—although it later had to return for one last offensive against the Khmer Rouge.

Efforts to secure lethal assistance, which perhaps contributed to Sihanouk's decision to renege on his previous commitments to break with the Khmer Rouge, may thus have doomed the Paris conference. U.S. officials may have come "home from Paris depressed, even bitter at the temperamental prince whose leadership role we had been championing," as Rodman wrote.[19] But blaming Sihanouk overlooks the administration's unwillingness to support his moves away from the Khmer Rouge, despite its strong criticism of the Khmer Rouge. According to knowledgeable sources, at Paris Sihanouk refused to break with China and its Khmer Rouge protégés and instead ally with Hun Sen because he lacked international—and especially American—support. "The United States opposed the alliance because it would have legitimatized the Hun Sen government. . . . Sihanouk," stated one well-informed observer, "looked around him in Paris and got cold feet." The American refusal to back Sihanouk's break with the Khmer Rouge, "more than any other single factor, doomed the conference," as two critics of American policy put it. The *New York Times* termed the administration's policy "bankrupt and immoral."[20]

Thus, the tentative change in American policy proved to be momentary and illusory. The United States continued to champion the NCR, to vote to seat the CGDK in the United Nations, to go along with China, to prevent international aid from reaching Cambodia, and to oppose all attempts to legitimatize Hun Sen's government. The United States was willing to include the SOC as part of the proposed quadripartite interim government (the others being the Khmer Rouge plus the two elements of the NCR), but Hun Sen had little interest in an arrangement that would dissolve his government prior to elections.

Critics pummeled the administration's position, particularly during a congressional hearing in September 1989. And over the next several months the United States did cooperate in efforts to find a formula to end the conflict. The first significant American involvement in this process was not by the administration, however, but by Solarz who in October 1989 conferred with Australian Foreign Minister Gareth Evans. Evans was seeking some formula for administering Cambodia prior to an election. The following month he presented his plan, which drew in part from the ideas of Solarz and Sihanouk. The foreign minister proposed that the United Nations provide an interim authority while preparing for elections, thus getting around the problems that a quadripartite authority posed. It also avoided dismantling Hun Sen's government but also made it clear that the SOC would not be entirely in charge of developments leading up to an election.

The Evans proposal set in motion new thinking about how a settlement might be reached. The Bush administration was helpful in urging a serious collaboration among the Perm 5. Beginning in January 1990 Perm 5 representatives met monthly to discuss options for settling the Cambodia problem. Although their initial meetings were stormy, they eventually agreed to try to bring about a comprehensive settlement, end outside military assistance, and involve the United Nations to assure sufficient internal security to allow a "neutral political environment." Rather than rely on some combination of existing structures, the Perm 5 began to consider establishing a "Supreme National Council" that would be the repository of Cambodian sovereignty during the transition period.[21]

The Cambodians themselves discussed these ideas at a third meeting in Jakarta in February 1990 (JIM III) and at Tokyo in June, but there was no final breakthrough. The CGDK did not want the SOC to survive intact prior to an election (even if it was partially supplanted by some kind of United Nations authority), and Hun Sen continued to see no reason why he should relinquish power prior to an election, since his government controlled most of the country. Nor did he want to have any settlement that gave the Khmer Rouge any significant role.

Although the administration was now more involved in seeking a political solution, its continuing support for the NCR and its reluctance to endorse a Hun Sen–Sihanouk coalition provoked considerable criticism. A particularly influential critical piece was an ABC documentary, "Peter Jennings Reporting from the Killing Fields," telecast on 26 April 1990. Among other

Two cartoons critical of American support for the Khmer Rouge. Jeff Danziger © 1989 and 1990, *The Christian Science Monitor* (www.csmonitor.com). All Rights Reserved.

things, the documentary appeared to confirm close military coordination between the NCR and the Khmer Rouge; and it revealed the existence of an American intelligence unit in Thailand that appeared to have ties to the Khmer Rouge. On film Sihanouk virtually admitted that the United States had given him arms. Assistant Secretary of State Richard Solomon stated that the United States did supply weapons for the NCR, then said he had misspoken. In sum, the documentary appeared to demonstrate that many of the critics' assertions were valid.

A recent scholarly account characterizes the Jennings report as "perhaps the most significant media event of the Bush period."[22] It is likely that it was a major factor in changing American policy. The documentary angered the Bush administration and its supporters, but they grudgingly acknowledged the program's importance. The following year the Robert F. Kennedy Center for Human Rights gave the documentary its first prize award for international reporting.

In sum, the critics had a powerful case. Faced with the contradictions in American policy and the growing public and congressional pressures, the administration began to consider changes. National Security Adviser Brent Scowcroft and Secretary of Defense Dick Cheney opposed change, but Baker was more open to new approaches. Back in November as the criticism was mounting, the administration made one small concession: for the first time it stated that the Khmer Rouge had committed genocide. Then on 24 May President Bush, hinting that a change was coming, stated that he was "uncomfortable" with a policy that assisted the Khmer Rouge in any way; the whole policy was under review.[23]

Although the United States had not yet changed its policy, it was beginning to shift course. The State Department and the CIA were now urging direct U.S. talks with Hun Sen, while also encouraging Sihanouk to join with him. A further indication that the administration was seriously considering a change came on 13 July when it accepted an offer from the SOC to cooperate in efforts to locate American MIAs from the Vietnam War. Although on the surface this was a humanitarian undertaking, it had important political implications. As Representative Atkins, a passionate critic, put it, "I am just delighted they are sending over this team."[24]

The seemingly dramatic shift finally came on 18 July 1990 when Baker, apparently having overcome opposition from Scowcroft and Cheney, announced that the United States would no longer recognize the CGDK, would open negotiations with Vietnam, and would provide humanitarian aid to the SOC. The primary goal now became to keep the Khmer Rouge from taking power, a goal that, Baker acknowledged, the United States had not been able to achieve with the former policy. The United States would no longer defer to the ASEAN countries and China on Cambodian matters.

The reasons for the reversal were complex. At the highest level they reflected the ending of the Cold War and a tentative joint Soviet-American approach to third world problems. Closer to home the growing domestic criticism of the administration's policy threatened to result in legislation that would seriously constrain administration options. There was also fear that the United States would be blamed if the Khmer Rouge managed to regain power, which seemed a distinct possibility in 1990 because of recent battlefield gains. Rodman expressed well the administration's dilemma. "Our trying to ride two horses—opposing both Phnom Penh and the Khmer Rouge—was a risky gamble," he recalled as he acknowledged the contradictions in American policy. "How could we possibly overthrow the one without removing the main barrier to the dominance of the other?"[25]

In effect the administration was acknowledging that the critics had mounted a persuasive attack on long-standing American policy that stretched back to Brzezinksi, and perhaps to Kissinger. As the critics charged, the United States, while opposing the Khmer Rouge rhetorically, was in effect supporting them. From the beginning, American funds helped sustain them on the Thai border. The United States also supported Chinese and Thai efforts to resuscitate the Khmer Rouge militarily as a means of countering the Vietnamese and their Cambodian allies. The United States provided covert aid to the Khmer Rouge's non-Communist allies, and possibly to the Khmer Rouge themselves; later it provided overt funds to the NCR and looked the other way when the NCR coordinated its military activities with the Khmer Rouge. On the diplomatic front, the United States followed the lead of ASEAN and China and always voted for Khmer Rouge representation at the United Nations. In terms of a peace settlement, the United States insisted that the Khmer Rouge have a role equal to the other "factions"—in particular the PRK/SOC—in whatever governmental structure emerged. It demonized Hun Sen and the PRK/SOC to such an extent that, as a senior Asian diplomat put it, "it came to the point that any move Hun Sen made, no matter how positive, was immediately discounted in Washington as a trick of the Vietnamese. . . . It has been obsessive and counterproductive."[26]

Briefly stated, geopolitical reasons related to the Cold War, and the desire to undercut Soviet influence anywhere in the world, explained most aspects of American policy. In pursuit of this goal the United States wanted to align with China against the Soviet Union and its perceived clients—Vietnam and the PRK. But there was also an emotional component. Successive American administrations found it hard to forgive Vietnam. As columnist William Pfaff put it, "The United States government has been punishing Communist Vietnam's leaders for having defeated the United States in the Vietnam War."[27]

But Baker's move did not represent a complete reversal of American policy. Although the administration had withdrawn support for the CGDK and was willing to talk to Vietnam, it still supported the NCR, wanted to see it prevail in any elections, and hoped to continue funding it. Thus Baker's move was, in part, a tactical change only. Consequently, the critics remained unconvinced of the administration's sincerity.

Intensive discussions to devise a framework for peace soon overshadowed other concerns. On 27 and 28 August 1990 the big powers drafted a framework document to serve as the basis for negotiations among the Cambodians. It urged the parties to assent to a long-discussed Supreme National Council (SNC)—"a unique legitimate body and source of authority in which, throughout the transitional period, national sovereignty and unity would be enshrined"—to prepare for an election. It fudged the question of bipartite or quadripartite representation by saying that the SNC should be "composed of representative individuals with authority among the Cambodian people . . . acceptable to each other," and it urged that Sihanouk be made SNC president. The document also called for a ceasefire and the creation of a United Nations Transitional Authority in Cambodia (UNTAC) to monitor the ceasefire and other military matters. Principles for elections were promulgated, along with provisions to protect human rights.[28]

The fact that all Perm 5 powers could agree on the document was itself remarkable and, as the *Jakarta Post* put it, clearly showed "that as far as the Cambodian conflict is concerned, the Cold War is definitely over."[29] Shortly thereafter U.S. diplomats in Laos met with SOC officials, and U.S. Ambassador to Indonesia John Monjo shook hands with Hun Sen himself, the photograph appearing on the front page of the *Jakarta Post*. The Monjo–Hun Sen encounter symbolized how much had changed so quickly in American diplomacy.

At Jakarta in September the peace process advanced significantly when the parties accepted the Perm 5's framework document, agreeing on an SNC headed by Sihanouk that would delegate to the United Nations "all powers necessary" to implement the agreement and conduct fair elections. This was a concession from Hun Sen, but the conference also agreed that Hun Sen's government could nominate six of the twelve members, the other six being divided equally among the three other factions—a division of power that China was no longer blocking.[30]

Despite the important steps taken by the Perm 5 and at Jakarta (and the results of the conference produced almost universal praise), a ceasefire had not been achieved, and agreement on details proved difficult, including the precise powers of the United Nations, the SNC's composition, and the circumstances under which Sihanouk could chair the new structure. Indeed the first attempted meeting of the SNC, held in Bangkok only a week after the Jakarta conference, ended in failure. The group did not convene again until December, when it met in Paris.

As for the United States, it continued to play a positive role by announcing that, for the first time in fifteen years, it would provide aid to Cambodia. However, this was not an administration initiative. Rather, in 1990 Congress had passed an emergency appropriation to assist Cambodian children "in areas controlled by the Phnom Penh government." Expenditure of these funds symbolized continuing American willingness, if grudging, to advance its new relationship with Hun Sen's government.[31] Shortly there-after the Khmer Rouge ambushed and murdered some fifty persons on a train 100 miles south of Phnom Penh, reminding the world of the group's brutality and the probable consequences should they ever again regain power. To many (though not yet to the U.S. government), backing Hun Sen's SOC seemed a reasonable alternative.

Despite the new American contacts with the SOC, it still remained American policy to dismantle Hun Sen's government, if this could be done without ensuring a Khmer Rouge victory. In fact the United States hoped to enlist Vietnam in such a quest as part of the price for ending the U.S. economic embargo and diplomatic isolation of that country. In addition to pressuring Vietnam, the American strategy was to give the United Nations as much power as possible in Cambodia, even as Hun Sen wanted the international body's role limited to providing humanitarian assistance and helping to organize elections.

When the Cambodians proved unable to achieve a ceasefire or advance toward a political settlement, the Perm 5 again stepped into the process and in November proposed a comprehensive peace plan, which gave the United Nations sweeping powers, including the right to take over Cambodian ministries. A large contingent of United Nations troops would also be sent to the country. The Khmer Rouge, which like the United States favored an extensive and intrusive U.N. role, applauded the plan, leading critics to fear that the United States and other members of the Perm 5 were intent primarily on ending Hun Sen's government. Although Hun Sen and the other Cambodian leaders accepted many aspects of the plan, the prime minister refused to have his government and his armed forces dismantled. "We would be better off isolated than dead," he said.[32] He also tried to insert a reference in the text about preventing the "genocidal regime" from returning to power. For the moment, progress toward a peace settlement stalled.

In February 1991 Hun Sen suffered a setback when a military coup in Thailand ousted Chatichai, who had been friendly to the SOC; shortly thereafter China announced that it was once again sending military supplies to the Khmer Rouge, something it had previously suspended. Perhaps due in part to these developments, plus some modest gains made on the battlefield, the Phnom Penh government announced that it was willing to reopen the deadlocked negotiations. The United States responded with an important effort to reassure Phnom Penh and Hanoi that it understood and shared their concerns about a possible Khmer Rouge return and dramatically announced that it had suspended all aid to the NCR due to reports that it was cooperating with the Khmer Rouge. The United States dispatched American consultants to Phnom Penh to assess Cambodia's humanitarian needs.

Nevertheless, the SNC meeting in June 1991 resulted in little progress. Phnom Penh's insistence on strong measures to prevent a Khmer Rouge return to power was not met, and no agreement was reached. Hun Sen did meet Sihanouk outside of the SNC structure (Sihanouk had never been formally made a part of the SNC due to disagreements over how the council should be structured) and agreed that the prince should chair the SNC, with Hun Sen to be vice chair and the council to be expanded by two members, to fourteen. But Sihanouk could not persuade the Khmer Rouge to accept even this. The future looked bleak for a Cambodian settlement.

But soon thereafter important progress occurred. Sihanouk joined the SNC—not as chair but as a simple member; in June 1991 the SNC then met again in Pattaya, Thailand, and reached a number of agreements, thanks largely to the sagacious leadership of Sihanouk (who was finally elected to chair the SNC). The United States praised Sihanouk for his "wisdom" and "moral influence." Later in July the SNC convened in, of all places, Beijing, indicating that the Chinese leadership was being more conciliatory. The parties agreed about representation at the United Nations (Hun Sen was appointed one of the delegates) and, more importantly, agreed to stop the arms flow and to allow the United Nations to monitor a ceasefire (which had been in place for about two months on a voluntary basis). The only major issue yet to be resolved involved disarming the factional armies. That issue was settled in August when the parties agreed that 70 percent of the armed forces would be demobilized and the remaining 30 percent would regroup and disarm under U.N. supervision. Sihanouk was so pleased with the outcome of the meeting that he "led the dinner orchestra in renditions of his original Khmer and French love songs."[33] Suddenly Cambodia's future looked bright again.

None of these recent developments, it might be noted, owed much to the United States. The Bush administration, uncertain about the domestic political consequences of conciliation with Vietnam and aid to the SOC, was mostly on the sidelines, repeating the mantra that the Perm 5 plan had to be accepted and implemented in every detail. Only after Sihanouk charged the Americans with being obstructionists did the United States reluctantly accept the compromises reached by the Cambodian parties.

The stage was now set for the momentous final agreement reached in October 1991 at the Paris conference. The SOC ceded considerable power to UNTAC, which took on the role of monitoring the ceasefire, demobilizing and disarming the factional armed forces, repatriating refugees in the border camps, de-mining large areas of the country, ensuring that human rights were protected (a provision that was inserted at the insistence of the United States), and preparing for the elections to take place in April 1993 that would determine who would lead the country in the postwar era. Secretary General Javier

Pérez de Cuellar described the U.N. undertaking as "probably the most important and most complex in the history of the United Nations."[34]

The final settlement resulted from years of discussions and negotiations among the Cambodian parties, the Perm 5, Indonesia, Australia, France, and Japan. No party got everything it wanted. Hun Sen thought the United Nations had too much power. On the other hand American and Chinese efforts to dissolve the SOC were not successful. The quadripartite plan also was essentially abandoned in favor of a solution that gave the SOC representation equal to that of the other three parties combined. References to genocide were removed, and the Khmer Rouge remained a party to the peace settlement. But they did not have representation equal to Hun Sen's, and they, along with the other factions, were required to demobilize or disarm under U.N. supervision. The whole process, which concluded with the Paris accords, appeared to have achieved a remarkable settlement.

The Americans played a role in bringing about the settlement and shaped it in important (and arguably negative) ways, but they were not the determining factor. The most important American contribution was the "Baker shift" in July 1990, in which the United States withdrew support for the CGDK and made some gestures in support of Hun Sen and the Vietnamese. This reflected in part a new team in the State Department that was not so wedded to the policies of the past. However, the shift also resulted from external pressure, and the Bush administration was not fully committed to the new course. Although it did put more emphasis on preventing the Khmer Rouge from returning to power, it still desired a solution that would also result in the dissolution of the SOC. Thus Baker himself acknowledged that what had changed were the tactics, not the goal. Partly one senses that the president and others in high positions in the administration had not gotten over the defeat in Vietnam. It was galling to them to reconcile with Vietnam and its supposed client in Phnom Penh. The administration was also uncertain of the domestic political ramifications of a rapprochement with Vietnam. The changing international situation (as the Cold War ended and the Soviet-Chinese rift began to heal) was an important contextual factor in the final settlement, and the Cambodian parties themselves (including at crucial points Sihanouk himself), plus the Indonesians, crafted the compromises needed to bring about a settlement.

Many Americans, even those who had been critical of the American approach, hoped that the accords offered a chance to end Cambodia's suffering. But the agreement did not meet with universal praise. Many of those associated with nongovernmental organizations that had worked for years in Cambodia, or on the Cambodian issue, criticized the accords, primarily because they included the Khmer Rouge in a significant way. Those who shared such views soon founded the Campaign to Oppose the Return of the Khmer Rouge (CORKR). Such misgivings lingered for years.

A related criticism was that the accords were not fundamentally intended to advance the good of the Cambodians. As the respected Cambodian journalist and government official Khieu Kanharith put it, "The U.N. plan was mapped out not for the Cambodian people but to please the superpowers." A Hun Sen–Sihanouk alliance might have done that, for example, but the big powers, including the United States, had discouraged that prospect. Hun Sen remains resentful of the Perm 5's insistence on including the Khmer Rouge.[35]

In any event, with the settlement in place the United States proceeded to improve its relations with Cambodia. It promised to end its economic embargo against the country, support aid projects, and open a liaison office in Phnom Penh. Charles Twining opened the liaison office on 11 November 1991 (the same day that the first contingent of lightly armed United Nations troops entered Phnom Penh). But the administration was slow to lift the embargo, resulting in congressional criticism, and skepticism remained about ultimate American intentions. In view of past American policy and the horrendous record of the Khmer Rouge, such skepticism of American policy was understandable. But it may be that over the long run the settlement and subsequent American policy contributed to the Khmer Rouge's eventual demise. "What the Khmer Rouge feared most was contamination of their cadre and population with materialism and independent views," Ambassador Quinn recalled. Thus by including language in the Paris agreement that all zones must be open, the parties may have put the Khmer Rouge on the road to ultimate extinction.[36]

Following this premise, during the period when the peace agreement was being implemented (1991–1993) the United States shaped its assistance programs to give priority to constructing roads in rural areas where the Khmer Rouge were operating. Opening up the countryside to outside influences would undermine the Khmer Rouge. "If we neglect the countryside and put all of our resources in Phnom Penh," Charles Twining said, "then the Khmer Rouge can come back again." This policy was not coordinated with Hun Sen, but the two governments shared the goal of thwarting the Khmer Rouge. No official American would have any dealings whatsoever with Khmer Rouge officials, even those on the SNC, said Twining.[37] The United States also contributed substantial funds to the U.N. operations in Cambodia (it had agreed to pay 30 percent of the cost), some of which were aimed at keeping the Khmer Rouge in line. And at least on the surface, the United States warmed to Hun Sen's government.

Meanwhile the Khmer Rouge showed increasing signs that they would not comply with the agreements. Their obstruction led to renewed calls to bypass them altogether, to hold elections without them and, if necessary, to arm the government to take on the rebels. Others disagreed, arguing that isolating the Khmer Rouge would only promote their cause. However, as it became clear that the Khmer Rouge was going to repudiate their commitments, many of those who had urged a cautious approach changed their minds. At the end of November 1992 the Security Council banned the export of oil to the Khmer Rouge and the import of lumber from their zones and threatened to take further action if they refused to abide by U.N. agreements. The Khmer Rouge responded by abducting U.N. personnel.

Although Khmer Rouge behavior exasperated and angered the United States, this did not translate into political support for Hun Sen and his Cambodian People's Party (CPP). Although no longer demonizing the CPP, the Americans still opposed it and hoped that in the election the two non-Communist parties would prevail. Reports began to circulate of serious human rights violations by the SOC. While not quite as bad as the Khmer Rouge, Hun Sen and his government were pictured as corrupt, brutal, and still under the Vietnamese thumb.[38]

In any event, after a "scathing verbal attack" on UNTAC (to say nothing of actual deadly attacks on U.N. personnel and ethnic Vietnamese), the Khmer Rouge definitively opted out of the electoral process—a disastrous choice that completely discredited them.[39] When the elections were held on 28 May 1993, almost 90 percent of eligible voters defied Khmer Rouge threats by taking part. The turnout was "beyond our wildest expectations," stated an American U.N. election official. The election was peaceful and impressive, evidence enough of the Cambodians' deep desire to end the interminable conflict. Some speculated that the Khmer Rouge remained quiescent because they feared that the United States would intervene militarily if they tried to disrupt the elections.[40]

The United States had become reconciled to a CPP victory as voters chose representatives to a constituent assembly, which was to write a new constitution for the country, and had announced ahead of time that it was prepared to accept the results. It was surprised, and pleased, when Sihanouk's FUNCINPEC emerged with 45.47 percent of the vote to 38.22 percent for the CPP. In terms of seats in the assembly, FUNCINPEC received fifty-eight to the CPP's fifty-one. Other parties garnered eleven.

At first the CPP, in a state of shock, threatened not to accept the results. One CPP supporter (Sihanouk's son Prince Norodom Chakrapong) attempted to organize a secessionist movement in several provinces. Then on 3 June (well before the official vote tally was announced on 10 June), Sihanouk announced that he was forming an interim government, with himself as prime minister and commander of the military, and with Ranariddh and Hun Sen as deputy prime ministers. The CPP quickly accepted this arrangement, but FUNCINPEC was ambivalent, while Ranariddh himself angrily rejected his father's proposal. Although Sihanouk seems to have announced this move after encouragement from French, Russian, and Japanese officials, the United States objected. While reportedly outraged by the

American position, Sihanouk backed down. But within two weeks a similar arrangement had emerged. The new Constituent Assembly restored Sihanouk as chief of state (after first declaring his ouster in 1970 to have been illegal), and Sihanouk in turn proposed an interim coalition government in which Ranariddh and Hun Sen would cochair the Council of Ministers. Subsequent negotiations led to a government structure in which the CPP and FUNCINPEC shared power, with two minor parties also being allowed to name four ministers.

Despite its opposition to Sihanouk's original proposal, the United States supported this very similar arrangement. Although such an arrangement was not envisaged in the Paris accords, it represented a Cambodian solution that brought about a measure of stability, further isolated the Khmer Rouge, and established the conditions that would bring in significant amounts of international assistance.

The United States professed that it would not interfere in internal Cambodian affairs, but the new Bill Clinton administration did make its views known, particularly on the question of Khmer Rouge participation in the government. When Sihanouk attempted to open a dialogue with the Khmer Rouge, the United States protested, telling the prince that it would not support his government, or provide aid, if the Khmer Rouge were given a role in the new government.

American interference upset Sihanouk. "I am more and more angered by these incessant warnings from the Americans, which have made me even more ill than I was in the recent past," he said.[41] So that he would not be forced into a mental asylum, Sihanouk said, he would cancel a proposed meeting with Khieu Samphan. Responding to strongly negative reactions from Cambodians and ASEAN, the Americans backed off some, saying that limited Khmer Rouge participation might be acceptable, and shortly thereafter Sihanouk authorized talks with DK officials.

In September the Constituent Assembly approved a new constitution, and Sihanouk was once again crowned king, a position he had abdicated in 1955. He quickly named Ranariddh first prime minister and Hun Sen second prime minister. In most respects, the new constitutional government was the same as the interim one. Two days later an emotional Yasushi Akashi, the head of UNTAC, bid farewell to Cambodia. The United Nations Transitional Authority in Cambodia was over. By the end of the month the United States had opened an embassy and appointed Charles Twining as the first American ambassador to serve in Phnom Penh since John Gunther Dean left under emergency conditions in 1975.

In many respects the efforts to achieve a settlement of the Cambodian imbroglio had achieved truly remarkable results. The major powers, the Security Council, ASEAN, and the international community in general had agreed on a plan to end the conflict. They had entrusted the United Nations with an enormous post–Cold War task: to organize an election and rebuild a country. They had ended outside support of various Cambodian factions (probably the strongest argument for including the Khmer Rouge in the peace process, since otherwise China would probably not have agreed to stop supporting the rebels). In the end, the Khmer Rouge, probably sensing a humiliating defeat at the ballot box, had rejected the process and isolated themselves, thus preparing the groundwork for their ultimate demise. The Cambodian people valiantly rejected them. And in the end, a coalition of Hun Sen's and Sihanouk's forces emerged, eventually giving the country needed stability.

Not that the UNTAC experience was perfect. No one had ever been through such an experience before, and there were many problems. The United Nations did not have experienced people to deal with such matters as visas or customs or even to monitor human rights. Despite Akashi's protests, some of those sent knew nothing of Cambodia and its people. Some of the peacekeeping troops abused the population.

If in the end the UNTAC mission was generally positive, such a result was attained at the cost of forcing the SOC to turn over much of its authority to the United Nations during the transition period and incorporating the Khmer Rouge into the process. Proponents of the latter approach, such as Kenneth Quinn, make a strong case that including them ultimately led to the group's dissolution. "This effort to destroy the Khmer Rouge is perhaps the only instance in which the US has been intimately involved which has led to the complete destruction of a terrorist organization," he points out. But at the time the critics accurately pointed out that the coalition government that emerged after the elections "*never* required the inclusion or appeasement of Khmer Rouge leaders."[42] Indeed some prominent scholars thought the entire U.N. operation actually strengthened the Khmer Rouge, despite that group's decision not to contest the elections. The alternative of the international community's uniting behind the SOC, perhaps encouraging an alliance between Hun Sen and Sihanouk, was rejected. In any event, the United States fully supported the new government.

One continuing American objective was to prevent a return to the killing fields. When the Khmer Rouge threatened a resurgence in 1994, some urged the United States to coordinate a multilateral effort to provide training and equipment to the Cambodian military. The United States had already provided funds to help integrate Khmer Rouge defectors into the Cambodian military and was providing some equipment and instructors for military construction. In light of the renewed Khmer Rouge offensive, the Americans spoke with Australia, France, and Indonesia about joining together with the United States to provide more assistance, including munitions. Though it did not in the end send lethal aid, the United States sent forty-four military advisers to assist in nonlethal areas. The United States also protested Thailand's continuing contacts with the Khmer Rouge. The Thais should be continually reminded that they were "undermining a neighbor" as well as the "costly work of the international community" in Cambodia, wrote former Ambassador to Thailand Morton Abramowitz.[43] The United States wanted the Khmer Rouge cut off.

The Americans hoped that, with their assistance, Cambodia would ultimately become a "peaceful, stable, progressive" country.[44] The United States therefore opposed efforts to weaken or topple the government, beginning with Prince Chakrapong's abortive effort to overthrow the government in July 1994. With strong support from Senator John McCain (R-AZ), Congress considered granting Cambodia Most Favored Nation trade status. (Congress, however, delayed granting Cambodia that status until 1996.) The Americans also supported Cambodia's efforts to join ASEAN. (Membership was approved in 1997 but delayed until 1998 due to Hun Sen's "coup" in July 1997.)

Probably the most important American contribution in the years after the elections was its economic aid, much of which continued to be aimed at constructing, reopening, repairing, and de-mining roads in areas where the Khmer Rouge continued to operate. Such projects were coordinated with Hun Sen's government. One of the more historically significant was the reconstruction of the American highway (Highway 4) from Phnom Penh to Sihanoukville.

Such efforts did not immediately end the Khmer Rouge threat. For much of 1994, the situation seemed bleak. The rebels made impressive military gains and recaptured their stronghold of Pailin, largely because of corruption and incompetence on the part of the government's military, which had taken the city only a month before. In September Sihanouk himself warned tourists not to come to his war-torn country. But by the end of the year conditions had brightened considerably. Visitors to the capital remarked on the palpable change in attitudes and the increase in business activity since spring. Ambassador Twining was especially optimistic, noting the increase in economic activity, and not just in Phnom Penh. "Drive down to Kampot . . . , or drive down to Sihanoukville, or drive down to Svay Rieng, or drive up to Kompong Thom," he suggested. Homes were being built in areas that had been insecure only a few months before. On the road to Battambang "there was more traffic . . . than I have seen *ever*. And that shows that there's something happening."[45]

Optimistic predictions are always dangerous in the Cambodian context. Twining was careful to note that important problems still remained, in particular the critical need of bringing services to the people who had lived in Khmer Rouge areas. There remained the possibility of a disaffected populace developing once again. But Twining's optimism has proved to be largely warranted. In December 1995 Cambodia hosted an international Ramayana festival at Angkor Wat. For several days, dance troupes from India and all countries of Southeast Asia performed the traditional Hindu epic on a floodlit stage in front of Cambodia's national symbol. The event symbolized Cambodia's return to health.

Although the Khmer Rouge continued to cause problems for some time to come, they never again regained the strength they had momentarily shown in 1994. Indeed, they soon began to implode. The new American ambassador, Kenneth Quinn, who arrived in 1996, continued to work closely with the Cambodian government to help repair roads and de-mine areas in Khmer Rouge zones. Considerable attention was devoted to upgrading Highway 10, which went to Pailin. That same year Khmer Rouge units near Pailin revolted against Pol Pot when Nuon Chea and other Khmer Rouge leaders ordered them to end their commercial contacts with the Thais—thus vindicating the American decision to insist on opening Khmer Rouge zones to outside influences.

In 1996 the first significant defections of Khmer Rouge troops to the government began. In June 1997 Pol Pot ordered the assassination of his former deputy and colleague in murder, Son Sen. The next month the Khmer Rouge leader was arrested by his own people and subjected to a show trial, witnessed by *Far Eastern Economic Review* correspondent Nate Thayer. The next spring Pol Pot died, reportedly despondent at the demise of his movement. After some last internecine battles, the Khmer Rouge nearly ceased to exist.

Politically, the Cambodian government has persevered, though with numerous serious strains. The Khmer Rouge also figured in this development. Prior to their collapse, thousands of Khmer Rouge had negotiated surrenders with the government. But Ranariddh in particular had courted the Khmer Rouge for support as he prepared for general elections scheduled for 1998, which angered Hun Sen. In June 1997 the dispute became violent when fighting between military units loyal to the rival factions took place on the streets of Phnom Penh. On 4 July Ranariddh went to Paris, and the following day fighting again broke out between forces loyal to both leaders. Who fired the first shot remains in dispute; American officials believed that neither side intended to ignite a military conflict. Still, the events were commonly portrayed as a Hun Sen coup, a belief strengthened when two high-level FUNCINPEC officials were murdered. Hun Sen denied that his actions amounted to a coup. He remained committed, he said, to the existing governmental structure and invited FUNCINPEC to name a replacement for Ranariddh. Sihanouk refused to condemn Hun Sen or support Ranariddh, and in mid-July FUNCINPEC member Ung Hout replaced Ranariddh. "This is enough to show to the world that there has been no coup d'etat," Hun Sen commented.[46]

The United States reduced its embassy staff and temporarily suspended aid to the country but nevertheless "judged the coup cautiously," given Ranariddh's efforts to gain Khmer Rouge support.[47] Like most other countries, the United States came to accept Hun Sen's action as a fait accompli. Instead of intervening strongly, the United States supported ASEAN's efforts to resolve the crisis, while encouraging Hun Sen to allow open elections.

Serious factional fighting continued in parts of Cambodia for several months. Lending some credence to Hun Sen's allegations about Ranariddh (whom he threatened to put on trial if he returned to the country), the royalist forces made common cause with the remnants of the Khmer Rouge. On the other hand, about 100 political opponents of the government were killed over the next several months. Hun Sen's supporters were widely suspected of committing the crimes, a suspicion that deepened when no one was arrested. The civil conflict was resolved in a peculiarly Cambodian way: in March 1998 Ranariddh was tried in absentia and convicted of arms smuggling and plotting a coup. He was sentenced to 35 years in prison and ordered to pay a $50 million fine. Then by prearrangement, his father the king pardoned him, thus allowing him to come back to Cambodia and contest the elections scheduled for July. According to Quinn, the United States played an important role in the settlement behind the scenes.

The question for the United States and other countries was whether the elections would be fair and free. Given the ruling party's entrenched position, its control of the media, and acts of intimidation, some observers doubted that genuinely impartial elections could be held. As a result, the United States continued to suspend aid, even for such popular programs as narcotics interdiction. It also cut back funds intended to help with the election process.

But there were other voices as well, particularly as the official time for opening political campaigns approached. European Union officials thought a fair and free election possible, as did Hun Sen opponent Kassie Neou. Shortly before the elections Assistant Secretary of State Stanley Roth told a Senate subcommittee that "fair and free elections could conceivably be held."[48]

On 26 July 1998 a large number of international observers watched as 94 percent of eligible Cambodians voted. The CPP received 41.2 percent to FUNCINPEC's 31.5 percent. Another opposition group, the Sam Rainsy party, received 14.2 percent. Had the opposition united (as a leading member of the United States Congress had passionately urged them to do), they would probably have been able to control the new government.

Most international observers thought the elections themselves were reasonably fair and represented a genuine expression of Cambodian opinion. Even so, at first the opposition parties protested the elections, and there was some violence. But by mid-November differences had been resolved. Hun Sen became the sole prime minister, Ranariddh became president of the National Assembly, and several opposition figures received amnesty. The CPP and FUNCINPEC agreed to share power over the interior and defense ministries, and the other ministries were divided between them. As for the United States, the Bill Clinton administration accepted the election results, nominated Kent Wiedemann as the new American ambassador (a person opposed by both Ranariddh and Sam Rainsy), and restored aid. ASEAN postponed admission of Cambodia to the organization but admitted the country the following year.

At the end of the year Khmer Rouge leaders Khieu Samphan and Nuon Chea surrendered to the government. The Khmer Rouge barely existed. The last holdout, the notorious "butcher" Ta Mok, was captured in March 1999. He died in July 2006 while awaiting trial. That was the end of the Khmer Rouge.

Despite the demise of the mass murderers, Cambodia is still impoverished and is troubled with corruption, drug trafficking, human rights problems, uncounted land mines, environmental degradation, HIV/AIDS, and other problems. It may, therefore, be too much to say that it now approximates that "peaceful, stable, progressive" country that Ambassador Twining hoped would emerge. But the elections did bring about political stability and created a climate for economic growth. For the first time in thirty years, Cambodia was at peace. Though beset by great challenges, Cambodia seems to be on the slow road to recovery—and this time it is doing so with the support of the United States. "I feel we have a good relationship," Hun Sen told a reporter in March 1999, "compared with the last two decades in which we seemed to be enemies."[49]

Epilogue

HUN SEN WAS CORRECT: by the end of the 1990s relations between the United States and Cambodia were reasonably good. In some respects, relations have continued to improve, notably in the area of textile exports. Cambodia has worked to achieve labor standards approved by the International Labor Organization (ILO), with the result that the United States increased its quota of goods imported from Cambodia's emerging textile industry. The World Trade Organization (WTO) rules ended the quota system in 2004, but American firms have continued to import substantial quantities of Cambodian textiles—specifically because Cambodian factories meet ILO standards. The Gap is a particularly important buyer.

On the other hand, when George W. Bush assumed power in 2001, a shriller tone marked administration comments about Communist and post-Communist regimes. There was much talk about regime change in various parts of the world, including Vietnam and Cambodia. This rhetoric emboldened those in the United States who had long detested Hun Sen and his cohorts. In the post–PRK period, some of this resentment went back to the elections of 1993, which FUNCIPEC won but which nevertheless resulted in a compromise that allowed Hun Sen and the CPP to retain considerable power. But the most immediate source of anger can be traced to a vicious grenade attack on a Sam Rainsy Party campaign rally in 1997 in which at least sixteen persons died. Others lost limbs. One American, Ron Abney, who was director of the International Republican Institute's (IRI) Cambodia program, was seriously wounded as well. From that day on Abney, who blames Hun Sen for the attack, "was 'full time' on Cambodia."[1] He has since sued Hun Sen in an American court. The critics believe that the response of Ambassador Quinn and the State Department to these events was pusillanimous.

The IRI, like its Democratic Party twin, the National Democratic Institute, receives public funds from the National Endowment for Democracy to promote democracy abroad. In Cambodia the IRI provides democratic training and is widely viewed as being against the CPP and in favor of the Sam Rainsy Party. Critics charge that it is really working for regime change.

In any event, with a new administration in Washington, those who wanted regime change had more influence. Their leader in Congress has been Senator Mitch McConnell (R-KY). McConnell urges the State Department to stand up to CPP bullying during elections. He also regularly introduces resolutions remembering the grenade attack of 1997, urging the FBI to return to Phnom Penh to continue a previously begun investigation into the attack, and inserting into the *Congressional Record* the names of those who died. He often condemns Hun Sen for one lapse or another, while referring back to the events of 1997 and sometimes mentioning Abney by name. Despite the opinion of most international observers, he finds none of the elections in Cambodia credible.

The critics of Hun Sen have succeeded in restricting aid to Cambodia, most of which must be funneled through nongovernmental organizations (NGOs) rather than through the government. Aid will be increased, the critics say publicly, if there is a change of government. Under McConnell's influence, American representatives to international lending agencies are admonished not to vote for loans to Cambodia. Removing Hun Sen seems to take precedence over all other considerations, including even a trial of Khmer Rouge leaders.

Calls in the United States, Australia, and elsewhere to create an international tribunal to try the Khmer Rouge stretch back to the early 1980s.[2] But not until 1997 did the United Nations begin to investigate the feasibility of creating a court. In 1999 U.N. officials began serious talks with the Cambodian government about establishing a judicial process. Progress has been agonizingly slow, however. China has been less than enthusiastic, and Hun Sen has vacillated. Cambodian authorities want a court dominated by Cambodian jurists, but foreign experts consider the Cambodian court system too prone to political influence; they want international jurists to have the final say. Tortuous negotiations ensued between Cambodian and U.N. officials. In 2003 an agreement was finally reached on a framework for a tribunal, which came to be called the Extraordinary Chambers in the Courts of Cambodia. Only in 2006 was an accord reached on all details and funding assured for the trials, which are now likely to take place in 2007.

What has been the American position on this? In 1994 Congress passed the Cambodian Genocide Justice Act, placing the United States officially on record in support of a Khmer Rouge tribunal, and at one time the United States appropriated $3 million in support of a U.N.–sponsored court. It has also generously supported the Documentation Center of Cambodia, which has painstakingly gathered evidence of Khmer Rouge crimes. However, those opposed to Hun Sen have come out in opposition to the trial—unless the tribunal also prosecutes Hun Sen, something that Republicans in the House of Representatives called for in 1998.[3] After the elections of 2003, which returned Hun Sen to power, Congress blocked American funding for the Khmer Rouge tribunal.[4] Since then McConnell has regularly introduced legislation prohibiting American funding while urging those who have promised funding to reconsider.

There is a reasoned argument against the tribunal, supported by such worthy organizations as Human Rights Watch and Amnesty International, which in 2003 argued that there were insufficient safeguards against Cambodian government interference with the court. McConnell and others have similar concerns, though one suspects that their primary fear is that a successful trial might bolster the status of Hun Sen. Others argue that a trial will be meaningless unless it investigates the roles of China, the United States, and even Sihanouk, all of which were involved with the Khmer Rouge. But to wait for perfection may mean no trial at all. For Youk Chhang, the respected director of the Documentation Center, there is no question but that the trials should be held soon, even if the court and the judicial process are not perfect. "For the victims . . . I think the issue is how do we move on," he stated. "The tribunal, to me, is the last solution to Cambodia's genocide."[5]

There is some evidence that American policy has moderated. Some former opponents of the trial have changed their mind, and in January 2006 when the U.S. Senate strongly condemned a Hun Sen crackdown on the opposition, it did not repeat previous calls to prohibit American funding for the tribunal. The Congress has in fact dropped legislative restrictions on U.S. financial assistance, and there is some hope that if the tribunal meets international standards (which is possible), American funding may materialize. The State Department, too, appears to be more supportive than in the past. Indeed, late in July 2006 Ambassador to Cambodia Joseph Mussomeli criticized those opposed to a tribunal and urged that the trials start just as soon as possible.

There are other straws in the wind that the bilateral relationship is beginning to improve. In July 2006 the two countries signed a trade and investment framework agreement (TIFA), intended to increase trade and investment connections. Bilateral trade has already increased substantially since 2005, when the United States helped facilitate Cambodia's entrance into the WTO. Important as economic matters are, the Bush administration's overriding concern is the war on terror, and its approach to Southeast Asia has emphasized that factor. (This has put it at some disadvantage with respect to China, which is engaged in a "charm offensive" to attract the loyalties of Southeast Asian nations. With its nonhectoring approach, China has made many friends in the region.) The United States has from time to time noted the growing influence of Islam in Cambodia and has feared that terrorist cells might prosper there. However, Hun Sen has proven to be an ally in the war on terror, with the result that relations have improved, even to the point that military assistance might be resumed.

Despite what appears to be a general improvement in relations in recent months, the critics will doubtless continue to condemn Hun Sen, though a note of resignation is apparent. Particularly disheartening to them was the defection of Prince Ranariddh, head of the opposition FUNCINPEC Party. In 2004 Ranariddh, who has had a stormy relationship with Hun Sen and who had the support of Americans opposed to the CPP, arrived at an agreement with Hun Sen and became president of the National Assembly, causing considerable outrage among the American critics of Hun Sen. "I don't know what causes a man to look you in the eye and say that, 'I'll never do something because it's against all my principles in life,' and then change his mind," lamented Ron Abney.[6] McConnell concluded that Ranariddh had gone over to the dark side and "cast his lot with CPP hardliners."[7]

Responsible critics of the Cambodian government are right to call attention to its abuses of human rights and pressure it to be more transparent and allow more dissent and free discussion of issues. Yet Hun Sen's rule differs little from that of Sihanouk. As Margaret Slocomb wrote in 2003, "Cambodian political society functions today in much the same way as it always has despite the trappings of multi-party democracy which have largely been imposed on it by the process of the peace settlement, globalization and the need for external assistance to fund its development agenda."[8]

The Khmer Rouge regime was so monstrous that strong efforts to modify its behavior were justified (although no one stood up to it until Vietnam finally invaded). Despite what the critics sometimes say, the Hun Sen government, whatever its lapses, has little in common with the Khmer Rouge regime. Thus in a way analogous to the tribunal issue, the question is whether it is better in general to accept an imperfect government, but one that has brought a considerable measure of peace and stability to the country along with some political diversity, or to push for a new regime—with unanticipated, and perhaps negative, consequences.

Ever since Woodrow Wilson tried unsuccessfully to control the Mexican Revolution in the interests of spreading democracy, ideologically driven foreign policies have produced problematic results. Perhaps in situations short of genocide or the truly awful suppression of human rights, it is best to heed the words of one of the wisest of the American secretaries of state, John Quincy Adams, who urged his countrymen to wish democratic reform and freedom well but not to go on crusades to change the world. The United States, he stated, "will commend the general cause [of freedom] by the countenance of her voice, and the benignant sympathy of her example." But she should not enlist "under other banners than her own" because to do so would "involve herself beyond the power of extrication, in all the wars of interest and intrigue, of individual avarice, envy, and ambition, which assume the colors and usurp the standard of freedom. The fundamental maxims of her policy would insensibly change from *liberty* to *force*. . . . She would become the dictatress of the world. She would be no longer the ruler of her own spirit."

The bilateral relationship has come a long way since the 1980s, when the United States was funding armed resistance to Hun Sen. Hopefully both countries will adopt reasonable approaches so that the relationship can continue to be friendly and constructive. Cambodia, having endured so much, deserves no less.

Abbreviations

AID	U.S. Agency for International Development
ANS	Armée Nationale Sihanoukiste
ARVN	South Vietnamese Army
ASEAN	Association of Southeast Asian Nations
Carter Papers	Jimmy Carter Papers, Jimmy Carter Presidential Library, Atlanta, GA
CDF	Central Decimal File
CFPF	Central Foreign Policy File
CGDK	Coalition Government of Democratic Kampuchea
CIDG	Civilian Irregular Defense Groups
CIA	Central Intelligence Agency
CINCPAC	Commander in Chief, Pacific
CMAA	Christian and Missionary Alliance Archives, Colorado Springs, CO
CNO	Chief of Naval Operations
CO	Country
CORKR	Campaign to Oppose the Return of the Khmer Rouge
COSVN	Central Office for South Vietnam
CPP	Cambodian People's Party
DCC	Documentation Center of Cambodia records, Phnom Penh, Cambodia
DK	Democratic Kampuchea
EXAF	External Affairs Office (Canberra, Australia, unless otherwise indicated)
FANK	Force Armée Nationale Khmère (Khmer National Armed Forces)

FBIS	Foreign Broadcase Information Services
FO	Foreign Office
Ford Papers	Gerald R. Ford Papers, Gerald R. Ford Library, Ann Arbor, MI
FRUS	Department of State, *Foreign Relations of the United States.* Washington, DC: Government Printing Office
FUNCINPEC	National United Front for an Independent, Neutral, Peaceful, and Cooperative Cambodia
FUNK	Front Uni National de Kampuchea (National United Front of Kampuchea)
GKR	Government of the Khmer Republic
GRUNK	Government Royal d'Union Nationale de Kampuchea
GVN	Government of Vietnam
HAKOF	Henry A. Kissenger Office Files
Hutchinson Papers	Edward Hutchinson Papers, Gerald Ford Library, Ann Arbor, MI
ICC	International Commission for Supervision and Control
ICRC	International Committee of the Red Cross
JCS	Joint Chiefs of Staff
Johnson Papers	Lyndon B. Johnson Papers, Lyndon B. Johnson Library, Austin, TX
LCU	Landing Craft Utility
MAAG	Military Assistance Advisory Group
MACV	Military Assistance Command, Vietnam
MEDT	Military Equipment Delivery Team
Melby Papers	John F. Melby Papers, Harry S. Truman Library, Independence, MO
MOLINAKA	Sihanouk's armed forces
NAII	National Archives II, College Park, MD
NAA	National Archives of Australia, Canberra
NAC	National Archives of Cambodia, Phnom Penh
NCR	Non-Communist Resistance

Nessen Papers	Ron Nessen Papers, Gerald R. Ford Library, Ann Arbor, MI
NIACT	Night Action
NLF	National Liberation Front
NPM	Nixon Presidential Materials, National Archives II, College Park, MD
NSC	National Security Council
NVA	North Vietnamese Army
NSF	National Security File
NSSM	National Security Study Memorandum
OCB	Operations Control Board
OF	Official File
PAVN	People's Army of Vietnam
PRK	People's Republic of Kampuchea
PSF	President's Secretary's File
RG	Record Group
SEA	Southeast Asia
SEATO	Southeast Asia Treaty Organization
SNC	Supreme National Council
SNF	Subject Numeric File
SOC	State of Cambodia
SS	Secretary of State
UNTAC	United Nations Transitional Authority in Cambodia
USDS	United States Department of State
USG	United States Government
VC	Viet Cong
WHCF	White House Central File
WHO	White House Office

Notes

1—Nineteenth- and Early Twentieth-Century Encounters

1. Milton Osborne, *The Mekong: Turbulent Past, Uncertain Future* (New York: Grove Press, 2000), 29.

2. Frank Vincent Jr., *The Land of the White Elephant: Travels, Adventures, and Discoveries in Burma, Siam, Cambodia, and Cochin-China* (4th ed., New York: Harper & Brothers, 1884), 221, 355.

3. Jacob E. Conner, "The Forgotten Ruins of Indo-China," *National Geographic* 23 (March 1912): 211.

4. Harry A. Franck, *East of Siam: Ramblings in the Five Divisions of French Indo-China* (New York: Century, 1926), 85.

5. Henry S. Waterman to Stanley H. Ford, 13 October 1931, U.S. Department of State, Records Relating to the Internal Affairs of France, 1910–1929, Microfilm 1442, reel 83 (U.S. Dept. of State records hereafter cited by microfilm and reel number—M1442, reel 83).

6. Letter from E. Matyus, 26 September 1938, in "Inventaire des Documents du Fonds Résident Supérieur," Phnom Penh, Paquet 1163, NAC.

7. Leland L. Smith, "Report on Cambodia," 15 June 1922, enclosed in Leland L. Smith to SS, 16 June 1922, Despatch 144, M560, reel 151.

8. Leland L. Smith, "The Future of COTTON in INDO-CHINA," 17 September 1923, M560, reel 152. Smith to SS, 28 August 1924, M560, reel 150.

9. Robert J. Casey, *Four Faces of Siva: The Detective Story of a Vanished Race* (London: George G. Hartop & Co., 1929), 268–69.

10. Mark Philip Bradley, *Imagining Vietnam and America: The Making of Postcolonial Vietnam, 1919–1950* (Chapel Hill: University of North Carolina Press, 2000).

11. E. F. Irwin, *With Christ in Indo-China: The Story of the Alliance Missions in French Indo-China and Eastern Siam* (Harrisburg, PA: Christian Publications, 1937), 5.

12. Arthur L. Hammond, "Manuscript History of Missionary Work in Cambodia" (manuscript), 14, CMAA.

13. Christian and Missionary Alliance, *Fifty-Third Year Annual Report of the General Council at Asheville, N.C. May 16–20, 1940 for the Year Ended December Thirty-First, 1939* (n.p., n.d.), 48.

14. *Light in Their Dwellings: A History of Forty Years of Missions in Cambodia* (Phnom Penh: Gospel Press of Cambodia, n.d.), 14–15.

15. Mrs. N. M. Cressman, "In Cambodia," *Alliance Weekly*, 22 September 1928, 616.

16. Christian and Missionary Alliance, *The Thirty-Fourth Annual Report of the Christian and Missionary Alliance for the Year 1930* (New York: [Christian and Missionary Alliance], 1931), 43.

17. David Chandler, *A History of Cambodia* (3rd ed.; Boulder, CO: Westview, 2000), 163.

18. Leland L. Smith, "The Political Situation in Indo-China," 28 August 1924, M560, reel 152.

19. John S. Sawin, "The Christian and Missionary Alliance in Indo-China, Pre 1911–1924, Vol I" (manuscript), 281, CMAA.

20. David Ellison, "The Gospel in Every Province," *Alliance Weekly*, 29 June 1929. Mrs. Gordon H. Smith, "The First Native General Conference in Cambodia," ibid., 11 October 1930, 667. Hammond, "Manuscript History," 27. Alfred C. Snead, *Missionary Atlas: A Manual of the Foreign Work of the Christian and Missionary Alliance* (Harrisburg, PA: Christian Publications, 1936), 39.

21. Alfred C. Snead, "Report of the Foreign Department," *Thirty-Ninth Annual Report of the Christian and Missionary Alliance for the Year 1935* (New York: n.p., 1936), 21. Paul Gunter, "Only One of Cambodia's Millions!" *Alliance Weekly*, 1 October 1927, 649.

2—Cambodia

1. David W. Ellison, "Under New Masters," *Alliance Weekly*, 28 November 1942, 760.

2. Floyd Peterson to "Dear Folks," 10 June 1942, RG 809–Cambodia, Box 4, folder 19, CMAA.

3. *Light in Their Dwellings: A History of Forty Years of Missions in Cambodia* (Phnom Penh: The Gospel Press of Cambodia, n.d.), 33.

4. Ben Kiernan, *How Pol Pot Came to Power* (London: Verso, 1985), 57.

5. David P. Chandler, *The Tragedy of Cambodian History: Politics, War, and Revolution Since 1945* (New Haven and London: Yale University Press, 1991), 43.

6. "Regional Repercussions of Indochinese Conflict," in Southeast Asia Regional Conference, 21–26 June 1948, Bangkok, Siam: Section VI: "Regional Repercussions of Continued Hostility in Indochina," Melby Papers, Box 9, folder 2. "Southeast Asia Conference, Monday, June 21, 1948," Southeast Asia Regional Conference, Bangkok, Siam, Melby Papers, Box 9, folder 1.

7. "A Report to the National Security Council by the Secretary of State on U.S. Policy toward Southeast Asia" (NSC-51), 1 July 1949, 6, Truman Papers, PSF—Subject File, National Security Council (Reports-5-Somers), Box 198, folder "Reports—to NSC for Information."

8. Kiernan, *How Pol Pot*, 60–61. For a study of the influence of Vietnamese communists on the Issarak movement, see Motoo Furuta, "The Indochina Communist Party's Division into Three Parties: Vietnamese Communist Policy toward Cambodia and Laos, 1948–1951," in Takashi Shiraishi and Motoo Furuta, eds., *Indochina in the 1940s and 1950s* (Ithaca, NY: Cornell University Southeast Asia Program, 1992), 143–64.

9. "A Report to the National Security Council by the Secretary of State on U.S. Policy Toward Southeast Asia," (NSC-51), 1 July 1949, 7–14.

10. Carlos Romulo to Dean Acheson, 2 March 1950, Acheson Papers, Box 75.

11. John F. Melby to John Davies, 31 August 1950, Box 12, Melby Papers. Melby to William S. B. Lacy, 29 September 1950, ibid. George Kennan to Acheson, 21 August 1950, Acheson Papers, Box 67.

12. Don V. Catlett to SS, 6 December 1950, 751H.00/12-650, RG 59, Indochina 1950–1954.

13. Christian and Missionary Alliance, *Sixty-Fourth Year Annual Report for 1950 and Minutes of the General Council Held at St. Louis, Missouri May 16–21, 1951* (N.p., n.d.), 90.

14. Catlett to SS, 19 December 1951, 751H.00/12–1951, RG 59, Indochina 1950–1954.

15. Michael James, "King, Here, Warns Cambodia May Rise," *New York Times*, 19 April 1953, 1.

16. Francis R. Valeo, Oral History Interview by Donald Ritchie, 3 July 1985–11 March 1986, 100, Kennedy Library.

17. Memorandum of Conversation, Philip W. Bonsal and Nong Kimny, 13 May 1953, 751H.00/5-1353, RG 59, Indochina 1950–1954.

18. Montllor's remark is from a conversation with an Australian official, reported in Australian legation, Saigon, 1 July 1953, Savingram 17, A1838/280, Control Symbol 3106/2/1 Part 2, NAA.

19. Donald Heath to SS, 4 July 1953, Tel. 21, 751H.00/7-453, RG 59, Indochina 1950–1954.

20. Montllor to SS, 10 September 1953, Tel. 30, 751H.00/9-1053, RG 59, Indochina 1950–1954.

21. Heath to SS, 12 September 1953, Tel. 439, 751H.00/9-1253, RG 59, Indochina 1950–1954 (also in FRUS 1952–54, 13:798–800).

22. John Foster Dulles to USDS, 19 February 1954, in FRUS 1952–1954, 15:416.

23. The Geneva Agreements with respect to Cambodia are in FRUS 1952–1954, 16:1531–39.

24. "Cambodia," *Alliance Weekly*, 30 June 1954, 9. Harry Taylor, "Unprecedented Opportunities," ibid., 5 May 1954, 9.

3—From Optimism to the Year of Troubles

1. OCB, "Analysis of Internal Security Situation in Cambodia and Recommended Action," 16 November 1955, 4, Eisenhower Papers, WHO, NSC Staff: Papers, 1948–1961, OCB Central File, Box 39, folder OCB 091, Indo-China (file #5)(2).

2. Unsigned NSC document, "Cambodia," 13 [undated but ca. 1 June 1955; a note indicates that a copy was sent to Elmer Staats on 2 June 1955], Eisenhower Papers, WHO, NSC Staff: Papers, 1948–61, OCB Central File, Box 39, folder OCT 091, Indo-China (file #4)(2). Subsequent versions of this paper omitted this passage and put a possible training role in the context of a future request from the Cambodian government.

3. Robert McClintock to USDS, 16 June 1955, Tel. 1216, 751H.00/6-6155. McClintock to USDS, 18 June 1955, Despatch 1240, 751H.00/6-1855; both in RG 59, Indochina 1955–59, reel 20.

4. Chandler, *Tragedy*, 83.

5. McClintock to Kenneth T. Young, 21 June 1955, FRUS 1955–1957, 21:457.

6. McClintock to SS, 28 November 1955, Tel. 649, 751H.00 (W)/11-2655, RG 59, Indochina 1955–59, reel 26. CNO to CINCPAC and CHMAAG Cambodia, 28 December 1955, RG 218, Geographic File, 1954–56, 092 Asia (6-25-48) (2), Sec. 18, Box 9, NA.

7. "Le Prince Sihanouk expose sans ambages la position du Cambodge vis-à-vis de la France et des Etats-Unis," *Le Monde*, 11 January 1956, enclosed in Robert P. Joyce to USDS, 13 January 1956, Despatch 1344, 751H.00/1-1356, RG 59, Indochina 1955–59, reel 21.

8. McClintock to SS, 2 March 1956, Tel. 1126, 751H.00/3-256, RG 59, Indochina 1955–59, reel 21.

9. Clipping, "Cambodia's Premier Backs Neutrality," *New York Times*, datelined February 18, Stanton Papers.

10. Felix B. Stump to George Lodoen, 22 March 1956, FRUS 1955–1957, 21: 500–501. Stump to Lodoen [3/28/55], quoted in McClintock to USDS, 30 March 1956, ibid., 505.

11. McClintock to Stump, 30 March 1956, FRUS 1955–1957, 21:506–7.

12. G. McMurtrie Godley to SS, 18 March 1956, 751H.00/3-1856, Despatch 1216, RG 59, Indochina 1955–59, reel 21.

13. McClintock to Arthur W. Radford, 27 July 1956, FRUS 1955–1957, 21:539. Robertson to McClintock, 21 August 1956, ibid., 549.

14. 295th Meeting of the NSC, 30 August 1956, 12, NSC Staff: Papers, 1954–61, Eisenhower Papers, Special Staff File Series, Box 8.

15. Dillon Anderson to Dwight D. Eisenhower, 28 August 1956, Eisenhower Papers, WHO, NSC Staff: Papers, 1954–61, Special Staff File Series, Box 7, folder Southeast Asia (2).

16. NSC, "U.S. Policy in Mainland Southeast Asia," NSC 5612/1, 5 September 1956, p. 9, Declassified Documents Series.

17. Australian Legation Phnom Penh to EXAF, 15 October 1956, Savingram 50, Series A1838/280, Control Symbol 3016/7/1A Part. 1, NAA.

18. Francis R. Valeo, Oral History Interview by Donald Ritchie, 3 July 1985–11 March 1986, 109–10, John F. Kennedy Library, Boston, MA.

19. OCB, "Outline Plan of Operations with Respect to Cambodia," FRUS 1955–1957, 21:559–62.

20. OCB, "Progress Report on Southeast Asia (NSC 5612/1)," 10, 6 November 1957, Eisenhower Papers, WHO, Office of the Special Assistant for National Security Affairs Records 1952–61, NSC series, Policy Papers Subseries, Box 18, folder NSC 5612/1.

21. Francis Stuart to EXAF, 17 January 1958, Memorandum 20, Series No. A1838/280, Control Symbol 3016/2/1 Part 8, NAA.

22. Memorandum of Conversation, Pierre Mathivet and Edmond Kellogg, 21 February 1958, enclosed in Kellogg to USDS, 11 March 1958, Despatch 256, 751H.00/3-1158, RG 59, Indochina 1955–59, reel 21.

23. Carl W. Strom to SS, 28 March 1958, Despatch 1014, 751H.00/3-2858, RG 59, Indochina 1955–59, reel 21.

24. Stuart, diary entry for 16 May 1958, in Stuart to John P. Quinn, 27 May 1958, Series No. 1838/280, Control Symbol 3016/7/1A Part 1, NAA.

25. Strom to USDS, 7 July 1958, FRUS 1958–1960, 116:233. Elbridge Durbrow to USDS, 9 July 1958, ibid., 235–36.

26. Strom to USDS, 25 July 1958, ibid., 16:243.

27. Memorandum of Conversation, Walter S. Robertson et al., 5 August 1958, ibid., 244–46.

28. Australian Legation Phnom Penh to EXAF, 9 September 1958, Savingram 35, Series No. A1838/280, Control Symbol 3016/2/1 Part 9, NAA.

29. Stuart to Secretary EXAF, 7 November 1958, Memorandum 400, Series No. A1838/280, Control Symbol 3016/7/1A Part 1, NAA.

30. Memorandum of Conversation, Durbrow and Ngo Dinh Nhu, 13 November 1958, FRUS 1958–1960, 16:264.

31. Sihanouk told this to the Australian minister. See Australian Legation Phnom Penh to EXAF, 27 January 1959, Savingram 3, Series No. A 1838/280, Control Symbol 3016/2/1 Part 9, NAA.

32. Australian Legation Phnom Penh to EXAF, 21 July 1958, Savingram 21, Series No. A1838/280, Control Symbol 3016/2/1 Part 9, NAA.

33. Memorandum of Conversation, Charles Meyer and Robert S. Barrett IV, 17 January 1959, enclosed in Robert S. Barrett to USDS, 21 January 1959, Despatch 259, 751H.00/1-2159, RG 59, Indochina 1955–59, reel 22.

34. Strom to SS, 13 February 1959, Despatch G-116, 751H.00/2-1359, RG 59, Indochina 1955–59, reel 22.

35. Stuart to James Plimsoll, 15 January 1959, Series A1838/276, Control Symbol TS383/12/1, NAA.

36. Australian Legation Phnom Penh to EXAF, 25 February 1959, Savingram 10, Series No. A1838/280, Control Symbol 3016/2/1 Part 10, NAA.

37. "Communique by the Royal Government," attached to Australian Legation Phnom Penh to EXAF, 25 February 1959, Savingram 10; Australian Legation Phnom Penh to EXAF, 3 March 1959, Savingram 13; both in Series No. A1838/280, Control Symbol 3016/2/1 Part 10, NAA.

38. Strom to USDS, 3 March 1959, FRUS 1958–1960, 16:295–97. Strom to USDS, 3 March 1959, ibid., 295–97.

39. Strom to William C. Trimble, 8 September 1959, Trimble Papers, Box 3, folder Chron Phnom Penh, April–May 1959.

40. Oral History Interview with William C. Trimble by Dennis J. O'Brien, 12 August 1969, 4–7, Kennedy Library.

41. Parsons to Trimble, 8 May 1959, Trimble Papers, Box 3, folder Chron Phnom Penh, April–May 1959.

42. Dowling (for J. Graham Parsons) to USDS, 5 May 1959, FRUS 1958–1960, 16: 310–13.

43. Trimble Diary Entries, 20 and 21 July 1959, Trimble Papers. Milton E. Osborne to EXAF, 30 July 1959, Memorandum 315, Series No. A1838/280, Control Symbol 3016/2/1 Part 11, NAA.

44. Australian Legation Phnom Penh to EXAF, 1 October 1959, Savingram 28, Series No. A1945/24, Control Symbol 248/4/13, NAA.

45. Richard E. Usher to John M. Steeves, 11 March 1960, FRUS 1958–1960, 16:356.

46. George Ball to U.S. Embassy Paris, 8 July 1964, Tel. 145, RG 59, CFPF 1964–1966, Box 1970, folder POL 15-1 7/1/64, NAII.

47. C. Douglas Dillon to USDS, 17 December 1959, FRUS 1958–1960, 16:348.

48. Trimble to Durbrow, 10 February 1960, Trimble Papers, Box 3, folder Chron File, Jan.–Feb.–March 1960.

49. OCB, "Special Report on U.S. Policy in Mainland Southeast Asia (NSC 5809)," 10 February 1960, Eisenhower Papers, WHO, Office of the Special Assistant for National Security Affairs: Records 1952–61, NSC Series, Policy Papers Subseries, Box 25, folder NSC 5809—Policy in Southeast Asia (1).

50. Trimble to Parsons, 22 August 1960, Trimble Papers, Box 4, folder CHRON file, Aug.–Dec. 1960.

51. Daniel V. Anderson to Parsons, 13 May 1960, FRUS 1958–1960, 16:360–61. Australian High Commission London to EXAF, 24 May 1960, Tel. 2284, Series No. A1945/24, Control Symbol 248/4/13, NAA.

52. Australian Embassy Phnom Penh to Secretary EXAF, 26 May 1960, Memorandum 182, Series A1838/280, Control Symbol 3016/2/1 Part 12, NAA. Steeves to Christian Herter, 18 June 1960, FRUS 1958–1960, 16:364.

53. Australian Embassy Phnom Penh to EXAF, 15 June 1960, Tel. 138, Series No. A1838/280, Control Symbol 3106/2/1 Part 12, NAA. State Department officials made this statement to a United Kingdom representative, according to the Australians.

54. C. M. Westergren, "The Problems & Difficulties of Distribution," *Cambodia* Vol. 8, No. 4, 1960, 6–7, 10 (copy in RG 809—Cambodia, Box 3, folder Cambodian Field Periodicals, 1953–1962, C&MA Archives). Clifford M. Westergren, "A Valiant Veteran," *Alliance Witness*, 14 December 1960, 11. Christian and Missionary Alliance, *Seventy-Fourth Year Annual Report for 1960 and Minutes of the General Council held at Columbus, Ohio, May 17–21, 1961* (N.p., n.d.), 107.

55. Steeves, quoted in Australian Mission to the U.N. to EXAF, 27 September 1960, Tel. UN 1049, Series No. A1838/280, Control Symbol 3016/7/1 Part 2, NAA.

56. John C. Monjo to USDS, 3 November 1960, Tel. 131, 751H.11/11–360, RG 59, CDF 1960–63, Box 1751, NAII.

57. Steeves to Trimble, 21 October 1960, FRUS 1958–1960, 16:386.

58. Sihanouk to Dwight Eisenhower, 12 November 1960, Eisenhower Papers, Ann Whitman File, International Series, Box 5, folder Cambodia (1).

4—A Casualty of War

1. Australian Embassy Phnom Penh to EXAF, 5 June 1961, Savingram 13, Series A1838/280, Control Symbol 3016/2/1 Part 13, NAA. Trimble to John F. Kennedy, 14 July 1961, Trimble Papers, Box 4, folder Chron, Phnom Penh, April–Sept., 1961.

2. Walt Rostow to Kennedy, 25 July 1961, Kennedy Papers, NSF-Regional Security SEA, Box 231.

3. Memorandum of Conversation, 25 September 1961, FRUS 1961–63, 23:165.

4. "Talk by Prince Norodom Sihanouk . . . to the Asia Society New York," 26 September 1961, 9, Trimble Papers.

5. Information on Sarit's comments comes from Thomas Hirschfeld, who was then serving in the Phnom Penh embassy. Hirschfeld e-mail message to author, 13 October 2001.

6. "Translation of Prince Sihanouk's Speech of October 26, at Kompong Speu. . . ," Trimble Papers, Box 2, folder *La Dépêche*. Trimble to SS, 30 October 1961, No. 329, 751H.11/10-3061, RG 59, CDF 1960–63, Box 1751, NAII. Trimble to SS, 27 October 1961, Tel. 315, Trimble Papers.

7. Clifford M. Westergren, "Missionaries and Governmental Authority," *Alliance Witness*, 15 November 1961, 7.

8. USDS to American Embassy Phnom Penh, 30 October 1961, Tel. 388, 751H.11/10-3061, RG 59, CDF, 1960–63, Box 1751, NAII. Australian Embassy Washington D.C. to EXAF, 31 October 1961, Series No. A1209/128, Control Symbol 1961/1304, NAA.

9. Edward H. Scherrer to Harry D. Felt, 15 November 1961, FRUS 1961–63, 23:176.

10. Roger Hilsman to Averell Harriman, 7 August 1962, Research Memorandum RFE-35, Kennedy Papers, NSF:CO:Cambodia, Box 16, folder 7/16/62–8/7/62.

11. Trimble to SS, 19 January 1962, No. 490, 751H.00/1-1962, RG 59, CDF 1960–63, Box 1750, NAII.

12. Trimble to SS, 25 January 1962, Tel. 500, Kennedy Papers, NSF:CO:Cambodia, Box 16, folder 1/18/62–3/28/62.

13. Sihanouk quoted in Trimble to SS, 17 February 1962, Tel. 548, Kennedy Papers, NSF:CO:Cambodia, Box 16, folder 1/18/62–3/28/62.

14. Charles F. Moore to SS, 16 June 1962, Tel. 751, Kennedy Papers, NSF:CO:Cambodia, Box 16.

15. Dean Rusk to U.S. Embassy Bangkok, 18 June 1962, Tel. NIACT 2018, 751H.022/6-1862, RG 59, CDF 1960–63, Box 1751, NAII.

16. Philip D. Sprouse to SS, 14 August 1962, Tel. 104, Kennedy Papers, NSF:CO:Cambodia, Box 16, folder 8/8/62–8/15/62.

17. Sprouse to SS, 18 August 1962, Tel. 131, Kennedy Papers, NSF:CO:Cambodia, folder 8/16/62–8/19/62. According to Thomas Hirschfeld, the American diplomat who requested Chu's release, the Cambodians pulled out Chu's fingernails. Hirschfeld e-mail message to author, 13 October 2001.

18. Herbert Gordon to USDS, 17 January 1962, Airgram A-339, 751H.11/1-1763, RG 59, CDF 1960–63, Box 1752, NAII.

19. Noël St. Clair Deschamps to Secretary, EXAF, 3 October 1963, Memorandum 494, Series No. 1838/280, Control Symbol 3016/7/1 Part 3, NAA. Deschamps to Secretary, EXAF, 10 October 1963, Memorandum 509, Series No. 1838/280, Control Symbol 3016/7/1 Part 3, NAA. Sprouse to SS, 4 October 1963, Tel. 265, RG 59, CFPF 1963, Box 3846, NAII.

20. Sprouse to SS, 13 November 1963, Tel. 350, Kennedy Papers, NSF:CO:Cambodia, Box 17, folder 11/8/63–11/16/63. Australian Embassy Washington D.C. to EXAF, 16 November 1963, Tel. 3105, Series No. A1838/280, Control Symbol 3016/2/1 Part 15, NAA.

21. Sprouse to SS, 16 November 1963, Tel. 375, Kennedy Papers, NSF:CO:Cambodia, Box 17, folder 11/17/63–11/19/63.

22. Sprouse to SS, 20 November 1963, Tel. 381, Kennedy Papers, NSF:CO:Cambodia, Box 17, folder 11/20/63–11/22/63.

23. Memorandum of Conversation, Kennedy, Hilsman, 20 November 1963, 11:12 a.m., Hilsman Papers, Countries: Cambodia, Box 1.

24. Memorandum of Telephone Conversation between Harriman and Hilsman, 21 November 1963, FRUS 1961–63, 23:259.

25. Sprouse to SS, 18 January 1964, Tel. 702, RG 59, CFPF 1964–1966, Box 1974, folder Political Affairs & Rels CAMB-US, NAII.
26. Australian Embassy Washington to EXAF, 19 December 1963, Tel. 3383, Series No. 1838/280, Control Symbol 3016/2/1 Part 15, NAA.
27. Memorandum of a Telephone Conversation, Harriman and Acheson, 9 December 1963, FRUS 1961–63, 23:282.
28. Sihanouk speech 9 December 1963, ibid., 281–82.
29. Sprouse to SS, 12 December 1963, Tel. 491, Johnson Papers, NSF-CO., Box 236, folder Cambodia Cables, Vol. I. Sprouse to SS, 13 December 1963, Tel. 497, Johnson Papers, NSF-CO., Box 236, folder Cambodia Cables, Vol. I. Research Memorandum RFE-100, Thomas L. Hughes, Bureau of Intelligence and Research, to Rusk, 19 December 1963, Thomson Papers, Southeast Asia Box 21, folder S.E. Asia, Cambodia 1959–1966.
30. Sprouse to SS, 12 December 1963, Tel. 500, Johnson Papers, NSF-CO., Box 236, folder Cambodia Cables, Vol. I.
31. Milton Osborne, Sihanouk: Prince of Light, Prince of Darkness (Honolulu: University of Hawaii Press, 1994), 164.
32. Sprouse to SS, 12 February 1964, Tel. 776, RG 59, CFPF 1964–1966, Box 1974, folder Political Affairs & Rels CAMB-US 1/1/64, NAII.
33. "SEATO Brief—Cambodia," n.d., Series No. A1838/280, Control Symbol 3016/2/1 Part 16, NAA.
34. Interview with Ambassador Noël St. Clair Deschamps by Kenton J. Clymer, 19–20 June 1999, at the Commonwealth Club, Canberra, ACT, Australia. Institute of Oral History, University of Texas at El Paso.
35. Deschamps to Keith Waller, 24 March 1964, Series No. A1838/280, Control Symbol 3016/2/1 Part 16, NAA.
36. Rusk to U.S. Embassy Saigon, 9 January 1964, Tel. 1050, Johnson Papers, NSF-Country File, Box 236, folder Cambodia Cables, Vol I.
37. [Canadian ICC Commissioner] Phnom Penh to EXAF, Ottawa, 20 March 1964, Series No. 1838/280, Control Symbol 3016/2/1 Part 16, NAA.
38. Michael Forrestal, Memorandum for the President, 21 March 1964, Johnson Papers, WHCF-Confidential File, Box 7, folder CO 40—Cambodia. Bergesen to USDS, 27 March 1964, Airgram A-487, RG 59, CFPF 1964–1966, Box 1967, folder POL 2-1, NAA.
39. Deschamps to EXAF, 21 March 1964, Tel. 116, Series No. 1838/280, Control Symbol 3016/2/1 Part 16, NAA.
40. Deschamps to Keith Waller, 24 March 1964, Series No. 1838/280, Control Symbol 3016/2/1 Part 16, NAA.
41. Sihanouk, letter to Time, in USDS to U.S. Embassy Phnom Penh, 6 May 1964, Airgram CA-11531, RG 59, CFPF 1964–1966, Box 1969, POL 15-1 CAMB 4/1/64, NAII.
42. Ian E. Nicholson to Secretary EXAF, 10 February 1965, Memorandum 84, Series No. 1838/334, Control Symbol 3016/11/161 Part 6, NAA.
43. Alf E. Bergesen to Hirschfeld, 6 November 1964, RG 59, CFPF 1964–1966, Box 1974, folder Political Affairs & Rels CAMB-US 7/1/64, NAII.
44. Mike Mansfield to Johnson, 9 December 1964, Johnson Papers, WHCF-Confidential File, Box 44, folder CO 312-Vietnam (1964–1965).
45. EXAF to Deschamps, 3 December 1974, Tel. 259, Series No. A1209/128, Control Symbol 61/1304, NAA.
46. James C. Thomson Jr. to Harriman, 4 August 1966, Thomson Papers, SEA, Box 21, folder S.E. Asia Cambodia 1959–1966.
47. L. Douglas Heck to USDS, 11 February 1965, Airgram A-844, RG 59, SNF 1964–1966, Box 1970, folder POL 15-1, NAII.
48. Bergesen to USDS, 9 March 1965, Airgram A-200, RG 59, SNF 1964–1966, Box 1967, folder POL 2-1, NAII.

49. Bergesen to SS, 25 April 1965, Tel. 632, Johnson Papers, NSF-Country File, Box 236, folder Cambodia Cables Vol III 8/64–6/65.

50. Rusk to U.S. Embassies Bangkok and Vientiane, 26 April 1965, Tel. 1794 (to Bangkok), RG 59, SNF 1964–1966, Box 1969, folder POL 8 Neutralism Non-Alignment CAMB, NAII.

51. CIA, Office of Current Intelligence, Intelligence Memorandum 1201/65, 26 April 1965, Johnson Papers, NSF-Country File, Box 236, folder Cambodia Cables, Vol. III.

52. Bergesen to SS, 26 April 1965, Tels. 636 and 637, RG 59, SNF 1964–66, Box 1970, folder POL 23 CAMB Internal Security, Counter-Insurgency, 1/1/64, NAII.

53. Bergesen to SS, 26 April 1965, Tels. 638 and 639, RG 59, SNF 1964–66, Box 1970, folder POL 23 CAMB Internal Security, Counter-Insurgency, 1/1/64, NAII.

54. Charles Bohlen to SS, 13 May 1965, Tel. 6451, RG 59, SNF 1964–1966, Box 1969, folder POL 8 Neutralism Non-Alignment CAMB, NAII.

5—Prelude to Tragedy

1. Interview with Ambassador Deschamps. Rusk to Paul Hasluck, 4 September 1965, in personal possession of Noël Deschamps.

2. Robert Shaplen, "Letter from Cambodia," *New Yorker,* 17 September 1966, 6.

3. Deschamps to Secretary EXAF, 30 June 1967, Memorandum 325, Series No. A1838/280, Control Symbol 3016/7/1 Part 6, NAII.

4. Deschamps to Secretary EXAF, 22 December 1965, Memorandum 574, Series No. A1838/334, Control Symbol 3016/11/161 Part 7, NAA.

5. Qiang Zhai, "China and the Cambodian Conflict, 1970–1975" (unpublished manuscript), 6–7. Qiang Zhai, communication with the author, 18 September 2001. The evidence for the 10 percent agreement in 1964 comes from interviews conducted by Nayan Chanda and David Chandler. The evidence for the agreement in 1965 allowing Vietnamese communist forces to take refuge in Cambodia, to establish base camps there, and to allow the passage of materials sent from China is a published summary of the military agreement. See Marie Alexandrine Martin, *Cambodia: A Shattered Society* (Berkeley: University of California Press, 1994), 92–93.

6. Johnson's handwritten notes on Rostow to Johnson, 20 June 1966, Johnson Papers, Box 237, folder NSF-Country File, folder Cambodia Vol. IV. Stanley Karnow, "U.S. Curbs Operations at Cambodia Border," *Washington Post,* 22 June 1966.

7. Deschamps to EXAF, 21 June 1966, Tel. 346, Series A1838/280, Control Symbol 3016/7/1 Part 7, NAA. Rostow to Johnson, 19 July 1966, Johnson Papers, NSF—Country File, Box 237, folder Cambodia Vol. IV.

8. Henry Cabot Lodge to SS, 5 August 1966, Tel. 2804, RG 59, SNF 1964–66, folder POL 32-1 CAMB-VIETS 6/1/66, NAII. W. Walton Butterworth to SS, 6 August 1966, Tel. 197, RG 59, SNF 1964–66, Box 1979, folder POL 32-1 CAMB-VIETS 6/1/66, NAII.

9. Quoted in Butterworth to SS, 6 August 1966, Tel. 197, RG 59, SNF 1964–66, Box 1979, folder POL 32-1 CAMB-VIETS 6/1/66, NAII.

10. Australian Embassy Phnom Penh to EXAF, 12 August 1966, Tel. 497, Series No. A1838/334, Control Symbol 3016/11/161 Part 9, NAA.

11. Cited in Deschamps to EXAF, 9 August 1966, Tel. 482, Series No. A1838/334, Control Symbol 3016/11/161 Part 9, NAA.

12. Shaplen, "Letter from Cambodia," 2. R. H. Robertson to P. C. J. Curtis, 7 December 1966, Series No. A1838/334, Control Symbol 3016/11/161 Part 11, NAA.

13. Australian Embassy Phnom Penh to EXAF, 12 October 1966, Tel. 691, Series No. A1838/334, Control Symbol 3016/11/161 Part 10, NAA.

14. Australian Embassy Paris to EXAF, 28 February 1967, Savingram 9, Series No. 1838/334, Control Symbol 3016/11/161 Part 11, NAA.

15. Deschamps to EXAF, 12 January 1967, Tel. 32, Prime Minister's Department, Series No. A1209/80, Control Symbol 67/7031, NAA.

16. Forrestal to Rusk, 8 November 1967, Declassified Documents Series 1996070101946.

17. William Westmoreland to Earl Wheeler, 5 December 1967, Tel. JCS 660/5, Johnson Papers, NSF, Country File: Vietnam, folder Vietnam/Cambodia 5E (1) a, Boxes 92–94.

18. "Notes of the President's Meeting with Secretary Rusk, Secretary McNamara, General Wheeler, CIA Director Helms, Clark Clifford, Abe Fortas, Walt Rostow, George Christian, Tom Johnson," 5 December 1967, Johnson Papers, Tom Johnson's Notes of Meetings, Box 1.

19. Australian Embassy Phnom Penh to EXAF, 8 January 1968, Tel. 34, Series No. 1838/280, Control Symbol 3016/9/4 Part 9, NAA.

20. New Zealand Embassy Washington D.C. to EXAF Wellington, 6 January 1968, Tel. 31, Series No. 1838/387, Control Symbol 3016/11/161 Part 14, NAA.

21. USDS, "The Bowles Mission to Cambodia January 8–12, 1968," 20 May 1968, RG 59, SNF 1967–1969, Box 2609, folder POL 7 US-BOWLES 1/1/68, NAII.

22. Bowles–Son Sann Joint Communique, in U.S. Embassy Bangkok to SS, 12 January 1968, Tel. 411, RG 59, SNF 1967–1969, Box 1804, folder POL 27-14 CAMB 1/1/68, NAII. Some in the State Department regretted Bowles's use of the word "aggression" since it seemed to imply that American actions in the past constituted aggression.

23. Quoted in George Ball to SS, 3 July 1968, Tel. 5849, RG 59, SNF 1967–1969, Box 1934, folder POL 32-1 CAMB-VIET S 7/1/68, NAII.

24. Godley, quoted in Australian Embassy Washington D.C. to EXAF, 16 September 1968, Tel. 4571, Series No. A1838/280, Control Symbol 3016/10/1/2/3 Part 1, NAA. Rostow to Johnson, 16 September 1968, Johnson Papers, NSF-Country File, Box 237. Memorandum of Conversations, Deschamps and Edwin M. Cronk, 27 September 1968, enclosed in Cronk to USDS, 9 October 1968, Airgram A-809, RG 59, SNF 1967–1969, Box 1803, folder Political Affairs & Rels CAMB 1/1/67, NAA.

25. "Press conference by Prince Sihanouk on 8 August in Damnak Chamcar Mon Palace, Phnom Penh," 12 August 1968, Series No. 1838/280, Control Symbol 3016/10/1/2/3 Part 1, NAA.

26. Deschamps to EXAF, 11 November 1968, Tel. 1449, Series No. 1838/357, Control Symbol 250/10/7/12 Part 3, NAA.

27. "Talk by Prince Sihanouk with Buddhist Monks at the Monastery of Po Veal in Battambang Province on the Occasion of the late Venerable Iv Tuot, Buddhist Patriarch of Battambang, on 25 December 1968," FBIS 23, Johnson Papers, NSF-Country File: Vietnam, Boxes 92–94, folder Vietnam/Cambodia 5E (3) 11/68–1/69.

28. Deschamps to EXAF, 31 December 1968, Tel. 1701, Series No. A1838/280, Control Symbol 3016/2/1 Part 22, NAA.

6—Richard Nixon and Cambodia

1. Mike Mansfield to Richard Nixon, 2 May 1969, NPM, WHCF-CO Files, folder CO 26 Cambodia, 6/1/70.

2. Interview with Ambassador Deschamps.

3. Taylor Branch, "The Scandal That Got Away," [MORE] Magazine, October 1973, 17.

4. Handwritten note by Mr. Pocock on Australian Embassy Phnom Penh to EXAF, 15 August 1969, Tel. 1509, Series No. 1838/334, Control Symbol 3016/11/161 Part 19, NAA.

5. C. G. Woodard to Secretary EXAF 21 July 1969, Memo 867/69, Series No. A1838/334, Control Symbol 3106/11/161 Part 19, NAA.

6. Lloyd M. Rives to USDS, 8 September 1969, Airgram A-9, Declassified Documents Series.

7. Earle G. Wheeler to Secretary of Defense, 11 April 1969, CM-4101-69, Declassified Documents Series.

8. Wheeler to Secretary of Defense, 9 April 1969, JCSM-207-69, Declassified Documents Series. Wheeler to Secretary of Defense, 11 April 1969, CM-4101-69, Declassified Documents Series. Kissinger, quoted in William Shawcross, *Sideshow: Kissinger, Nixon and the Destruction of Cambodia,* 2nd ed. (New York: Simon & Schuster, 1987), 28. Nixon, presidential news conference, 22 August 1973, quoted in Impeachment Inquiry Staff Committee on the Judiciary of the House of Representative, "Statement of Information Concerning the Bombing of Cambodia," Hutchinson Papers, Box 35, folder Statement—Concerning the Bombing of Cambodia.

9. Sour Bun Sou, "One Aspect of Negative Effect of American Bombing . . . ," 4 January 2000, unpublished manuscript, DCC. Truong Nhu Tang, *A Viet Cong Memoir* (New York: Vintage Books, 1985), 182.

10. Australian Embassy Phnom Penh to EXAF, 23 December 1969, Tel. 2129, Series No. A1838/334, Control Symbol 3016/11/161 Part 21, NAA.

11. Sour Bun Sou, "One Aspect of Negative Effect of American Bombing." Truong Nhu Tang, *Viet Cong Memoir,* 185. Arnold Isaacs, *Without Honor: Defeat in Vietnam and Cambodia* (Baltimore: Johns Hopkins University Press, 1983), 195.

12. "Cambodian Perspectives," March 1975, Ford Papers, Robert K. Wolthius Files, Box 1, folder Cambodian Fact Sheet; Evacuation of Phnom Penh.

13. Leonard Unger (for Bowles) to SS, 10 January 1968, Tel. 8561, RG 59, SNF 1967–1969, Box 2610, folder POL 7 US-Bowles 1/1/67, NAII.

14. Samuel R. Berger to SS, 5 April 1969, Tel. 6520, RG 59, SNF 1967–1969, Box 1930, folder Political Affairs & Rels CAMB-US 1/1/69, NAII.

15. Henry Kissinger, *White House Years* (Boston: Little, Brown, 1979), 251. A FBIS translation of the press conference is included in NPM, NSC files, Box 11 (HAKOF), folder Cambodia—Cambodia Bombing, NAII.

16. FBIS translation of the press conference, NPM, NSC files, Box 11 (HAKOF), folder Cambodia—Cambodia Bombing, NAII. Kissinger, *White House Years,* 251.

17. Mansfield to Sihanouk, 6 September 1973, RG 59, SNF 1967–1969, Box 2155, folder POL 15, CAMB 8/30/73, NAII.

18. Nixon to Sihanouk, in William Rogers to U.S. Embassies Bangkok, Saigon, and Vientiane, 15 February 1969, Tel. 24759, RG 59, SNF 1967–1969, Box 1930, File Political Affairs & Rels. CAMB-US 1/1/69, NAII.

19. Rogers to U.S. Embassies Bangkok, Saigon, and Vientiane, 15 February 1969, Tel. 24759, RG 59, SNF 1967–1969, Box 1930, folder Political Affairs & Rels CAMB-US, 1/1/69, NAII.

20. Interview with Ambassador Deschamps.

21. Australian Embassy Phnom Penh to Australian Embassy Washington, 29 May 1969, Tel. 375, Series No. A1838/361, Control Symbol 589/21/3/1 Part 1, NAA.

22. Bunker to SS, 7 September 1971, Tel. 14311, RG 59, SNF 1970–73, Box 2155H, folder POL 27-10 CAMB, NAII.

23. Rives to SS in Australian Embassy Phnom Penh to Australian Embassy Washington, 29 November 1969, Tel. 943 (U.S. Tel. 202), Series No. A1838/334, Control Symbol 3016/11/161 Part 21, NAA.

24. Marshall Green to Rogers, 26 November 1969, 18443, RG 59, SNF 1967–1969, Box 1931, folder POL 31-1, CAMB-US, 1/1/68, NAII.

25. Graeme Feakes to EXAF, 8 September 1969, Tel. 1634, Series No. A1838/334, Control Symbol 3016/11/161 Part 19, NAA.

26. Rives to SS in Australian Embassy Phnom Penh to Australian Embassy Washington, 25 November 1969, Tel. 913 (to EXAF 1989), Series No. A1838/334, Control Symbol 3016/11/161 Part 21, NAA.

27. Memorandum of Conversation, Suharto and Nixon, 26 May 1970, enclosed in Alexander M. Haig to Theodore L. Eliot Jr., 3 June 1970, RG 59, SNF 1970–73, Box 2372, folder POL 7 INDON 6/1/70, NAII.

28. H. R. Haldeman, *The Haldeman Diaries: Inside the White House* (New York: G. P. Putnam, 1994), 143.

29. Walter Isaacson, *Kissinger: A Biography* (New York: Simon & Schuster, 1992), 273. I am grateful to columnist William Pfaff for calling this quotation to my attention. See William Pfaff, "Cambodia Invasion Reminder of U.S. Political Use of Military," *Chicago Tribune*, 23 April 2000.

30. *Antara*, quoted in Francis Joseph Galbraith to SS, 23 April 1970, Tel. 2872, RG 59, SNF 1970–1973, Box 2372, folder POL 7 INDON 4/1/70, NAII.

31. U.S. Embassy Jakarta to SS, 26 April 1970, Tel. 2931, RG 59, SNF 1970–1973, Box 2372, folder POL 7 INDON 4/1/70, NAII.

32. USDS to U.S. Embassies Bangkok, Jakarta, Phnom Penh, and Saigon, 23 April 1970, Tel. 61378, RG 59, SNF 1970–1973, Box 2155J, folder POL 27 CAMB-KHMER 4/20/70, NAII.

33. Berger to SS, 5 May 1970, Tel. 6853, NPM, NSC Files, Box 589, Cambodian Operations (1970), folder CAMBODIA NODIS/KHMER, NAII.

34. Intelligence Brief INRB-94, 13 April 1970, RG 59, SNF 1970–1973, Box 2817, folder POL 27 VIET S 4/1/70, NAII.

35. See Haldeman's handwritten notes of a meeting with Rogers, Laird, Kissinger, and the president in the Executive Office Building, 27 April 1970, in NPM, Haldeman Handwritten Notes, Box 41, folder H. Notes 4/70–6/70 [4/1/70–5/5/70], Part I, NAII.

36. "Address to the Nation on the Situation in Southeast Asia. April 30, 1970," *Public Papers of the Presidents of the United States: Richard Nixon, 1970* (Washington, DC: Government Printing Office, 1971), 407.

37. Haldeman Handwritten Notes, 2 May [1970], NPM, NSC Files, Box 41, folder H. Notes from 4/70–6/70 [5/1–5/5/70], Part I, NAII.

38. Galbraith to SS, 1 May 1970, Tel. 3116, RG 59, SNF 1970–1973, Box 2155B, folder POL 27 CAMB 5/1/70, NAII. Memorandum of Conversation, Suharto, Nixon, Kissinger, 26 May 1970, enclosed in Haig to Eliot, 3 June 1970, RG 59, SNF 1970–73, Box 2372, folder POL 7 INDON 6/1/70, NAII.

39. Christopher Emmet, "The Missing Element in the Cambodian Debate" (typescript), n.d., Ford Papers, Vice Presidential Papers, Box 1970, folder Foreign Affairs.

40. Harlan Cleveland to Nixon, 4 May 1970, RG 59, SNF 1970–1973, Box 2155D, folder POL 27 CAMB 5/13/70, NAII.

41. Haldeman Notes, 3 May 1970, NPM, Haldeman Handwritten Notes, Box 41, folder H. Notes from 4/70–6/70 [4/1/70–5/5/70], Part I, NAII.

42. Haldeman to Lyn Nofziger, 14 May 1970, NPM, Haldeman Handwritten Notes, Box 60, Office & Memoranda Files: Alpha Name, folder 5/70–6/70 N–Z, NAII.

43. Haldeman Notes, 7 May, 13 May 1970, NPM, Haldeman Handwritten Notes, Box 41, folder H. Notes 4/70–6/70 [5/6/70–6/30/70], Part II, NAII.

44. Rives to SS, 8 June 1970, Tel. 1171, NPM, Box 589, NSC Files: Cambodia Operations (1970), folder Cambodia: NODIS/KHMER, CHRON Vol. III, NAII.

45. U.S. Embassy Phnom Penh to SS, 9 June 1970, Tel. 1176, Nixon Papers, Box 589, NSC Files: Cambodian Operations (1970), folder Cambodia: NODIS/KHMER, CHRON Vol. III: 5/26/70–6/10/70, NAII.

46. "Washington Special Actions Group Meeting with the President," 15 June 1970, in Kissinger to U. Alexis Johnson, David Packard, Thomas H. Moorer, and Richard Helms, 17 June 1970, NPM, NSC Files, Box 13, folder Cambodia, NAII.

47. Galbraith to SS, 18 May 1970, Tel. 3599, RG 59, SNF 1970–1973, Box 2372, folder POL 7 INDO 5/16/70, NAII.

48. Emory Swank to SS, 20 May 1972, Tel. 3074, SNF 1970–1973, Box 1694, folder DEF 13 CAMB 1/1/70, NAII.

49. Transcript, Senior Review Group Meeting, 15 September 1970, Ford Papers, National Security Adviser, NSC Staff for East Asian and Pacific Affairs: Convenience

Files, Box 2, folder Cambodia—NSSM 99 (1).

50. Transcript, Senior Review Group Meeting, 15 September 1970, Ford Papers, National Security Adviser, NSC Staff for East Asian and Pacific Affairs: Convenience Files, Box 2, folder Cambodia—NSSM 99 (1).

51. Kissinger, Press Briefing, 30 June 1970, p. 3, NPM, NSC files, Box 586, folder Cambodia—White Paper, Final Report, 3 June 70, NAII.

52. James G. Lowenstein and Richard M. Moose, "Cambodia: December 1970," *Congressional Record—Senate,* 16 December 1970, S 20290.

53. Diary Entry, Merle Graven, 31 October 1970, RG 809—Cambodia, Box 4, folder 10, CMAA. Rives to SS (for Swank), 18 August 1970, Tel. 2037, RG 59, SNF 1970–1973, Box 2155M, folder POL 1 CAMB-US, NAII.

7—Sticking with Lon Nol

1. Swank to SS, 11 November 1972, Tel. 7801, RG 59, SNF 1970–73, Box 2155A, folder POL 15-1 CAMB 6/22/72, NAII.

2. Lon Nol to Nixon, 31 December 1970, enclosed in U.S. Embassy Phnom Penh to USDS, 6 January 1971, Airgram A-4, RG 59, SNF 1970–73, Box 2155F, folder POL 27 CAMB 1/1/71, NAII.

3. Swank to SS, 7 January 1971, Tel. 72, RG 59, SNF 1970–73, Box 2155F, folder POL 27 CAMB 1/1/71, NAII.

4. Swank to SS, 22 January 1971, Tel. 280, RG 59, SNF 1970–73, Box 2155F, folder POL 27 CAMB 1/1/71, NAII.

5. Jack W. Lydman to SS, 10 January 1971, Tel. 548, RG 59, SNF 1970–73, Box 2154, folder POL 7 CAMB 1/1/71, NAII.

6. Haldeman Notes, 29 January 1971, 8 February 1971, 9 February 1971, NPM, Haldeman Handwritten Notes, Box 43, folder H. Notes January–March 1971, Part I [1/1/71–2/15/71], NAII.

7. Haldeman Notes, 19 February 1971, Box 43, folder H. Notes January–March 1971, Part II [2/15/71–3/10/71], NAII. It is possible that the comments about Kissinger's staff are Haig's rather than Nixon's. The notes are not entirely clear on this point.

8. Memorandum of Conversation with Sim Var, 13 July 1971, U.S. Embassy Phnom Penh to USDS, 13 July 1971, Airgram A-101, RG 59, SNF 1970–73, Box 2155J, folder POL CAMB-INDIA, NAII.

9. Sam Adams, "Vietnam Cover-Up: Playing War with Numbers," *Harper's,* May 1975, 72. Because of his estimates respecting both the Viet Cong and the Khmer insurgents, Adams was progressively isolated within the agency and eventually resigned. He contended that there was strong political pressure to keep the numbers unrealistically—and dishonestly—low.

10. USDS to U.S. Embassy Phnom Penh, 3 July 1971, Tel. 120357, RG 59, SNF 1970–73, Box 1852, folder DEF 19 US-CAMB 1/1/71, NAII.

11. Wilfred P. Deac, *Road to the Killing Fields: The Cambodia War of 1970–1975* (College Station, TX: Texas A & M University Press, 1997), 114–17.

12. Swank to SS, 25 July 1971, Tel. 3606, RG 59, SNF 1970–73, Box 2155G, folder POL 27 CAMB 5/1/71, NAII.

13. U.S. Embassy Rome to SS, 14 December 1971, Tel. 7829, RG 59, SNF 1970–73, Box 2155L, folder POL 30-2 CAMB 1/2/71, NAII.

14. Beam to SS, 21 January 1972, Tel. 638, RG 59, SNF 1970–73, Box 2155L, folder POL CAMB-US 1/32 [sic]/72, NAII.

15. Quoted in Chandler, *Tragedy,* 213.

16. Swank to SS, 4 February 1972, Tel. 722, RG 59, SNF 1970–73, Box 2155G, folder POL 27 CAMB 1/1/72, NAII.

17. Swank to SS, 24 February 1972, Tel. 1068, RG 59, SNF 1970–73, Box 2155M, folder POL CAMB VIET N, NAII.

18. Telegram to U.S. Embassy Phnom Penh, attached to R. T. Curran, Memorandum for the Record, 6 March 1972, RG 59, SNF 1970–73, Box 2155G, folder POL 27 CAMB 1/1/72, NAII.

19. Swank to SS, 10 March 1972, Tel. 1420, RG 59, SNF 1970–73, Box 2155H, folder POL 27-14 CAMB, NAII.

20. "Cambodia: Military Assessment," NSSM 152, 20 April 1972, Ford Papers, National Security Adviser: NSC Staff for East Asian and Pacific Affairs: Convenience Files, Box 2, folder CAMB—NSSM 152 (3).

21. "Cambodia: Political Stability and Prospects for Change and Implications for the Military Situation," NSSM 152, 24 April 1972, Ford Papers, National Security Adviser: NSC Staff for East Asian and Pacific Affairs: Convenience Files, Box 2, folder CAMB—NSSM 152 (5).

22. Thomas Enders to SS, 17 September 1972, Tel. 6191, RG 59, SNF 1970–1973, Box 2155A, folder POL 15-1 CAMB 6/22/72, NAII.

23. Chandler, *Tragedy*, 221. Swank to USDS, 20 February 1973, Airgram A-29, RG 59, SNF 1970–1973, Box 2155H, folder POL 27 CAMB 3/15/73, NAII.

24. Justin J. Corfield, *Khmers Stand Up! A History of the Cambodian Government 1970–1975* (Melbourne: Monash University Centre of Southeast Asian Studies, 1994), 150–51.

25. Enders to SS, 5 October 1972, Tel. 6766, RG 59, SNF 1970–1973, Box 2155, folder POL 15 CAMB 12/8/70, NAII.

26. Enders to SS, 7 October 1972, Tel. 6812, RG 59, SNF 1970–73, Box 2155H, folder POL 27 CAMB 7/1/72, NAII.

27. Briefing Paper, "Cambodia: Issues and Talking Points," enclosed in Theodore L. Eliot Jr. to Kissinger, 27 January 1973, NPM, NSC Files, Box 952, folder Vice-President's SEA Visit, 1/28/73–2/10/73 [1 of 3], NAII.

28. William Shawcross, "The Third Indochina War," *New York Review of Books*, 6 April 1978, 16.

29. "Cambodia Background," enclosed with Kissinger to Spiro Agnew, 30 January 1973, NPM, NSC Files, Box 952, folder Vice-President's SEA Visit, 1/28/73–2/10/73 [2 of 3], NAII.

30. Memorandum of Conversation, Lon Nol, Hang Tun Hak, Alexander Haig, Emory Swank, Thomas Enders, and John Negroponte, 12 November 1972; included in Negroponte to Haig, n.d., Ford Papers, National Security Adviser, NSC East Asian and Pacific Affairs Staff: Files (1969), 1973–1976, Box 15, folder Lon Nol (1) [Cambodia].

31. Shawcross, "The Third Indochina War," 22.

32. Swank to SS, 13 February 1973, Tel. 1319, RG 59, SNF 1970–73, Box 2155I, folder POL 30-2 CAMB 2/2/73, NAII. David L. Osborn to SS, 13 February 1973, Tel. 1425, RG 59, SNF 1970–73, Box 2155I, folder POL 27-14 CAMB 11/30/72, NAII.

33. Memcon, Zhou Enlai, Henry Kissinger, et al., 16 February 1973, in William Burr, ed., *The Kissinger Transcripts: The Top Secret Talks with Beijing and Moscow* (New York: New Press, 1998), 104–5.

34. Swank to SS, 6 March 1973, Tel. 2027, RG 59, SNF 1970–73, Box 2155, folder POL 15 CAMB 1/25/73, NAII.

35. USDS to U.S. Embassy Phnom Penh (Green to Swank), 8 March 1973, Tel. 43233, RG 59, SNF 1970–73, Box 2155, folder POL 15 CAMB 1/25/73, NAII.

36. Swank to SS (eyes only for Green), 9 March 1973, Tel. 2141, RG 59, SNF 1970–73, Box 2155, folder POL 15 CAMB 1/25/73, NAII.

37. USDS to US Embassy Phnom Penh, 15 March 1973, Tel. 47710, RG 59, SNF 1970–73, Box 2155A, folder POL 15-1 CAMB 1/3/73, NAII.

38. Swank to SS, 16 March 1973, Tel. 2355, RG 59, SNF 1970–73, Box 2155, folder POL 15 CAMB 1/25/73, NAII.

39. Swank to SS, 20 March 1973, Tel. 2507, RG 59, SNF 1970–73, Box 2153, folder POL 2 CAMB 1/2/73, NAII.

40. Swank to SS, 31 March 1973, Tel. 3016, RG 59, SNF 1970–73, Box 2155A, folder POL 15-1 CAMB 1/3/73, NAII.

41. Henry Kissinger, *Years of Upheaval* (Boston: Little, Brown, 1982), 346–47.

42. "Cambodian Negotiations—1973," Ford Papers, National Security Adviser, Kissinger-Scowcroft West Wing Office Files, 1969–1977, Box 1. Kissinger, *Years of Upheaval*, 350.

43. Osborn to SS, 27 April 1973, Tel. 4141, RG 59, SNF 1970–73, Box 2155I, folder POL 30-2 CAMB 2/2/73, NAII.

44. Deac, *Road to the Killing Fields,* 159.

45. Graven, Report on Conditions, 17 July 1973; T. G. Mangham Jr. to L. L. King, 25 July 1973; [Graven ?] to T. Grady Mangham, 7 August 1973, all in C&MA Records, RG 809–CAMB Box 4, folder 14, CMAA.

46. Ben Kiernan, "The Impact on Cambodia of the U.S. Intervention in Vietnam," in Jayne S. Werner and Luu Doan Huynh, eds., *The Vietnam War: Vietnamese and American Perspectives* (New York: Armonk, 1993), 216–29.

47. "Presidential Authority to Continue United States Air Combat Operations in Cambodia," enclosed in Eliot to John M. Dunn, 26 April 1973, RG 59, SNF 1970–73, Box 2155H, folder POL 27 CAMB 4/10/73, NAII.

48. *Hearing before the House Armed Services Committee,* 8 May 1973 (H.A.S.C. No. 93–10), 14–17. Copy in Ford Papers, Vice-Presidential Papers, Box 138, folder CAMB. "What Is the Real Situation in Cambodia?" enclosed in Gerald R. Ford and Elford A. Cederberg to Congressional Republicans, 8 May 1973, Ford Congressional Papers, Robert Hartman Files, 1965–1973, Subject File, Biographies (GRF), Box 1220, folder CAMB 1973.

49. Joint Chiefs of Staff, "Cambodia Assessment," enclosed in Robert N. Ginsburgh to the Secretary of Defense, 28 August 1974, Ford Papers, National Security Adviser, Presidential Country Files for East Asia and the Pacific, 1974–1977, Box 2, folder CAMB (2).

50. Kenneth Quinn, e-mail message to the author, 30 December 2002.

51. William E. Timmons to Nixon, 10 May 1973, NPM, Haldeman Files, Box 281, Staff Member and Office Files, folder L. Higby-Misc [Misc. Correspondence, 1972–1973], NAII.

52. Stuart W. Rockwell to SS, 30 May 1973, Tel. 2454, RG 59, SNF 1970–73, Box 2155I, folder POL 30-2 CAMB 2/2/73, NAII.

53. Richard W. Murphy to SS, 31 May 1973, Tel. 452, RG 59, SNF 1970–73, Box 2155I, folder POL 27-14 CAMB 11/30/72, NAII.

54. USDS to U.S. Embassy Conakry, 19 May 1973, Tel. 96590, RG 59, SNF 1970–73, Box 2155I, folder POL 27-14 CAMB 11/30/72, NAII. Murphy to SS, 16 June 1973, Tel. 480, RG 59, SNF 1970–73, Box 2155I, folder POL 27-14 CAMB 11/30/72, NAII. Memorandum of Conversation, Kissinger, Brent Scowcroft et al., 19 July 1973, in Burr, ed., *The Kissinger Transcripts,* 152.

55. "Cambodian Negotiations—1973," Ford Papers, National Security Adviser, Kissinger-Scowcroft West Wing Office Files, 1969–1977, Box 1. Kissinger, *White House Years,* 351–52.

56. Kissinger, *Years of Upheaval,* 352.

57. Kissinger, *White House Years,* 352–55.

58. Ibid., 354. "Cambodian Negotiations—1973," Ford Papers, National Security Adviser, Kissinger-Scowcroft West Wing Office Files, 1969–1977, Box 1.

59. Burr, ed., *The Kissinger Transcripts,* 147.

60. Kissinger, *White House Years,* 363–64.

61. Burr, ed., *The Kissinger Transcripts,* 149–51.

62. The Habib press conference is recorded in SS to U.S. Embassy Phnom Penh, 5 March 1975, Tel. 49889, DCC.

63. Kissinger, *White House Years*, 361–62.

64. Memorandum of Conversation, Lew Kuan Yew, Kissinger et al., 4 August 1973, Ford Papers, NSC Convenience Files, Copies of Materials from the U.S. Embassy Saigon: 1963–75 (1976), Box 10, folder Memcon Singapore, 8/4/73 (1).

65. Oral remarks of Cambodian ambassador Um Sim, in Richard T. Kennedy to Kissinger, 28 August 1973, NPM, WHCF-CO Files, Box 14, folder CO26 CAMB 1/1/73, NAII.

66. Memorandum of Conversation, Lew Kuan Yew, Kissinger et al., 4 August 1973, Ford Papers, NSC Convenience Files, Copies of Materials from the U.S. Embassy Saigon: 1963–75 (1976), Box 10, folder Memcon Singapore, 8/4/73 (1).

67. Deac, *Road to the Killing Fields*, 180.

68. Memorandum of Conversation, Long Boret, Kissinger et al., 4 October 1973, RG 59, SNF 1970–73, Box 2155, folder POL 15 CAMB 8/30/73, NAII.

69. Memorandum of Conversation, Kissinger, Zhou et al., 13 November 1973, in Burr, ed., *The Kissinger Transcripts*, 203. Memorandum of Conversation, Kissinger, Zhou et al., 14 November 1973, in ibid., 208.

70. Memorandum of Conversation, Kissinger, Zhou et al., 13 November 1973, in ibid., 203.

71. "Few Tears for Richard Nixon in Cambodia," *Cambodia Daily*, 25 April 1994. The publisher of this newspaper was Bernard Krisher, whose article in *Newsweek* in 1965 was the ostensible cause of the break in diplomatic relations.

8—Dénouement

1. Enders to Graham Martin, 7 January 1974, Tel. 747, Ford Papers, NSC Convenience Files, Copies of Materials from the U.S. Embassy, Saigon: 1968–75 (1976), Box 7, folder Saigon to Washington, 1/7/74–12/3/74.

2. Ambassador Bryce Harland, New Zealand Embassy Beijing, to Secretary of Foreign Affairs, 10 April 1974, in DCC. Cross to SS, 28 May 1974, Tel. 5974, Ford Papers, National Security Adviser, NSC Vietnam Information Group: Intelligence and Other Reports, 1967–1975, folder Cambodian Communist Terrorism 1973–75 (3).

3. Martin to Kissinger, 21 June 1974, Tels. 0622 and 0617 (Martin Channel), Ford Papers, NSC Convenience Files, Copies of Materials from the U.S. Embassy, Saigon: 1968–75 (1976), Box 6, folder Saigon to Washington, 1/12/74–11/21/74 (3).

4. W. Richard Smyser to Kissinger, 6 September 1974, Ford Papers, National Security Adviser, Presidential Country Files for East Asia and the Pacific, 1974–1977, Box 2, folder CAMB (1).

5. Jim B. to Les [Aspin?], 18 October [1974], Ford Papers, National Security Adviser, Presidential Country Files for East Asia and the Pacific, 1974–1977, Box 2, folder CAMB (3).

6. Smyser to Kissinger, 13 September 1974, Ford Papers, National Security Adviser, Presidential Country Files for East Asia and the Pacific, 1974–1977, Box 2, folder CAMB (1).

7. Memorandum of Conversation, Adam Malik, Ford, Kissinger et al., 25 September 1974, Ford Papers, National Security Adviser: Memoranda of Conversations, Box 6, folder 9/25/74—Ford, Kissinger . . . Malik.

8. John Gunther Dean to U.S. Legation Peking, 25 November 1974, Tel. 15663, Ford Papers, National Security Adviser, Presidential Country Files for East Asia and the Pacific, 1974–1977, Box 4, folder CAMB—State Department Telegrams to SECSTATE-NODIS (1).

9. Memorandum of Conversation, Deng Xiaoping, Henry Kissinger et al., 27 November 1974, 3:36 p.m.–5:45 p.m., RG 59, Policy Planning Staff (Director's Files), 1969–77, Box 371, "Secretary Kissinger's Talks in China, 25–29 Nov. 1974," NAII.

10. Memorandum of Conversation, Deng Xiaoping, Henry Kissinger et al., 27

November 1974, 3:36 p.m.–5:45 p.m., RG 59, Policy Planning Staff (Director's Files), 1969–77, Box 371, folder Secretary Kissinger's Talks in China, 11/25–29/74, NAII.

11. Memorandum for the Record, Ford, Nelson Rockefeller, James R. Schlesinger, George Brown, Bipartisan Congressional Leadership, 28 January 1975, Ford Papers, National Security Adviser, Memoranda of Conversations, 1973–1977, Box 8, folder 1/8/75—Ford, Kissinger, Rockefeller, Bipartisan Congressional Leadership. "Summary of Negotiating Efforts on Cambodia," Nessen Papers, Box 12, folder Indochina-Cambodia.

12. This account of the French intervention is taken from Shawcross, *Sideshow,* 335–43. The documentary record, not available to Shawcross, confirms his analysis of the initiative.

13. Memorandum of Conversation, Ford, Kissinger, Scowcroft, 11 April 1975, Ford Papers, National Security Adviser, Memoranda of Conversations, Box 10, folder 4/11/75—Ford, Kissinger. Shawcross, *Sideshow,* 343.

14. Dean to SS, 4 February 1975, Tel. 2113, Ford Papers, National Security Adviser, Presidential Country Files for East Asia and the Pacific, 1974–1977, Box 4, folder CAMB—State Department Telegrams to SECSTATE-EXDIS (1). Dean to SS, 4 February 1975, Tel. 2129, Ford Papers, National Security Adviser, Presidential Country Files for East Asia and the Pacific, 1974–1977, Box 4, folder CAMB—State Department Telegrams to SECSTATE-EXDIS (1).

15. Dean to SS, 6 February 1975, Tel. 2287, Ford Papers, National Security Adviser, Presidential Country Files for East Asia and the Pacific, 1974–1977, Box 4, folder CAMB—State Department Telegrams to SECSTATE-NODIS (2).

16. Kissinger to U.S. Embassy Phnom Penh, 7 February 1975, Tel. 28530, Ford Papers, National Security Adviser, Presidential Country Files for East Asia and the Pacific, 1974–1977, Box 4, folder CAMB—State Department Telegrams from SECSTATE-NODIS.

17. Dean to SS, 18 February 1975, Tel. 3041, Ford Papers, National Security Adviser, Presidential Country Files for East Asia and the Pacific, 1974–1977, Box 4, folder CAMB—State Department Telegrams to SECSTATE-NODIS (2).

18. Memorandum of Conversation, Ford, Kissinger, Scowcroft, 20 February 1975, Ford Papers, National Security Adviser, Memoranda of Conversation, Box 9, folder 2/20/75—Ford, Kissinger.

19. "Supplement to the Report called 'Cambodian Medical Services Program,'" 5 March 1975, RG 809–Cambodia, Box 4, folder 15, CMAA. A. Eugene Hall to T. G. Mangham Jr., 1 March 1975, RG 809–Cambodia, Box 4, folder 15, CMAA.

20. Wolfgang Lehman to Scowcroft, 17 February 1975, Tel. 0668 Via Martin Channel, Ford Papers, National Security Adviser, Backchannel Messages, 1974–1977, folder Martin Channel 2/75–Incoming.

21. Dean to SS, 26 February 1975, Ford Papers, National Security Adviser, Presidential Country Files for East Asia and the Pacific, 1974–1977, Box 4, folder CAMB—State Department Telegrams to SECSTATE-NODIS (2).

22. For a contrary interpretation of Sihanouk's response, see Deac, *Road to the Killing Fields,* 218.

23. *New York Times,* 27 February 1975, 3.

24. Dean to SS, 19 March 1975, Tel. 5021, Ford Papers, National Security Adviser, Presidential Country Files for East Asia and the Pacific, 1974–1977, Box 4, folder CAMB—State Department Telegrams from SECSTATE-NODIS (4).

25. Memorandum of Conversation, Ford, Kissinger, Scowcroft, 8 April 1975, Ford Papers, Memoranda of Conversation, 1973–1977, Box 10, folder 4/8/75—Ford, Kissinger.

26. Dean to SS, 12 April 1975, Tel. 6134, Ford Papers, National Security Adviser, Presidential Country Files for East Asia and the Pacific, 1974–1977, Box 4, folder CAMB—State Department Telegrams to SECSTATE-NODIS (6).

27. Deac, *Road to the Killing Fields,* 6.

28. John F. Guilmartin Jr., *A Very Short War: The* Mayaguez *and the Battle of Koh Tang* (College Station, TX: Texas A & M University Press, 1995), 55–56. The subsequent account of the battle is taken primarily from Guilmartin's detailed work, as well as from "Chronology of Events of the *Mayaguez* Incident," Ford Papers, National Security Adviser, Memoranda of Conversations, 1973–1977, Box 11, folder 5/14/75—Ford, Kissinger Bipartisan Congressional Leadership.

29. Phelin Kyne and Chea Sotheacheath, "Tragedy of Errors: The *Mayaguez* Incident Remembered," *Phnom Penh Post,* 12–25 May 2000, 8–9.

30. Statement of Senator Mike Mansfield, enclosed in William T. Kendall to Max Friedersdorf, 7 April 1975, Ford Papers, National Security Adviser, Presidential Country Files for East Asia and the Pacific, 1974–1977, Box 3, folder CAMB (15). Ford, draft speech, enclosed in Scowcroft to Lawrence Eagleburger, 8 April 1975, Ford Papers, National Security Adviser, Presidential Country Files for East Asia and the Pacific, 1974–1977, Box 3, folder CAMB (15).

31. The information in this and the following paragraphs comes from Kenneth M. Quinn, "The Khmer Krahom Program to Create a Communist Society in Southern Cambodia," 19 February 1974, enclosed in Lehman to USDS, 20 February 1974, Airgram A-008, DCC.

32. Extracts from a letter from E. Eugene Hall to Christian and Missionary Alliance Headquarters, 14 May 1975, RG 809–Cambodia, Box 4, folder 15, CMAA.

33. Pam Moeun, "My Break for Freedom," *Alliance Witness,* 14 January 1976, 16.

34. Quoted in Sheldon Neuringer, *The Carter Administration, Human Rights and the Agony of Cambodia* (Lewiston, NY: Edwin Mellen, 1993), 18.

35. Thomas J. Barnes to Kissinger, 16 October 1975, Ford Papers, National Security Adviser, Presidential Country Files for East Asia and the Pacific, 1974–1977, Box 3, folder CAMB (19).

36. Memorandum of Conversation, Henry Kissinger, Chatichai Choonhavan et al., 26 November 1975, posted on Yale Genocide Project website <www.yale.edu/cgp>.

37. Memorandum of Conversation, J. Malcolm Fraser, Ford, Kissinger et al., 27 July 1976, Ford Papers, National Security Adviser, Memoranda of Conversation, Box 20, folder 7/27/76—Ford, Kissinger, . . . Fraser.

9—Jimmy Carter, Human Rights, and Cambodia

1. Jimmy Carter, *Keeping Faith: Memoirs of a President* (New York: Bantam Books, 1982), 144.

2. Douglas Brinkley, "The Rising Stock of Jimmy Carter: The 'Hands On' Legacy of Our Thirty-Ninth President," *Diplomatic History* 20 (Fall 1996): 521.

3. Congress, House, Committee on International Relations, *Human Rights in Cambodia: Hearing before the Subcommittee on International Organization,* 95th Cong., 1st sess., 3 May 1977, 14.

4. U.S. Congress, *Human Rights in Cambodia: Hearing Before the Subcommittee on International Organization,* 3 May 1977, 95th Congress, 1st sess. (Washington, DC: U.S. Government Printing Office, 1977), 32, 47.

5. Paul B. Hentze to Theodore Shackley, 9 January 1978, Carter Papers, National Security Affairs, Staff Materials, Horn/Special, Box 1. Bennet to Mazzoli, 31 January 1975, Carter Papers, WHCF-CO Files, 81, Box CO-40.

6. "Human Rights Violations in Cambodia." Statement by the President, 21 April 1978, Carter Papers, WHCF-CO Files, 81, Box CO-40. Zbigniew Brzezinski to Cyrus Vance, 28 April 1978, Carter Papers, Vertical File, Cambodian Directives.

7. Carter's comments on Brzezinski to Carter, 13 October 1978, Carter Library, Brzezinski Donated Material, Subject File, Box 42, folder Weekly Reports 9/78–12/78.

8. Eugene L. Stockwell, "Record of Conversation with Prime Minister Pham Van Dong of the Socialist Republic of Vietnam," 26 October 1979, Carter Papers, Presidential Commission on Hunger, General Records—Subject File, Box 11, folder CAMB (2).

9. *Chicago Tribune,* 29 August 1995.

10. Bureau of Public Affairs, "Current Situation in Indochina," *Current Policy,* June 1979, No. 71.

11. Zbigniew Brzezinski, *Power and Principle: Memoirs of a National Security Adviser, 1977–1981* (New York: Farrar, Straus, Giroux, 1983), 410.

12. Michael Oksenberg and William Odom to Brzezinski, 19 February 1979, Carter Library, Brzezinski Donated Material, Geographical File, Box 10, folder "Sino-Vietnamese Conflict, 2/17/79–2/21/79." B. Lynn Pascoe to Edward F. Snyder and Gretchen Eich, 5 April 1979, Carter Papers, WHCF-National Security-Defense, Box ND-48, folder General ND16/CO 172, 1/20/77–1/20/81.

13. Qiang Zhai, communication to the author, 1 May 2001. I am grateful to Qiang Zhai for his assessment of Carter's letter to Deng and American policy surrounding the Chinese invasion.

14. Stephen Solarz et al. to Carter, 22 February 1979, Carter Papers, WHCF-National Security and Defense, Box ND-47, folder Executive, ND 16/CO-172, 1/1/78–4/30/79.

15. "Statement by Honorable Cyrus R. Vance, Secretary of State, before the House Judiciary Subcommittee on Immigration, Refugees and International Law," Carter Papers, WHCF-Countries, Box CO-66, folder Executive CO 172 4/1/79–1/20/81.

16. Monique Sihanouk to Carter, 26 October 1979, Carter Papers, WHCF, Foreign Affairs, Box FO-31, folder Executive FO3-2 (CO-81) 1/20/77–1/20/81. Former GKR Prime Minister In Tam sent a similar telegram of appreciation.

17. Don Oberdorfer, "Cambodia: Salvation Coming, but Slowly," *Washington Post,* 4 November 1979, A1. U.S. Department of State, Bureau of Public Affairs, "Senators' Report on Refugees, October 26, 1979," Special Report No. 59.

18. Jack Anderson, "State Dept. Obstructing Cambodia Aid," *Washington Post,* 29 October 1979, C27.

19. Richard Moe to Hamilton Jordan, 12 November 1979, Carter Papers, Chief of Staff Jordan, Box 41, folder CAMB.

20. Brzezinski to Director of CIA, 3 December 1979 [misdated 1985], Carter Papers, Vertical File, Cambodia Directives. The White House, "Statement on Kampuchea," 5 December 1979, WHCF-Foreign Affairs, Box FO-31, folder Executive FO3-2 (CO-81) 1/20/77–1/20/81.

21. Newspaper clipping, Mary McGrory, "Carter's Geopolitics Helps Keep Cambodia . . . ," *Washington Star,* December [day uncertain], [1979], Carter Papers, Presidential Commission on World Hunger, General Records, Box 11, folder CAMB (1).

22. Author's interview with Charles Twining, 27 December 1994, Phnom Penh.

23. Quoted in remarks by Richard Holbrooke in Bureau of Public Affairs, U.S. Department of State, "Kampuchea: The Never-Ending Tragedy in Indochina," 2 April 1980, *Current Policy* No. 156.

24. Sihanouk told this to the Italian journalist Oriana Fallaci. Shawcross, *Sideshow,* 321.

25. Vance to Carter, 14 January 1980, Carter Papers, Vertical File, folder "Cambodia Directives."

26. Sihanouk's letter is in Leonard Woodcock to SS, 7 April 1980, Tel. 3134, Carter Papers, WHCF-Country Files, CO-81, Box CO-40.

27. Cyrus Vance, *Hard Choices: Critical Years in America's Foreign Policy* (New York: Si-

mon and Schuster, 1983), 126–27. Lincoln Bloomfield to Brzezinski, 16 June 1980, Carter Papers, Brzezinski—Subject File, Box 23, folder Meetings: Muskie/Brown/Brzezinski 5/80–6/80.

28. Bloomfield to Brzezinski, 16 June 1980, Carter Papers, Brzezinski—Subject File, Box 23, folder Meetings: Muskie/Brown/Brzezinski 5/80–6/80.

29. Sam Brown to Edmund Muskie, 8 October 1980, Carter Papers, WHCF-International Organizations, Box IT-8, folder IT-86 1/1/80–1/20/81.

30. William Shawcross, *The Quality of Mercy: Cambodia, Holocaust and Modern Conscience* (New York: Simon and Schuster, 1984), 355.

31. Roger W. Sullivan to Brzezinski, 16 June 1980, Carter Papers, Brzezinski—Subject File, Box 23, folder Meetings: Muskie/Brown/Brzezinski 5/80–6/80. Brzezinski to David Aaron and Les Denend, 17 June 1980, Carter Library, Brzezinski Collection, Donated Historical Material: Subject File 01/1977–01/1981, Box 23, folder Meetings—Muskie/Brown/Brzezinski, 5/80–6/80.

32. John Pilger, "America's Second War in Indochina: Only the Allies Are New," *New Statesman*, 1 August 1980, 12.

10—Toward a New Beginning

1. "About This Issue," *Southeast Asia Chronicle*, No. 79, August 1981, 1.

2. James M. Scott, *Deciding to Intervene: The Reagan Doctrine and American Foreign Policy* (Durham: Duke University Press, 1996), 1–2.

3. Sihanouk's armed forces are sometimes referred to as MOLINAKA, although MOLINAKA was a sometimes independent force that from time to time allied with Sihanouk. I am grateful to Craig Etcheson for this clarification.

4. Paul Quinn-Judge, "Asia Allies Want Open US Aid for Kampuchean Guerrillas," *Christian Science Monitor*, 12 October 1984, 13.

5. "The Democratic Kampuchea Seat at the United Nations and American Interests," *Bearing before the Subcommittee on Asian and Pacific Affairs and on Human Rights and International Organizations of the Committee on Foreign Affairs of the House of Representatives, 97th Congress, 15 September 1982* (Washington, DC: U.S. Government Printing Office, 1983), 28–32.

6. Barbara Crossette, "U.S. Official Rules Out Arms for Cambodian Rebels," *New York Times*, 19 January 1985, 4.

7. Craig Etcheson, "US-Cambodia Relations in the 1980s: A Puzzle for Historians," 30. Paper presented at the 20th Annual Meeting of the Society for Historians of American Foreign Relations, Bentley College, Waltham, MA, 23–26 June 1994.

8. Jack Colhoun, "Back into the Indochina Tunnel," *The Guardian*, 24 April 1985.

9. Quoted in "Kampuchean Contra Aid: 'Here We Go Again,'" ibid., 5 June 1985.

10. David J. Scheffer, "Arming Cambodian Rebels: The Washington Debate," *Indochina Issues*, No. 58, June 1985, 6.

11. Quoted in Etcheson, "US-Cambodia Relations in the 1980s."

12. Information and quotations from the hearings come from Congress, House, Subcommittee on Asian and Pacific Affairs of the Committee on Foreign Affairs, *Hope for Cambodia: Preventing the Return of the Khmer Rouge and Aiding the Refugees: Hearing before the Subcommittee on Asian and Pacific Affairs of the Committee on Foreign Affairs*, 100th Cong., 2nd sess., 30 June and 28 July 1988.

13. Congress, House, Subcommittee on Asian and Pacific Affairs of the Committee on Foreign Affairs, *The Implications of Establishing Reciprocal Interest Sections with Vietnam: Hearing before the Subcommittee on Asian and Pacific Affairs of the Committee on Foreign Affairs*, 100th Cong., 2nd sess., 28 July 1988, 62.

14. John McAuliff and Mary Byrne McDonnell, "Ending the Cambodian Stalemate," *World Policy Review* 7, 1 (1990): 94.

15. Quoted in Kenton J. Clymer, "American Assistance to the Cambodian Resistance Forces," *Indochina Issues*, April 1990, No. 90, 6.

16. Author's interview with an important senatorial staffer, Summer 1989.

17. Ben Kiernan, "Cambodia's Missed Chance: Superpower Obstruction of a Viable Path to Power," *Indochina Newsletter*, Issue 72 (November–December 1991), 4.

18. Peter W. Rodman, *More Precious than Peace: The Cold War and the Struggle for the Third World* (New York: Charles Scribner's Sons, 1994), 468.

19. Ibid., 467–68.

20. Stan Sesser, "Report from Cambodia," *New Yorker*, 18 May 1992, 63. McAuliff and McDonnell, "Ending the Cambodian Stalemate," 79. "Bankrupt and Immoral on Cambodia," *New York Times*, 27 September 1989, A28.

21. MacAlister Brown and Joseph J. Zasloff, *Cambodia Confounds the Peacemakers 1979–1998* (Ithaca: Cornell University Press, 1998), 61. Typescript, "Statement of John R. Bolton, Assistant Secretary of State, Bureau of International Organization Affairs, before the Senate Foreign Relations Committee, February 28, 1990," in author's possession.

22. Christopher Brady, *United States Foreign Policy towards Cambodia, 1977–92: A Question of Realities* (New York: St. Martin's Press, 1999), 164.

23. *New York Times*, 25 May 1990, A4.

24. Clifford Krauss, "U.S. Policy on Cambodia Shifts a Bit," *New York Times*, 14 July 1990, 3.

25. Rodman, *More Precious than Peace*, 461.

26. Steven Erlanger, "Hanoi's Partial Victory," *New York Times*, 20 July 1990, A2.

27. William Pfaff, "Cambodia: Belated Good News," *Minneapolis Star Tribune*, 19 July 1990, 20A.

28. The text of the document is in *The United Nations and Cambodia, 1991–1995* (New York: United Nations Department of Public Information, 1995), 88–92.

29. "Cautious Steps to Peace," *Jakarta Post*, 3 September 1990.

30. The text of the Jakarta document is in *The United Nations and Cambodia, 1991–1995*, 93–94.

31. United States General Accounting Office, International Security and Affairs Division, *Cambodia: AID's Management of Humanitarian Programs*, GAO/NSIAD-91-260, 28 August 1991.

32. "Cambodian PM Boycotts Paris Meeting," *Jakarta Post*, 30 November 1990.

33. Brown and Zasloff, *Cambodia Confounds the Peacemakers*, 83. Richard H. Solomon, *Exiting Indochina: U.S. Leadership of the Cambodian Settlement & Normalization with Vietnam* (Washington, DC: United States Institute of Peace, 2000), 76–77.

34. "Cambodia: U.N. Is Given Chief Role in Making Sure Accord Is Respected," *Minneapolis Star Tribune*, 24 October 1991, 17A.

35. Sesser, "Report from Cambodia," 64.

36. E-mail message, Quinn to the author, 9 January 2003.

37. Philip Shenon, "U.S. Diplomat Warns of Return by Khmer Rouge," *New York Times*, 14 November 1991, A3.

38. This is not to deny that some of the allegations against the CPP were valid. See, for example, Brown and Zasloff, *Cambodia Confounds the Peacemakers*, 103–6, 146–47, and Judy Ledgerwood, "Patterns of CPP Violence during the UNTAC Period," in Judy Ledgerwood and Steve Heder, eds., *Propaganda, Politics, and Violence in Cambodia: Democratic Transition under United Nations Peace-Keeping* (Armonk, NY: M. E. Sharpe, 1996), 114–33.

39. "Cambodian Guerrillas Denounce UN Effort," *International Herald Tribune*, 17–18 April 1993.

40. "Giving Peace a Chance," *Newsweek*, 7 June 1993, 22.

41. "US Pressure Forces Sihanouk to Shun KR," *The Nation* [Bangkok], 21 July 1993.

42. E-mail message, Quinn to the author, 30 December 2002. Ben Kiernan, letter to the editor, *New York Times,* 29 October 1993, A28.

43. Morton Abramowitz, "Pol Pot's Best Pal: Thailand," *Washington Post,* 29 May 1994, C7.

44. Charles Twining, interview with the author, 27 December 1994, Phnom Penh, Cambodia.

45. Ibid.

46. "Cambodian Legislators Approve New Co-Premier," *Chicago Tribune,* 7 August 1997, 1:18.

47. Craig S. Smith, "Hun Sen Begins to Unify Cambodia, Pledging Election, Winning Over King," *Wall Street Journal,* 14 July 1997, A10.

48. Jim Wolf, "Free and Fair Elections Possible in Cambodia—US Official," Reuters dispatch, 10 June 1998 (in author's possession).

49. Terry McCarthy, "Hun Sen: Cambodia's Mr. Justice?" *Time* (on web), 22 March 1999 <www.time.com/asia>.

Epilogue

1. "Political Warhorse no Stranger to Hardball Democracy," *Phnom Penh Post,* 12 April 2004.

2. On the early efforts, see Ben Kiernan, ed., *Genocide and Democracy in Cambodia: The Khmer Rouge, the United Nations and the International Community* (New Haven, CT: Yale University Southeast Asia Studies, 1993) and Tom Fawthrop and Helen Jarvis, *Getting Away with Genocide? Elusive Justice and the Khmer Rouge Tribunal* (Ann Arbor, MI: Pluto Press, 2004).

3. Craig Etcheson, *After the Killing Fields: Lessons from the Cambodian Genocide* (Lubbock, TX: Texas Tech University Press, 2006), 147.

4. Ben Kiernan, "The Cambodian Genocide and Imperial Culture," posted on <www.yale.edu/cgp/KiernanCambodia30thAnniversaryEssay.doc>.

5. Samantha Brown, "Khmer Rouge Tribunal a Race against Time as Debates Rage," Agence France Presse, 14 April 2005, posted at <www.globalpolicy.org/intljustice/tribunals/cambodia/2005/0414farcical.htm>.

6. "Political Warhorse no Stranger to Hardball Diplomacy."

7. *Congressional Record—Senate,* 3 February 2005, 109th Congress, 1st Sess., 151: S 966.

8. Margaret Slocomb, *The People's Republic of Kampuchea 1979–1989: The Revolution after Pol Pot* (Chiang Mai, Thailand: Silkworm Books, 2003), ix.

Selected Bibliography

Unpublished Sources

Australia

National Archives of Australia, Canberra, ACT
Records of:
    Australian Embassy, Washington
    Department of Defence
    Department of External Affairs
    Prime Minister's Department

Cambodia

American Friends Service Committee Library:
    Newspaper Clipping File and Miscellaneous Materials

Cambodian National Archives:
    Records of the *Résident Supérieur*
    Miscellaneous Materials

United States

University of Bridgeport, Bridgeport, CT
Papers of:
    Stanton, Edwin M.

Jimmy Carter Presidential Library, Atlanta, GA
Papers of:
    Carter, Jimmy
    Brzezinski, Zbigniew (donated historical material, collection)

Christian and Missionary Alliance Archives, Colorado Springs, CO
    RG 809: Cambodia Records
    Annual Reports
    Miscellaneous Materials

Dwight D. Eisenhower Library, Abilene, KS
Papers of:
    Eisenhower, Dwight D.
    Seaton, Fred A.

Gerald R. Ford Library, Ann Arbor, MI
Papers of:
    Ford, Gerald R.

Hartmann, Robert T.
Hutchinson, Edward
Nessen, Ronald

Indochina Project, Washington, DC
Newspaper Clipping File and Miscellaneous Material

Lyndon B. Johnson Library, Austin, TX
Papers of:
    Bundy, McGeorge
    Johnson, Lyndon B.

John F. Kennedy Library, Boston, MA
Papers of:
    Hilsman, Roger
    Kennedy, John F.
    Thomson, James C., Jr.

Seeley G. Mudd Manuscript Library, Princeton University, Princeton, NJ
Papers of:
    Dulles, John Foster (State Department Microfilm Collection)
    Trimble, William C.

National Archives and National Archives II
    Despatches from United States Consuls in Saigon, 1889–1906, T-103 (microfilm)
    Confidential U.S. State Department Central Files, Indochina: Internal Affairs,
        1945–1959 (microfilm)
    Confidential U.S. State Department Special Files, Southeast Asia, 1944–1958. 39 mi-
        crofilm reels. University Publications of America
    Richard M. Nixon Presidential Materials
    RG 59 General Records of the Department of State, Central Decimal File, 1960–1963
    RG 59 General Records of the Department of State, Central Foreign Policy File,
        1963–1969
    RG 59 General Records of the Department of State, Subject Numeric File, 1967–1973
    RG 218 Records of the U.S. Joint Chiefs of Staff, Geographic File, 1951–1958
    RG 218 Records of the U.S. Joint Chiefs of Staff, Central Decimal File, 1959–1963
    RG 319 Records of the Army Staff, Records of the General Staff, Records of the
        Deputy Chief of Staff of Military Operations (G-3), Security Classified General
        Correspondence, 1955–1960
    RG 472 Records of the United States Forces in Southeast Asia, Military Assistance
        and Advisory Group—Cambodia
    U.S. Department of State, Records Relating to the Internal Affairs of France,
        1910–1929, M560 (microfilm)
    U.S. Department of State, Records Relating to the Internal Affairs of France,
        1930–1939, M1442 (microfilm)

Harry S. Truman Library, Independence, MO
Papers of:
    Acheson, Dean
    Melby, John F.
    Truman, Harry S.

Selected Works

Ablin, David A., and Marlowe Hood, eds. *The Cambodian Agony*. Armonk, NY: M. E. Sharpe, 1990.

Alagappa, Muthiah. "Soviet Policy in Southeast Asia: towards Constructive Engagement." *Pacific Affairs* 63 (Autumn 1990): 321–50.

Becker, Elizabeth. *When the War Was Over: The Voices of Cambodia's Revolution and Its People*. New York: Simon and Schuster, 1986.

Brady, Christopher. *United States Foreign Policy towards Cambodia, 1977–92: A Question of Realities*. New York: St. Martin's Press, 1999.

Brands, H. W. *The Specter of Neutralism: The United States and the Emergence of the Third World, 1947–1960*. New York: Columbia University Press, 1989.

Brown, MacAlister, and Joseph J. Zasloff. *Cambodia Confounds the Peacemakers 1979–1998*. Ithaca: Cornell University Press, 1998.

Burr, William, ed. *The Kissinger Transcripts: The Top Secret Talks with Beijing and Moscow*. New York: New Press, 1998.

Chanda, Nayan. *Brother Enemy: The War after the War*. New York: Macmillan, 1986.

Chandler, David. *A History of Cambodia*. 3rd ed. Boulder, CO: Westview, 2000.

———. *Brother Number One: A Political Biography of Pol Pot*. Boulder, CO: Westview, 1992.

———. *The Tragedy of Cambodian History: Politics, War, and Revolution since 1945*. New Haven and London: Yale University Press, 1991.

Chandler, David, and Ben Kiernan, eds. *Revolution and Its Aftermath in Kampuchea: Eight Essays*. New Haven: Yale Center for International and Area Studies, 1983.

Chandler, David P., Ben Kiernan, and Chanthou Boua, eds. *Pol Pot Plans the Future: Confidential Documents from Democratic Kampuchea, 1976–1977*. New Haven: Yale University Southeast Asian Studies, 1988.

Clymer, Kenton. *The United States and Cambodia, 1870–1969: From Curiosity to Confrontation*. London: Routledge, 2004.

———. *The United States and Cambodia, 1969–2000: A Troubled Relationship*. London: Routledge, 2004.

Corfield, Justin. *Khmers Stand Up! A History of the Cambodian Government 1970–1975*. Melbourne: Monash University Centre of Southeast Asian Studies, 1994.

Deac, Wilfred P. *Road to the Killing Fields: The Cambodia War of 1970–1975*. College Station, TX: Texas A & M University Press, 1997.

Doyle, Michael W. *UN Peacekeeping in Cambodia: UNTAC's Civil Mandate*. Boulder, CO: Lynne Rienner, 1993.

Duiker, William J. *U.S. Containment and the Conflict in Indochina*. Stanford, CA: Stanford University Press, 1994.

Elliott, David W. P., ed. *The Third Indochina Conflict*. Boulder, CO: Westview, 1981.

Etcheson, Craig. *After the Killing Fields: Lessons from the Cambodian Genocide*. Lubbock, TX: Texas Tech University Press, 2006.

———. "The Reagan Doctrine in Cambodia: Design for a Research Project." Paper prepared for the Conference on the United States and Viet Nam: From War to Peace, University of Notre Dame, 2–4 December 1993.

———. *The Rise and Fall of Democratic Kampuchea*. Boulder, CO: Westview, 1984.

———. "US–Cambodia Relations in the 1980s: A Puzzle for Historians." Paper at the Society for Historians of American Foreign Relations, Bentley College, Waltham, MA, 23–26 June 1994.

———. "The U.S. Role in Negotiating Ad Hoc International Criminal Tribunals: The Case of Cambodia." Paper at the Society for Historians of American Foreign Relations, Washington, DC, 6–8 June 2003.

Fawthrop, Tom, and Helen Jarvis. *Getting away with Genocide? Elusive Justice and the Khmer Rouge Tribunal.* Ann Arbor, MI: Pluto Press, 2004.

Gottesman, Evan. *Cambodia after the Khmer Rouge: Inside the Politics of Nation Building.* New Haven, CT: Yale University Press, 2004.

Guilmartin, John F., Jr. *A Very Short War: The Mayaquez and the Battle of Koh Tang.* College Station: Texas A & M University Press, 1995.

Haas, Michael. *Cambodia, Pol Pot, and the United States: The Faustian Pact.* New York: Praeger, 1991.

Hall, D. G. E. *A History of South-East Asia.* 4th ed. London: Macmillan, 1981.

Heder, Steven, and Judy Ledgerwood, eds. *Propaganda, Politics, and Violence in Cambodia: Democratic Transition Under United Nations Peace-Keeping.* Armonk, NY: M. E. Sharpe, 1996.

Heininger, Janet. *Peacekeeping in Transition: The United States in Cambodia.* New York: Twentieth Century Fund, 1994.

Herring, George. *America's Longest War: The United States and Vietnam, 1950–1975.* 4th ed. New York: McGraw Hill, 2002.

Hildebrand, George C., and Gareth Porter. *Cambodia, Starvation and Revolution.* New York: Monthly Review Press, 1976.

Hitchens, Christopher. "The Case against Henry Kissinger: Crimes against Humanity." *Harper's,* March 2001, 49–74.

———. "The Case Against Henry Kissinger: The Making of a War Criminal." *Harper's,* February 2001, 33–58.

Hurst, Steven. *The Carter Administration and Vietnam.* New York: St. Martin's Press, 1996.

Isaacs, Arnold R. *Without Honor: Defeat in Vietnam and Cambodia.* Baltimore: Johns Hopkin's University Press, 1983.

Isaacson, Walter. *Kissinger: A Biography.* New York: Simon & Schuster, 1992.

Jackson, Karl D., ed. *Cambodia 1975–78: Rendezvous with Death.* Princeton, NJ: Princeton University Press, 1989.

Jeldres, Julio A. *The Royal House of Cambodia.* Phnom Penh: Monument Books, 2006.

Kamm, Henry. *Cambodia: Report from a Stricken Land.* New York: Arcade, 1998.

Kelly, Francis J. *Vietnam Studies: U.S. Army Special Forces 1961–1971.* Washington, DC: Department of the Army, 1985.

Kiernan, Ben. *How Pol Pot Came to Power: A History of Communism in Kampuchea, 1930–1975.* London: Verso, 1985.

———. "The Impact on Cambodia of the U.S. Intervention in Vietnam." In Jayne S. Werner, and Luu Doan Huynh, eds. *The Vietnam War: Vietnamese and American Perspectives,* 216–29. New York, Armonk, 1993.

———. *The Pol Pot Regime: Race, Power, and Genocide in Cambodia under the Khmer Rouge, 1975–79.* New Haven: Yale University Press, 1996.

———, ed. *Genocide and Democracy in Cambodia: The Khmer Rouge, the United Nations, and the International Community.* New Haven, CT: Yale University Southeast Asia Studies, 1993.

Kiernan, Ben, and Chanthou Boua, eds. *Peasants and Politics in Kampuchea 1942–1981.* New York: M. E. Sharpe, 1982.

Kimball, Jeffrey. *Nixon's Vietnam War.* Lawrence, KS: University Press of Kansas, 1998.

Kissinger, Henry. *Ending the Vietnam War: A History of America's Involvement in and Extrication From the Vietnam War.* New York: Simon & Schuster, 2003.

———. *White House Years.* Boston: Little, Brown, 1979.

———. *Years of Upheaval.* Boston: Little, Brown, 1982.

Ledgerwood, Judy, ed. *Cambodia Emerges from the Past: Eight Essays.* DeKalb, IL: Southeast Asia Publications, 2002.

Magistad, Mary Kay. "The Khmer Rouge: A Profile." *Indochina Issues,* no. 86 (December 1988): 1–7.

Martin, Marie Alexandrine. *Cambodia: A Shattered Society*. Berkeley: University of California Press, 1994.

McAuliff, John, and Mary Byrne McDonnell. "Ending the Cambodian Stalemate." *World Policy Journal* 7, no. 1 (1990): 71–105.

McMahon, Robert. *The Limits of Empire: The United States and Southeast Asia since World War II*. New York: Columbia University Press, 1999.

Morris, Stephen J. *Why Vietnam Invaded Cambodia: Political Culture and the Causes of War*. Stanford, CA: Stanford University Press, 1999.

Mysliwiec, Eva. *Punishing the Poor: The International Isolation of Kampuchea*. Oxford: Oxfam, 1988.

Neuringer, Sheldon Morris. *The Carter Administration, Human Rights and the Agony of Cambodia*. Lewiston, NY: Edwin Mellen, 1993.

Norodom Sihanouk, Prince. *My War with the CIA: The Memoirs of Prince Norodom Sihanouk*. London: Penguin Books, 1974.

———. *Le Rejet de l'Aide américaine: Trois exposés de S.A.R. le Prince Norodom Sihanouk*. Phnom-Penh: Ministére de l'Information, Royaume du Cambodge, 1964.

Osborne, Milton. *Sihanouk: Prince of Light, Prince of Darkness*. Honolulu, HI: University of Hawaii Press, 1994.

Peou, Sorpong. *Intervention and Change in Cambodia: Towards Democracy*. New York: St. Martin's Press, 2000.

Ponchaud, François. *La Cathédrale de la Rizière: 450 ans d'histoire de L'église au Cambodge*. Paris: Le Sarment: Fayard, 1990.

Porter, Gareth. "Cambodia: The Politics of Food." *Indochina Chronicle* no. 47, 1976.

Rodman, Peter W. *More Precious than Peace: The Cold War and the Struggle for the Third World*. New York: Charles Scribner's Sons, 1994.

Sardesai, D. K. *Southeast Asia Past and Present*. 2nd ed. Boulder, CO: Westview, 1989.

Sawin, John S. "The Christian and Missionary Alliance in Indo-China Pre-1911–1924," Vol. I. Christian and Missionary Alliance Archives. Unpublished.

———. "The Christian and Missionary Alliance in Indo-China 1925–1930," Vol. II. Christian and Missionary Alliance Archives. Unpublished.

Scott, James M. *Deciding to Intervene: The Reagan Doctrine and American Foreign Policy*. Durham: Duke University Press, 1996.

Shawcross, William. *The Quality of Mercy: Cambodia, Holocaust and Modern Conscience*. New York: Simon and Schuster, 1984.

———. *Sideshow: Kissinger, Nixon and the Destruction of Cambodia*. 2nd ed. New York: Simon & Schuster, 1987.

Short, Philip. *Pol Pot: Anatomy of a Nightmare*. New York: Henry Holt, 2005.

Slocomb, Margaret. *People's Republic of Kampuchea, 1979–1989: The Revolution after Pol Pot*. Chiang Mai, Thailand: Silkworm Books, 2004.

Solomon, Richard H. *Exiting Indochina: The Leadership of the Cambodian Settlement & Normalization with Vietnam*. Washington, DC: United States Institute of Peace, 2000.

U.S. Department of State, *Foreign Relations of the United States*. Washington, DC: Government Printing Office.

Index